ETHICS AND SOCIETY:
A Marxist Interpretation of Value

ETHICS
AND SOCIETY

A Marxist Interpretation

of Value

MILTON FISK

Professor of Philosophy, Indiana University

New York University Press. New York *and* London

First published in the U.S.A. in 1980 by
New York University Press
Washington Square
New York, NY 10003

©in the United Kingdom by Milton Fisk, 1980

Library of Congress Cataloging in Publication Data

Fisk, Milton.
 Ethics and society.

 Bibliography: p.
 Includes index.
 1. Socialist ethics. 2 Social ethics. I. Title.
BJ1388.F57 1980   170   79–3513
ISBN 0–8147–2564–3

Printed in Great Britain

For my children
Barth, Graham, Melany

The aim of this science is not knowledge but action.

Aristotle, *Nicomachean Ethics*

Contents

PART FIVE
A Prospectus for a Theory of Rights

Preface

THERE are two things this book tries to say. One is negative and the other positive. The negative thing is that many of the convictions people have about what they ought to do or what they have a right to do lack a basis in what they are themselves. To that extent these convictions are simply false. People are not altogether to blame for holding these false ethical beliefs since holding them results from social forces that control people's behaviour. Still, there are ways out of these beliefs. One way is through action; people break with an ethics imposed on them when they have to take action in order to realize their interests. Another way out is through thought; this involves taking a critical look at one's ethical convictions. A critical look will show that the only justification for some of those convictions is that they help control one's behaviour in a way that promotes some alien interest.

This leads to the positive thing this book says. It is that the correct basis for what is morally good, what one's duty is, what the right thing to do is, what is fair to do—in short, for ethical matters—is one's place in one's society. The correct basis is not the human person taken in isolation. Rather, the focus is on the groups in society to which a person belongs. There is good reason for this, since the person and the groups in society he or she belongs to are more intimately related than coffee and a cup it happens to be in. Indeed, what people are is in part determined by their places in society. So focussing on the social does not involve going beyond the human person. Many of us are unaccustomed to thinking in terms of an intimate connection between the personal and the social. But an ethics must deal with the social existence of human agents. Otherwise it will end by reinforcing false moral beliefs.

For purpose of contrast, it will be well to consider a view that minimizes the importance of the social. Individualism is not just a view that backs up the behaviour of the loner. It also holds that the nature of the human agent can be understood independently of the groups he or she happens to live in. So individualism is both ethics and metaphysics: it says something about both what we *may* do and what we really *are*. These two sides of it are connected, for to justify behaving as an individualist one can appeal to the view that one's nature is fully determinate apart from membership in any group.

Individualism is at the opposite pole from the positive view of this book. The core of this positive view is that ethics is a social study because the nature of the person is social. Yet individualism rejects the social nature of humans. In doing so it helps to keep alive the kind of society that has developed in western countries over the past three centuries. It is somewhat ironic, then, that this asocial view has deep social roots. But since it does, combatting it is not combatting an abstraction that exists only in philosophers' minds.

Individualism has been used to get people to accept a given kind of society and to reject other kinds of society. It has persuaded people to accept a society in which competitiveness has been a characteristic trait. Competitiveness has been used to perpetuate a high degree of inequality and to discourage the kind of cooperation that might challenge the privileged. In turn, this inequality and lack of cooperation keeps individualism alive. This backing does not prevent individualism from containing a false theory of what the human agent is and an ethics that is false for members of all the major groups in our society.

Since ethics has a social basis, a study of society is relevant to ethics. In particular, a study of society tells us two things that are of utmost importance for ethics. First, it tells us that within a society there are various groups having distinctive tendencies. That is, a society is not just a homogeneous collection of people. It has an internal structure in the form of various groups. These groups have their places within the society because of their distinctive tendencies. (Speaking here about the tendencies of a group is shorthand for speaking about the common tendencies people have because they are in the group.)

Second, such a study tells us that in a society like our own there are conflicts between many of the groups. Further, it tells us that conflicts between some of the groups are, whatever their origins, given their reason for present existence in terms of conflicts between others. The assumption here will be that conflicts between socio-economic classes sustain in this way conflicts between other groups. This assumption has been given strong confirmation in recent sociological literature.[1]

Both of these points are important in an ethics that does not isolate the human agent from society. Take first the point that society is not homogeneous. This will mean that it is not just the society, but also the groups within it, to which a person belongs that will be important to him or her. Basic dispositions, attitudes, and the ways needs are patterned will reflect membership in these groups. The basis for regarding these features as accidental would be the old individualist way of thinking, which does not see the social an essential to the self.

Ethics is not a form of sadism; it does not aim to thwart what is essential to people. Rather it must set out from an understanding of what human nature is and attempt to resolve conflicts on the basis of this understanding. This much can be agreed to even by those who hold fundamentally different views of what the nature of humans is. An individualist and a social ethics do not differ on the centrality of human nature; what they differ on is whether the social is essential to the self. The social ethics elaborated in this book incorporates the view that humans do not wander about in search of the basic social groups that fit them but instead they have no given nature that a group can fit well or poorly until they are first members of certain basic social groups. Alternative groups will shape humans differently, and the way this shaping takes place will be the subject of considerable discussion in the body of the book.

Now take the point that classes are 'primary' among groups—in the limited sense that conflicts among other groups are given their reason for present existence by conflicts among classes. This point will be crucial in attempting to show that the needs formed by membership in one's class take precedence over other needs when there is an incompatibility. No dire consequences result from this for the needs of, say, blacks and women, since it turns out that the needs of oppressed groups do not really conflict with the needs of lower classes. The key factor here is the necessity for cooperation between these oppressed groups and the lower classes if any of them is to achieve liberation.

Making these social points important in ethics yields a relativist ethics. This means that the ethics valid for one class or group need not be valid for some other class or group. Most of us have long believed that ethics is absolute, that there is a final arbiter of all disputes. But this belief itself must be analyzed from the perspective of the structure of our society. Does the conventional ethics that all groups are asked to accept advance the tendencies of some of those groups at the expense of others? Relativism in ethics enables us to look critically at the ethical principles we have been taught at school, from the media, or by self-styled objective scholars. Also it prevents us from replacing our old unexamined ethical principles with a new absolutism. When one finds that what one has believed has served the goals of an alien group, one might then be tempted to erect the goals of one's own group into ideals valid for all groups. But from the perspective of relativism, the lesson to be learned is that even the new principles are not valid on a basis that transcends one's group.

The conviction that there must be absolutes has been extensively cultivated. Consequently, relativism is frequently assumed wrong from the very outset. Yet only arguments against the crudest forms of relativism ever appear. For example, it is argued that if one is a relativist one must believe that might makes right, or that doing what one wants is doing what is right, or that what the group accepts is the standard of right.

There are many different forms of relativism. Responsibility need not be taken for the weaknesses of all of them. Only the form presented here needs to be defended. According to this form of relativism, might does *not* make right. The right thing to do is determined by a consideration of what ultimately, in view of the primacy of class, advances the realization of the tendencies of one's class. And that class may be weak rather than strong. What the individual wants is *not* always right. Such wants may be fashioned by propaganda that serves an alien class. The tendencies of the individual's own class may then conflict with what the individual wants. Here those tendencies determine what is right. Finally, what the group accepts as right need *not* be right. Here again the group's beliefs might have been formed under the influence of another group. The group might then be blind to its own interests. To determine what is right, these imposed beliefs must first be overcome.

The class relativist ethics developed here is an empirical ethics. It calls for a careful empirical study of the tendencies of classes and of the humans in them. This brings ethics down to earth without making it any easier. It counteracts the widespread belief that if ethics does not deal with otherworldly entities—with transcendent norms, the word of God, or the structure of pure spirit—then it is nothing at all. If disputes about what is right and wrong must be answered by reference to such otherworldly entities, then those disputes are necessarily fruitless, for there is no way of determining what those entities really are. These disputes can be settled only by forgetting otherworldly entities and appealing back to the sorts of things that are crucial in an empirical ethics, to things in our own spatio-temporal social existence.

In both method and motivation, the ethics elaborated here is a Marxist ethics. It emphasizes, as did Karl Marx, the social nature of the person, the class nature of society, the importance of exposing moral conceptions that serve the interests of alien groups, and the necessity of replacing them with moral conceptions that can be said, with some empirical warrant, to serve the interests of one's own group.[2] This need for moral critique and reconstruction is not based on an idle pursuit of the truth about matters ethical. Rather, it is based on the conviction that there is a need for fundamental change in a society that is marked by the oppression of large groups and the domination of large classes. Today the change that is needed is one that leads to socialism. Part of this change will be just such a moral critique and reconstruction.

Socialism means conflicting things to different people. Here it will mean a form of society controlled from below by those who are productive in it, in short, by workers. Moral critique and reconstruction on a mass scale will go on as part of the gathering movement for a change to socialism. To bear real fruit, efforts such as those in this book must be integrated into this movement. As part of the movement for socialism, the thoughts contained here can be instruments that hasten the process of moral critique and reconstruction that is already taking place in that movement.

Often Marxist writers segregate the Marxist from other traditions in the history of philosophy. But here the insights of Aristotle, Hobbes, Nietzsche, and Dewey are incorporated into the elaboration of class relativist ethics. Moreover, this position is developed from elementary considerations on which it is hoped rather broad agreement can be reached. To state these elementary matters, a neutral vocabulary, rather than a technical Marxist one, is required. With this procedure, readers can more easily determine where in the argument their disagreement arises. The conclusions are, to be sure, ones over which partisan feelings reach the boiling point. Nonetheless, by starting from elementary considerations phrased in a neutral vocabulary, the path to these conclusions is made accessible both to those who have no familiarity with Marxism and to those who have no prior knowledge of philosophy.

The ambiguity of the word *ethics* will soon cause trouble unless it is pointed out now. On the one hand, ethics is a systematic study. In this study one might inquire whether the right thing to do is the thing that would maximize happiness. And in the same study one might inquire whether membership in a class is important in determining obligation. After solving such general problems, ethics as a systematic study can be extended to include applications of their solutions to concrete problems, such as abortion, war resistance, and academic freedom.

Ethics conceived in this way as a systematic study is clearly different from *an* ethics, which, on the other hand, is a body of principles. Your ethics, as a body of principles, differs from that of a journeyman in a mediaeval guild. Not all things that are good, right, obligatory, or fair for you would be so for him. This is an ethics book in the sense of being a systematic study and not in the sense of presenting a set of principles of good, right, obligatory, and fair behaviour.

It is worth noting that the adjective *ethical* is ambiguous in a different way than the noun *ethics*. When one says that a certain practice is not ethical, one means it is bad. This is the first, positive sense of *ethical*. But when one speaks about ethical evaluation of behaviour, one certainly does not mean good evaluation, but only evaluation to determine whether something is good or bad, right or wrong, obligatory or forbidden, fair or unfair. This is the second, neutral sense of *ethical*. Here both good and bad are viewed as having ethical significance, both coming within the scope of ethical principles.

It is *ethical* in this neutral sense that will be used here. In this sense, one can say that human action has an ethical dimension, meaning that it is good or bad, right or wrong, obligatory or forbidden, fair or unfair. The terms in these pairs are rightly called ethical terms; thus if action can be described by any of these terms, it has an ethical dimension. In the same way, human life has an ethical dimension and is thus ethical life. Since the term *ethical* has the neutral sense here, this does not mean that human life is truly good, but only that it can be evaluated in ethical terms. Human life is ethical life since it is open to evaluation by some ethics. This connects *ethical* in the neutral sense with *ethics* in the sense of a body of principles. (The terms *morals* and *moral* admit of the same range of ambiguity.)

In due course, the key terms *good*, *right*, *obligatory*, and so on will be explained so as to make them relative to classes. In other ethical theories they get a different explanation. It will suffice now to explain them in a superficial way that allows for agreement on all sides. Something good to do need not be something mandatory, but it is worthwhile. Doing it is, thus, a sign of worthiness. Doing the right thing is doing the best thing that in the circumstances can be done, even though there may be no obligation there to do anything at all. Obligation leaves no alternative. Failing to do what one is obliged to do is not just to miss the possibility of doing something worthwhile; it is actually to make oneself blameworthy. *Having* the right to do something—as distinct from *doing* the right thing—implies at least that others are obligated to allow one to do that thing. So rights are backed up by obligations. Among other rights, people have a right to fair or just treatment.

Part One lays all the author's cards out on the table. This creates some difficulties, but the advantages outweigh them. Arguments for important points are given only in barest outline. The main thing about Part One is, then, the drift. It will create lots of questions, questions about how anyone could possibly hold such a view rather than about the general nature of the view.

The task of Parts Two and Three is to give fuller arguments for the class relativism outlined in Part I. Part Three gives the positive theory of human nature on which everything hinges. The view of human nature as changing, that is developed in Part Three, is an outgrowth of a more general view of natures developed elsewhere.[3] The negative work of criticizing several ethical views of an absolutist character is undertaken in Part Two. Absolutist views receive far less than equal space in this book. But in available ethical literature, they have monopolized all the space. Still, even in trying here to redress this imbalance, the opposition is not entirely neglected.

Parts Four and Five go beyond giving direct support to the outline of ethical relativism in Part One. They extend the relativist conception into areas that are important for a full development of ethics. Part Four develops a view of human action in order to deal with the nature of good character, rational choice, freedom, and responsibility. The social nature of human agents must be recognized to deal adequately with these matters. The theory of human action developed in Part Four belongs to a more abstract level but Part Five is intelligible without it.

Part Five discusses fairness, showing that what is fair cannot be decided abstractly but only in light of the actually existing ways people organize the struggle for existence. Even a revolutionary ethics does not advance an abstract ideal of fairness, but an ideal of fairness that is a response to current inequities.

The basic ideas around which this book is built were beginning to take shape in 1970 during a course in Marxist ethics. Michael Hebert provided critical support as these ideas began to develop sharper outlines in a series of articles. Extensive comments on the entire first draft were provided by Frank Thompson. Shin-Yun Yeh, Robert Morris, and David Seiferth pointed to weaknesses while assisting me in courses where the typescript was used. Separate drafts were typed by Kim Liford, Jenny Meadows, and Karen Durnil

MILTON FISK
November 1978
Bloomington, Indiana

Notes

1   For sources, see Charles H. Anderson, *The Political Economy of Class*, Prentice-Hall, Englewood Cliffs, N. J., 1974, Ch. 12.
2   Karl Marx and Frederick Engels, *The German Ideology* (written in 1845–46), International Publishers, New York, 1970, Part I.
3   Milton Fisk, *Nature and Necessity*, Indiana University Press, Bloomington, 1973, Ch. II, Sec. 3.

PART ONE

An Outline of Ethical Relativism

I
The Person and the Group

ETHICS is a field of study concerned with human action. There are, though, many ways of being concerned with human action, and ethics must be distinguished from the rest of them. One might be concerned with human action from the point of view of how it is affected by a low protein diet. Finding this out would be relevant to making ethical judgments about those who limit large numbers of people to such a diet. Nonetheless, the focus of ethics is not primarily the casual basis of behaviour.

This chapter defines the perspective from which ethics studies action. It was noted in the Preface that action has an ethical dimension if it can be described using the ethical terms good or bad, right or wrong, and so on. Now it is necessary to probe behind this merely terminological view of the matter. The claim to be defended here is that a person's action has an ethical dimension precisely because of conflicts between needs of the person and interests of the group or groups to which the person belongs. Action would lack an ethical dimension were there a complete harmony between the person and the group.

The short answer to our question is, then, that ethics is a study of the ethical dimension of action. A fuller answer includes an explanation of how action has an ethical dimension. It is given such a dimension by efforts of humans to guide action when there is conflict between the person and the group. The dimension ethics studies is not then a physical feature of action. It is through and through social.

1 **Harmony and conflict**   Suppose there is a perfect harmony between you and all of the groups to which you belong. Whatever you have a need to do is compatible with the interests of those groups. The interests of a group are not interests of some supra-human being. They are the interests people could be expected to have in virtue of the role they play that makes them members of the group. In a situation of harmony, whatever is imperative for the advancement of the interests characteristic of members of those groups either does not conflict with any of your needs or is just what you need to do anyway. If the well-being of the family

3

requires that roof repairs be made, then by some curious coincidence helping out in making those repairs fits right in with the complex of your own needs, so that no conflict is generated.

Philosophers, beginning in the western tradition with Plato,[1] have imagined that when all persons are properly developed there will be such a coincidence between their needs and the interests of at least the most important group they constitute. Conflict between the person and such a group is, for them, a sign that the person has not been developed to his or her full potential. Properly developed persons make the interests found in this group their own interests.

Before taking up the consequences of such a coincidence, a word needs to be said about the source of the conflict between person and group. It is not to be sought in a natural rebelliousness or selfishness in persons. The person whose needs conflict with the interests of his or her group is a person most of whose needs arise in a social context that involves more groups than this one. Groups beyond the one the person belongs to influence his or her character. On the one hand, standards whose acceptance is encouraged by the overall society are often a source of conflict with the person's own group. Acceptance of dominant standards by many blacks and women becomes a source of needs that conflict with the interests of the oppressed groups to which they belong. These needs are based on standards whose wide acceptance is useful to dominant groups and are not based on a fixed human nature. On the other hand, certain socially created conditions are a fertile source of needs that pit persons against their groups. In conditions of relative deprivation members of lower groups can be pitted against their groups by offers of favoured treatment. The need for better pay or more dignity is genuine enough but it arises here precisely because of the conditions of deprivation. It is not fixed in human nature apart from these conditions.

So long as some groups in society dominate others, the problem of conflict between person and group will remain. People in dominated groups will develop needs that reflect standards useful to the dominating groups of the society or conditions created by them. There will then be conflicts with the interests of the dominated groups arising from these needs. Plato's ideal of a coincidence between person and group can, then, be realized only when there is no domination between groups. Ironically, his own ideal state contained a thoroughgoing domination of lower by higher classes, which undercut a coincidence between needs of persons and lower-class group interests.

The question here is not so much whether such a coincidence is ever possible but whether, if it existed, action could still have an ethical dimension. In the absence of conflict or the threat of conflict between the needs of the person and the interests of the person's group, would there be ethical life? Would actions be good or bad, right or wrong, obligatory or forbidden?

First, there would be no occasion for the parent to press on the child the necessity of considering the welfare of others in the family. Any group's need for educated members could be met without the urgings of the teacher for greater diligence on the part of students. The discipline imposed by leaders would be replaced by the cooperative strivings of the rank and file to realize common interests. The use of authority in all these ways is characteristic of ethical life. Yet ethical authority would be irrelevant in a context in which person and group were in harmony.

Second, conscience is another aspect of the ethical side of humans that would cease to have a useful role. Conscience is the internal parent, teacher, and leader. Too much external authority tends to make human existence an oppressive affair, so after a little guidance from external ethical authority, one learns to become one's own ethical guide. By means of conscience, the group speaks to one about the limits of satisfying one's own needs without the necessity of a spokesperson for the group. But without a conflict between the person and the group, an internal spokesperson for the group would be superfluous.

The point is that where there is harmony there is no external or internal nagging, urging, commanding, or blaming. But in the absence of these things, goodness, right, and duty are not just hidden from us. They are simply not there to be found. This is explained by the fact that they are not natural but rather social features of action. No inner eye of reason is going to discover them where there is harmony between the group and person and hence where there has been no human effort to guide action through conflict. (In Section 2, an objection to this line of reasoning will be discussed.)

One of the consequences of this conclusion is that there is no ethical life on an island which I alone inhabit. There is no social group there, and hence no conflict between my needs and the interests of a group. If I have been taken out of a group environment and transported into exile on the island for the rest of my days, then I may well behave on the island in accordance with certain of the rules I followed before my exile began. Yet my life is no longer part of the ethical life of the old group. I might even develop new rules for my island existence; I would, for example, prohibit myself from swimming over the coral reef on the north side of the island in order to avoid cutting my legs. But such rules would aim simply at my own well-being. They would add an ethical dimension to my life only if I had to take care of myself for the sake of some group.

A second consequence is that conflicts within the person are not *of themselves* the subject of ethical deliberation. It is only when this internal conflict is related to a conflict between the needs the person feels and the interests of the group that the conditions exist for its being an ethical conflict. These conditions are normally met since—except on our island—it is virtually impossible to avoid describing the so-called inner conflict without relating it to group concerns. Should I indulge my longing for idleness or should I develop my potential for socially useful skills? But just to have stated the conflict is to have perceived it as one that goes beyond a conflict contained entirely within the person. The skills are ones that fit into a group purpose. Even if I describe them more neutrally as the skills of an X-ray technologist, there is no *ethical* resolution of the conflict apart from going beyond the needs the person feels and seeing these skills in relation to a social purpose.

A third consequence concerns conflicts of a lateral sort between groups themselves rather than those of the vertical sort between persons and groups. Suppose the interests of two groups conflict and that these groups have no members in common. Suppose further that there is harmony between these members and their respective groups. (This is an unlikely supposition since, where there are conflicting groups, persons in some of those groups may develop attitudes incompatible with the interests of their groups.) The group conflict would not be sufficient to make the lives of these people, who are in harmony with their groups, ethical. They all march in step with their groups and thus march into conflict with alien groups without nagging, urging, or commanding. Joining with one's group is an action with an ethical dimension, not because of the conflict between one's group and another group, but because of the possibility of conflict between one's needs and one's group's interests.

A final consequence concerns conflicts between persons. Am I in an ethical situation simply because my needs conflict with yours? The island does *not* become the scene of ethical life just by increasing the population from one to two. Only by being in a group do my relations with others—in or out of my group—become ethical. It is the discipline imposed by group membership that begins to regulate relations between persons. Without that discipline and the possibility of conflict it implies between the group and the person, interaction between persons has no more of an ethical character than interaction in the inanimate world.

2 Conformity to principles

Since comparison aids understanding, it is appropriate to sketch an alternative to this social view of the ethical, and then to outline the limitations of this alternative. On such a fundamental point as the nature of ethical life, this brief discussion will not be decisive. To decide which of these views of ethical life is correct, we should examine how each would make a difference in directing our behaviour. Even this book as a whole goes only part way toward showing what difference the social view of ethical life makes to behaviour.

The alternative is that the domain of human action has an ethical aspect because there are valid principles of human action. Thus my behaviour is part of ethical life if there are valid ethical principles that apply to what I do—that tell me that what I do is good or bad, is right or wrong, or is obligatory or forbidden. The idea is that *of themselves* principles of behaviour make the behaviour to which they apply ethical. It is not the context in which principles have their origin that makes them ethical principles and, through them, transmits an ethical dimension to human action. For my action to have an ethical dimension, it does not matter that what I do either advances or sets back the interests of a group I am in. Rather, what matters is that what I do either agrees with or conflicts with a set of principles for behaviour.

It becomes possible in this view for the exile on the island to fall within the ethical community. A conflict that is internal to the person can as such be an ethical one. This is all because participation in the ethical life is simply a matter of acting within the scope of ethical principles. Some of these principles may, of course, have a social content; they may tell me that I am not permitted to do just what I want when there is the good of the family to consider or that I cannot revel in idleness when the community needs productive labour. But the fact that human action has an ethical dimension depends, not on the social content of these principles, but solely on the fact that human action falls within their scope.

In our social conception of the ethical, the exile's committing suicide would *not* be a matter to be judged in ethical terms. Still there might be—in an appropriate sense of *be*—principles relating to suicide. Off hand, putting any suicide outside the ethical strikes most of us as strange. The reason, though, is that we are accustomed to questioning the rightness or wrongness of suicide in a social setting. There it is indeed an ethical matter. Judged by surface plausibility, ethics conceived in terms of principles seems then to be superior. Surface plausibility is though, never a final check.

More important than surface plausibility is an understanding of how principles give action an ethical dimension. Can one say how they do this without getting back to the social view of the ethical? In the alternative view, the principles are supposed to give action an ethical dimension simply by existing, by being there. Is this really the case, or do they confer an ethical dimension only because principles come out of the effort to guide people when there is conflict between the person and the group?

The argument below against the view that principles alone confer an ethical dimension is an argument that supports the more general view called 'historical materialism', to be discussed further in Chapter XI, Section 1. According to this general view, it is against the background of the social existence of humans that things such as principles, theories, civil laws, and institutions exist and change in the ways they do. These things are, then, never final in explanation. In particular, ethical principles, however valid, are not the basis for ethical life. It is rather against the background of the existence of persons in groups that there is such a thing as the ethical dimension of life and that it changes in certain ways.

Principles of good, right, or obligation exist within the course of human history. They are certainly not there in the way the Rocky Mountains are there. Still there are people who would deny this by claiming that principles are independent of the social life of humans. Even if their denial was true, it is not clear how principles could confer an ethical dimension on human action of themselves.

Suppose there was an entity that came about through some spiritual chemistry and that had somehow been interpreted as an ethical principle. It is difficult to see how it is any more relevant to ethical life than the Rockies themselves.[2] If there was an entity out in some fifth dimension—an otherworldly entity—that someone interpreted as having the meaning that one should not waste one's talents by idleness, then why should we consider 'obeying' such an entity and cultivating our talents? To say that we should would be like saying that we should obey whatever inscriptions the wind should happen to carve in the Gobi Desert.

Ethics would become a superstition if we were to obey entities found in another world, in nature, or in the mind simply because it is possible to interpret these entities as saying what moral imperatives say. For a disposition to be awed by things taken as symbols is a form of superstition. Finding the symbols *Thou shalt not kill!* engraved on a tablet might be taken as finding an expression of a principle forbidding killing. It might even be taken as the word of God. But should one obey it simply because the principle exists, or even because it exists in God's mind?

There are two parts to the answer. First, one can interpret inscriptions in the sand or on tablets as moral principles only if one is already familiar with moral principles. One must rely here on the use of principles in everyday interaction. Moral principles are never simply out there, but always there as part of efforts to come to grips with conflicts between persons and their groups. Even what is held to be the word of God cannot be read as a moral imperative outside of this social context.

Second, a principle by itself has no claim to giving action covered by it an ethical dimension. If I read in the wind-carved sands *Eat no fowl!*, I cannot say that eating fowl has thereby an ethical dimension. This principle has a claim to making action ethical only if eating fowl is a potential trouble point between certain persons and their groups. In short, the principle must be relevant to person-group conflict. It is then this conflict and not principles themselves that is the origin of ethical life. The word of God has ethical import not because of its alleged divine origin but because of its relevance to the conflict between people and groups.

3 Conceptions of the person   The real reason that ethics is social has not yet been discussed. So far it has been noted that certain things intimately associated with the ethical, such as external and internal authority, would disappear if there was harmony between the person and the group. But this says only that ethics must be social without explaining why.

Before outlining in Section 4 the view of the person that gives the needed explanation, it will be instructive to have before our eyes two extreme views of the person. Neither explains why the ethical depends on a tension between the person and the group.

In the first conception, the person is dependent on groups only in superficial and accidental respects. What might be called the 'core' person develops no matter what kind of group the person becomes a member of. The core person is the person in all essential respects. Your intelligence quotient, your income, your accent are, to be sure, conditioned by the specific kinds of groups you find yourself in. But these, it is held, are superficial traits of yourself; what you really are, your essential traits, your core self, shines through all the accidents of nationality, class, and family.[3] This is the 'atomic' conception of the core person. It treats the core person like a physical atom, an atom that is the same even in quite different combinations with other atoms.

From the point of view of the atomic person, a group is something quite alien, something that in no way conditions what the person really is. How then could a conflict between a person and a group take on an ethical significance?

The conflict between the atomic person and the group reduces to one like that between my desire to split an oak block and its resistance to being split due to the presence in it of a thick, tough knot. The group is just as much outside me as the oak block. The block's resistance to my axe blows hardly forces any ethical demands on me, though it may force me to stop chopping out of sheer exhaustion. Analogously, the group with which I am in conflict forces no ethical demands on me. Those who adopt the atomic view of the core person have themselves seen the force of the analogy. For them nations, classes, governments, families, and monopolies are to be tolerated only in so far as they promote the realization of persons, whose potentialities are formed independently of these social entities. The conflict between the person and a group is of concern, not because the person might hamper the group, but only because the group might stand in the way of the needs of the core person. The group, like the block, is an obstacle to will.

This atomic conception can preserve the ethical only by appeal to conflict within the person. For there can be no conflict of ethical significance with an entity like a group that remains utterly alien to the person. Only within the person can the needed interdependence be found between the poles of conflict. But is this enough for the conflict to be ethical?

The individual capitalist's need to get around government restrictions on economic enterprise for the sake of short-term profits with which to pay creditors is ultimately in conflict with his class's interest in protection from economic disaster by government measures aimed at avoiding depressions. The individual capitalist's need for gain conflicts with his class's interest in stability. But there will be an internal conflict only if the individual capitalist internalizes this class interest and thus feels a need for overall stability. In the atomic view of the core person, right and wrong can have their origin only in the conflict between the person's penchant for short-term gratification and the person's own more reflective need for long-term stability in overall living conditions. How are we to say now that there is a good and a bad side to this internal conflict? This would be easy enough if we could appeal to the fact that one side of the conflict represents the interests of other people who belong to the same group as the person experiencing the conflict. But such matters are accidental as far as the atomic core person is concerned. It is to the conflict in its internal dimensions that appeal must be made. Yet nothing internal gets us closer to the ethical; wanting profits and stability becomes no more an ethical dilemma than the child's wanting candy and ice cream with only a quarter in its pocket. To break out of the internal conflict and make it social will, though, lead back to the ethical only after abandoning the atomic person.

In the second conception, the person is entirely conditioned by his or her social context. There are no natural needs in the sense of needs that play a role in generating human action in any and every social setting. Even the person's biological make-up is by some mysterious mechanism totally dependent on social forces. There is no drive for food that is there to be moulded by social forces into certain distinctive eating habits, for the desire for food is itself dependent on those forces.

Where there is such a thoroughgoing dependence of the person on the social context, it cannot be claimed that the person has an independent existence that can be affected by the social context. The person is not external to social groups in a way that allows us to say that they can have a casual influence on the person. Instead, the person is so dependent on the group that he or she can be said to be a mere aspect of the group, in somewhat the same way that shapes and sizes are aspects of physical objects. In the 'aspect' view of the person, it is the social whole that has an independent and separate existence which is shared by persons. The person, then, has no call on the social whole to adjust to the person's desires.

In this view, the person cannot properly be said to act. For to act the person would have to have an independent existence. But here only the group exists of itself. Benito Mussolini, the Italian dictator, adopted the aspect view when he said, 'Fascism conceives of the state as an absolute in comparison with which all individuals or groups are relative . . . .'[4] The individual becomes relative in precisely the sense that everything he or she has is dependent on the overarching social entity. And so the aspect person is a part of a group in the way organs are parts of a living organism. Since, strictly speaking, it is the organism as a whole that acts, there is no question a person can raise as to what he or she should do. The organism acts and the person is a mere aspect of that action. If the person cannot act, there is no personal freedom. Ethics is, then, not possible for the person. The aspect view is then absurd as a foundation for an ethics of persons. (Both it and the atomic view are useful only by way of contrast for the view of persons to be developed in this book.)

The problem with the aspect view is just the reverse of that with the atomic view. The group was so alien to the atomic person that the group could have no call on the person to weigh the interests of the group against those of the person. The aspect person is so little distinguished from the group that the aspect person can have no call on the group to take into account the needs of the aspect person. Historically speaking, the atomic view is at the base of the 'individualist' tradition of democratic liberalism whereas the aspect view is at the base of the 'collectivist' tradition of various forms of totalitarianism. Neither view explains why the conflict between the self and the group should be important enough to be the point from which ethical life emerges.

4 The social person The conception of the person to be adopted here takes the best of both the atomic and the aspect views and rejects the worst in both of them. From the atomic view, this third view takes the idea that there is something to the person that does not depend on specific groups, something that is needed for social forces to act on. What this is will be spelled out in Chapter IX, Section 2, as a system of four survival needs that are basic among all needs. These are the needs for food, sex, human support, and deliberation. This view of the person rejects the idea—advocated by the atomic view—that the results of social forces in the person are always accidental additions, additions outside the core person. From the aspect view, then, the third view takes the idea that being in different epochs and being in different groups moulds the person in such a way that there are essential differences between the persons in these epochs and in these groups. But it rejects the idea—advocated by the aspect view—that there is nothing left of the person when it is stripped, in thought, of its specific social layers. It is natural to call this third view simply the 'social' conception of the person. The core of the social person includes a pattern of needs that is peculiar to a given epoch and to groups to which the person belongs, such as race and class. Though the pattern changes, some of the needs—the four survival needs—that are patterned do not change.

This conception of the person—to be developed fully in Part Three—puts a foundation under the view that conflict between person and group is what gives action an ethical dimension. Suppose you are a woman who has just been offered a sizeable increase in salary to assist the male employment officer in your workplace in reviewing job applicants. Pay in your current job classification is little above the legal minimum, and you have several dependents. You need the extra money from the new job to move to an adequate apartment in a safe area. This need does not stem from your nature in isolation but from the social conditions of deprivation. It became clear when the job was approved that it was to be a screen. Your being a woman would be used to protect management if it were charged with sexual discrimination in hiring. After all, with a woman reviewing applicants how could women be discriminated against? The old policy of employing women for only the lowest paying jobs would, in fact, not be changed.[5] Management had thought, perhaps mistakenly, that you would have no qualms about being its screen.

You need a better apartment, but as a woman you would support demands for non-discriminatory hiring. At least you would support these demands once the initiative had been taken by someone else in agitating for them. In supporting these demands, you would reveal that what you are has been formed by being a member of your sex. One of the interests of this group is an end to sexual discrimination in hiring. There is, then, a conflict between this interest of the group and your need for adequate housing, which is not based on selfishness but on social deprivation. The conflict exists because by taking the job you provide management with a cover for continuing discriminatory hiring.

The conflict is not with something alien like the oak block, for the group whose direction conflicts with your need for adequate housing is one that has been internalized by you. It is part of your core self that you would support demands for ending discrimination. This tendency to support those demands is a bridge between yourself and the group. It keeps the group from being alien like the oak block, as it is on the atomic view. The group interest has a call on you since this interest has partly formed what you are. In deciding what to do—to accept or to reject the job—you have an ethical question on your hands. Your need for a better place to live is not to be ignored, but neither is the need of the group for support for its goal, which you have internalized.

In sum, the social person, as the very expression implies, contains tendencies that are a bridge between the person and the group. Those tendencies are part of the core person but are also formed as a result of membership in the group.[6] In taking the group seriously one is indirectly taking one's person seriously. A conflict between the person and a group is not, then, a conflict between two alien entities, as was the case for the atomic view of persons. Yet it does not reduce to a conflict within one entity, since the bridge is one from the person to something distinct from the person, a group. From a conflict such as this it is natural that standards of an ethical sort should emerge. Since you do internalize the interest of women in ending discrimination, there is a genuine conflict within yourself. But it is only because this inner conflict reflects a conflict between your needs and group interest that it too can be characterized as ethical.

Nothing said so far determines how the conflict between your need and group interest is to be resolved. Neither the person nor the group has been given priority in deciding ethical matters. We must now ask how such a conflict is to be resolved.

Notes

1 Plato, *Republic* (written in the fourth century B. C.), trans. F. M. Cornford, Oxford University Press, New York, 1945, 421, 444, 586.
2 Plato refers to 'a pattern set up in the heavens' as a possible norm for a commonwealth, in *Republic* 592.
3 What you really are is, then, what you are in what used to be called a 'state of nature'. See John Locke, *Second Treatise of Government* (first published in 1690), Bobbs-Merrill, Indianapolis, 1952, Sec. 4.
4 Benito Mussolini, *The Political and Social Doctrine of Fascism*, trans. J. Soames, Hogarth, London, 1933, pp. 21-2.
5 See the anonymous article 'We usually don't hire married girls', in *The Capitalist System*, 2nd ed., eds R. C. Edwards, M. Reich, and T. E. Weisskopf, Prentice-Hall, Englewood Cliffs, N. J., 1978, pp. 13-15.
6 For a fuller development of this theme than will be attempted below in Part Three, see Lucien Sève, *Man in Marxist Theory and the Psychology of Personality*, trans. J. MacGreal, Harvester, Hassocks, 1978.

II

Ethical Naturalism

How are conflicts between the person and the group to be resolved? Are we to favour the person, the group, or each under different circumstances? Neither the *isolated* person nor the *alien* group is to be favoured by valid ethical principles. Fortunately, we deal in reality with a *social* person. The social person breaks down any sharp division between the person and the group. The social person has, as part of his or her nature, tendencies that act as a bridge to the group. This chapter advances the view that valid ethical principles must accord with the nature of the social person—with the core social person. Neither the person nor the group becomes the exclusive focus since the nature of the person is in part shaped by the group to which the person belongs.

To defend this view of valid ethical principles, it will be necessary to defend 'ethical naturalism'. The ethical naturalist holds that it is the nature of persons that is the basis for the validity of ethical principles. When backed up by a social theory of persons, ethical naturalism leads to the view that social factors enter into determining the validity of ethical principles.

1 Self-interest and enlightened self-interest There is a whole range of principles for ranking, in regard to rightness, the demands of the person and those of his or her group. Four of them will be mentioned, between which there are doubtless others. Only later, in Section 4, shall a decision be made between them. In this section, the first two, which give primacy to self-interest, will be discussed. In Section 2, the two that emphasize the group will be discussed. All four are very general since they are not ethical principles themselves. They are really standards for choosing entire sets of ethical principles, where each ethical principle, is understood to deal with a specific kind of action. These four general principles could then be called 'meta-principles'.

At the one extreme there is the principle of *selfishness*. This principle says it is right to act as the selfish person would act. The selfish person pursues what *appears* satisfying to that person. (This need not be what actually is satisfying to that person.) As a result the selfish person tends to avoid entanglements with groups. Such a person avoids getting involved in a group in a way that promises no obvious net payoff for him or herself.

It is assumed by the principle of selfishness that persons face groups as fully determined individuals. They know what they want and look to groups merely to see what the groups can offer in the way of satisfaction. This is clear since the principle of selfishness supposes that the person makes his or her choice about involvement with a group from a standpoint outside the group. If the person is convinced that the group can be manipulated for his or her already formed needs without any great sacrifice to the group, then that group becomes an appropriate tool for the selfish person. The selfish person rides a group to his or her own apparent satisfaction. The selfish person avoids entanglements with groups by determining, prior to getting involved with a group, that the apparent sacrifice needed to get the group's support is less than the apparent satisfaction coming to the person from the group.

Thomas Hobbes assumed that successful social organization had to begin with the assumption that the people to be organized are selfish. 'For no man gives but with intention of good to himself . . . ; if men *see* they shall be frustrated, there will be no beginning of benevolence or trust nor consequently of mutual help nor of reconciliation of one man to another.'[1] Hobbes was an optimist despite his assumption that people were selfish. He thought selfish people would 'see' that social organization, as opposed to social chaos which he called war, would have a net payoff.

Selfishness involves a certain blindness, or at least a certain lack of caution. The avoidance of those involvements with others that put demands on oneself with no obvious net payoff is many times the source of unsatisfying situations for the self. This results from the fact that the selfish person, who like anyone is fallible, pursues only what *appears* satisfying. One might have thought, for example, that being able to manipulate people would give one great satisfaction. But after getting over all of the hurdles in the way of having this power over others, one has in fact created a situation in which those one manipulates have sacrificed their self-respect and have become cringing animals. In manipulating them one feels disgust and satisfaction eludes one.

Next there is the possibility of adopting the principle of *enlightened self-interest*. The conviction that one can pursue what appears to lead to personal satisfaction and reach actual satisfaction is seen many times to have disastrous consequences. One then substitutes for this conviction the attitude that since humans are fallible entanglements with groups have a point. Groups can often act as a cushion by keeping the worst situations that might happen from being as bad as they otherwise might be. Groups are like insurance: when the worst happens, one is better off with them than without them. One comes to be willing to sacrifice what appears to be more satisfying personally for the security offered by the group. The amount of sacrifice for the group needed to gain this security would be more than the selfish person would be willing to make. Behaviour enabling one to gain this security would be right only according to the principle of enlightened self-interest.

If the worst happens to one's home—it is destroyed by fire or earthquake—, insurance makes that situation less dire than it would be without it. More generally, if one is unable to feel secure about one's life, freedom, and possessions without the support of others, then one might guard against losing such support by entering into cooperative efforts to realize the interests of the group. Thus John Locke was following the principle of enlightened self-interest when he approved the formation of a civil community, based on consent, as a means to 'a secure enjoyment of property' and to 'comfortable, safe, and peaceful living'.[2] Still, the selfish person might reason that it is better to risk the worst occurring than to make the personal sacrifice needed to gain the support of such a community.

In the view of enlightened self-interest, the person is, nonetheless, viewed as already constituted in his or her core before allegiance to the programme of any group is called for. The person is an atomic person. One surveys groups in terms of their ability to provide 'insurance' relative to an already given set of self-interests. As will be explained in Chapter VI, Section 1, core atomic persons with these interests seem to enter into a contract with one another for group protection. Thus the person is not antecedently social, but becomes social through accepting a group as a bulwark against catastrophe.

2 Group interest and selflessness The third and fourth principles for ranking, in regard to rightness, the person and the group begin with the person as part of a group. The third principle is difficult to differentiate from the second without reference back to the difference between the atomic and the social person. The third principle is based on the social view of the person, and it is the one to be adopted here. It can be called the principle of *group interest*. The fourth principle will be based on the erroneous aspect view of the person and will be called the *selflessness* principle.

Since a core person is social, groups will not be reviewed for choice by a person like so many suits in a shop. When it is a question of which of several competing clubs to join, the club that is chosen will, like a suit, be the one that seems to fit best. But let us talk about groups that are non-voluntary associations, such as a race and a class. The person has been formed by a group, such as his or her race or class, even before being fully aware of belonging to such a group. The goals that characterize the group are the ones that have shaped the person's own everyday responses prior to joining voluntary associations.[3] The characteristic features of one's class, say, influence one's attitudes, explicit evaluations, and basic personal aims.

What does this tell us about the resolution of person-group conflict? It tells us that one cannot go against one's group without at the same time going against what one has become. The principle of group interest has its plausibility on the basis of this coincidence between the group and human nature. It asserts that in a conflict between the person and the group the right thing to do will advance the characteristic interests of the group.

There are some qualifications that cannot be discussed in detail yet. First, persons will be influenced by groups other than those they belong to. This is important since it tells us about the source of needs that conflict with the interests of groups to which a person does belong. But it will be argued that most of these needs have only a precarious existence and are thus not part of the person's nature. The rest are such that only they can be eliminated in forming a coherent human nature out of one that is rent with conflict. Second, groups too will be influenced by groups external to them. This can lead to features that tend in directions opposite to the characteristic interests of groups. The principle of group interest asserts the primacy of the characteristic interests of groups and not of features imposed on them in conflict with other groups.

The important thing about the group-interest principle is that the group is appealed to in resolving conflict only because the person is formed in groups. The group is also appealed to in resolving conflict in the case in which enlightened self-interest has led one to identify with a group. But the reason for the appeal is clearly different; the group is appealed to because the principle of enlightened self-interest refers us to groups as sources of security. Yet as sources of security the groups protect personal interests with which, as in the atomic view of the self, they have only a contingent connection.

Not all groups are important for ethical life. Class, race, nation, sex, and family are important, whereas sophomores, wearers of size eleven shoes, and gardeners are less important, if important at all. Moreover, among the important groups, class is preeminent since, as will be argued in Chapter IV, class domination provides the basis for continuing racial and other forms of domination. In natural science, the important kinds of entities are those for which the fundamental laws get formulated. Those entities have the capacities that underlie the behaviour we observe. Thus molecules are more important than clouds in thermodynamics, and electrons more important than lightning in the theory of electricity. In a theory of society, the important kinds of groups will appear in the fundamental explanations of conflicts within society. In the Preface, it was noted that a theory of society was relevant to ethics because ethics deals with group conflict. Obviously, then, the kinds of groups important for a theory of society will be the ones important in ethics.

It is not merely enlightened self-interest that gets us to identify with the struggles of the important groups. The person already pursues some goals because of being formed in one or more of these important groups. The purpose of pursuing these goals is not, then, merely to help us realize pre-social goals, as it would be if the purpose was enlightened self-interest. Rather, the social person pursues, among other things, a characteristic patterning in realizing pre-social needs. This patterning is not simply for the sake of the pre-social needs, but is something aimed at by persons shaped in certain groups. The goal of improving educational opportunity and that of shortening the working day are pursued to realize the needs for food, sex, support, and deliberation in a distinctive interrelationship. Group existence makes the need for the patterning part of the person. The patterning is not freely chosen as a means of insuring against catastrophe.

The fourth and final principle—the principle of selflessness—goes one step further and requires that conflicts between the person and the group be resolved by submerging the person entirely within the group. This is the extreme selflessness of the aspect view of the person. Here the group is given a destiny of its own that determines the destinies of its members. To realize this destiny, the members must sacrifice themselves. Mussolini thought that fascism correctly perceived that the individual was nothing and that all that mattered was duty to the higher goal of the state. Under this principle of selflessness, the overarching group is personified in the crown, in the dictator, or in an elite. In practice, then, this kind of selflessness turns out to be a denial of person for a single leader or an elite, not for a large group that includes oneself.

How, though, does selflessness differ from our third standard, the principle of group interest? Primarily by the fact that selflessness means, in principle at least, limiting one's role to supporting something beyond persons altogether, whereas in deciding conflicts by what was called group interest one decides in favour of supporting the realization of the social persons in a group. On the third view, then, when one supports the group, one can recognize that one supports the realization of one's self, not as on the fourth view the immolation of the self.

3   The postulates of ethical naturalism   We shall determine which of the above four meta-principles is valid against the background of ethical naturalism. The task of this section is to explain what ethical naturalism is.

When we are taught an ethics, most teachers give us the impression that it has the backing of the highest authority. Each principle in the ethics is, we come to think, a command from on high. This impression is deepened by the fact that those who instruct us in ethical codes are for us figures of authority themselves; they are parents, school teachers, or political leaders. And they use their own authority in the teaching of an ethics to convey to us the idea that its principles are backed by something stronger than even their own authority. For a time we are content to regard these rules as these teachers would have us regard them. But when their authority recedes into the past, we wonder what it is that provides a backing for ethical principles. Just why are they so authoritative?

So long as we accept an ethical code as most of our teachers would have us accept it—as authoritative to the highest degree—we are likely to be unsatisfied with any account of its authoritativeness that restricts itself to familiar factors of life. We shall, then, be pushed in the direction of higher realities than those with which we are familiar. The code becomes endowed with an eternal existence in a realm transcending our world.

Yet when the authority of our teachers recedes, we are more likely to be impressed by another aspect of ethical codes. We are likely to be impressed with the fact that a given ethical code serves a *purpose* within the confines of a certain social organization that it could not serve outside those confines. It then appears to us that the authority of the code does not carry beyond those confines. With this discovery, we are more likely to look for the basis of its authoritativeness in terms of the familiar factors of life.

Once we look to familiar factors of life, we have the beginnings of a naturalistic viewpoint in the study of ethics. We end up rejecting the view that the authority of an ethical code can be explained only in terms of a spiritual structure hidden in our minds, or only in terms of pure ideals that do not exist in the space-time world but in some fifth dimension that runs off from it, or in terms of the commands of God. In short, we end up saying that ethical life—life as evaluated in ethical terms—can be fully accounted for without appeal to the supranatural. Ethical naturalism has as its *first postulate*:

I   Ethical life and all that on which it depends is totally encompassed within the universe of people, their groups, and the material things they use.

Not just the authority but also the origin and the validity of ethical codes are matters to be accounted for in this universe of people, groups, and things.

Some people believe in the existence of a separate realm of entities that is more basic than the universe of people, groups, and things. The universe is seen by them as derivative from these 'higher' entities. The familiar universe is either made out of spiritual structures hidden in our minds. Or it is an image of those pure ideals in our mythical fifth dimension. Or it is the creation of God. The general world-view these people adopt, which puts people, groups, and things in a derivative or secondary position, is called 'idealism'. The view that puts this familiar universe in the basic or primary position is 'materialism', in a broad sense. The naturalistic view of ethics is, then, a form of materialism, whereas non-naturalism in ethics is a form of idealism. Both non-naturalism in ethics and idealism introduce entities 'higher' than people, groups, and material things.

The first postulate of naturalism tells us to look at the world of people, groups, and things, but it does not tell us what to look for. In deciding ethical principles we do not want to concentrate simply on the image people have of themselves. We know that this is often misleading as to what they really are. This is not because people are inherently prone to error about themselves, but because people live in a world of conflicting groups. The more powerful among the conflicting groups have a decisive influence on communication and education. They are, then, able to build up in people a distorted image of what they are. So the factors the pollster concentrates on, in order to determine the image people have of themselves, cannot be the only ones that the ethical naturalist is interested in.

This leads to the *second postulate* of ethical naturalism:

II   Human nature is the ultimate basis for the origin, the authority, and the validity of ethical principles.

Thus the ethical naturalism put forward here is a humanistic kind of naturalism. The nature of the human person is the focus of ethical study. A set of principles governing the good, right, obligatory, and fair is not something that grows up and gets its credentials outside human life in a blind physical or technical struggle. But at the same time this is not an abstract humanism. It does not put a human nature which is formed independently of the social and material forces around the person at the centre of the study of ethical life. It is a humanism that accepts the social conception of the person according to which part of any person's nature is formed through the membership in groups.

The second postulate, when joined with the social view of the person, tells us that the validity of an ethical principle depends on its not being contrary to what a person is as formed in a given social and material context. Of course, this gives rise to the difficult question as to how one tells what accords with what one really is. If the pollster cannot find out by superficial empirical methods, then what methods will do? It is not what people will say so much as what they are willing to do in a collective way that is the index of what they are.

Out of a fear created by constant harassment, the people of a certain group may have appeared to be passive, docile, and contented. Conditions may arise, though, which create among them a sense of collective power that overcomes that fear. Emboldened by this sense of power, they act in ways that enable them to see what their needs actually are. Struggle is their method for gaining self-knowledge. Through struggle it becomes clear to them that the old code of docility was not the product of what they actually were. It was the joint product of their own fear in face of intimidation and of the intimidator's propaganda about them. The old code was not valid; its authority derived from the dominant position of people outside their group; and its origin was oppression. Their proper ethics, whether they be blacks or women, becomes an ethics of overcoming this oppression.

The most compelling reason for holding the naturalistic approach to ethics is that it accords with a reasonable conception of the kind of knowing that guides practical activity. Such knowing is an aspect of doing. It is not something that belongs in a compartment separate from doing.

Suppose knowing an ethical principle were a matter of putting one's self in relation to an otherworldly realm. It is hard to see how knowing this principle could be an aspect of practical activity. If it could not be, then, ethical knowledge could never play the role it should play of guiding activity. Merely finding some entity in another world calls for no action. Even if that entity is interpreted as an imperative there is no call to obey it just because it is out there. In short, such knowing would be purely contemplative and not an aspect of doing.

If, however, ethical naturalism is correct, an ethical code emerges within the familiar universe where persons struggle in a material and social context. It functions to expedite the winning of that struggle. Its validity is then to be judged in terms of whether it furthers or impedes the realization of the possibilities opened up by the nature the person has in that context. As John Dewey, the American naturalist philosopher, put it, 'When the belief that knowledge is active and operative takes hold of men, the ideal realm is no longer something aloof and separate; it is rather that collection of imagined possibilities that stimulates men to new efforts and realizations'.[4] In the naturalist view, different material and social conditions create different possibilities for the person and thereby give rise to different ethical codes. Knowing these codes is part of taking these possibilities in hand and shaping a future. The validity of these codes is not a matter that is separable from their origins. For they will not be valid if they thwart the realization of these possibilities.

4   Choosing among principles   Does ethical naturalism, as defined by the two postulates of Section 3, tell us which of the four meta-principles for deciding between the person and the group, enumerated in Sections 1 and 2, is to be adopted? The answer is that, when the social theory of the person is assumed, ethical naturalism eliminates three of the four meta-principles, leaving only the principle of group interest.

To support the principle of *selfishness* would be, from the point of view of ethical naturalism, to suppose that the core person is what it is independent of group membership. Since, however, the core person is a product of social interaction, selfishness would lead to behaviour that ultimately makes the realization of many of the important possibilities for the person impossible. The reason is simply that by avoiding group entanglements the person forfeits the realization of those among his or her possibilities that depend on cooperation and mutual understanding. The selfish person is not, then, acting naturally but rather acting in a way that puts obstacles before the most natural ways of action for a social person.

This argument against selfishness does not suppose that humans, considered in abstraction from groups, have as a fixed part of their nature a feeling of benevolence for other humans, as was supposed by the British philosopher David Hume.[5] Rather, benevolence or fellow feeling is a consequence of the social view of the person, not a starting point for it. It is not because people have fellow feelings that they join together in groups. It is rather because what they are involves them in practical relations with one another that they develop fellow feeling. The selfish person puts obstacles in the way of those practical relations and thus thwarts the realization of human nature. Benevolence, however, often promotes its realization.

The principle of *enlightened self-interest* might seem to get around the problem of realizing the group aspect of human nature. For this principle encourages group involvement for the sake of realizing the atomic person. By encouraging group involvement it seems to insist on the realization of the group aspect of human nature as well.

The appearances are, though, deceptive. In reality no person is ever a mere pre-social entity looking for a group that is most likely to advance its pre-social needs. Any person is already a social being. This has the important consequence that the group a person might choose as best for realizing his or her pre-social needs could be one that blocks the social needs that person already has. Thus enlightened self-interest could easily lead to a one-sided development of the human individual, realizing pre-social at the expense of already acquired social needs.

This is in fact what happens when people accept reforms that do not fundamentally alter the fact that they are being dominated by others. Return to our woman employee of Chapter I, Section 4. Her unfulfilled need for a better apartment is a consequence of a system of inequality, and is thus socially conditioned. But behind this lies a need for shelter that is not socially conditioned. Once we artificially abstract this pre-social need from the context of social inequality, she can be considered as someone who might take care of the pre-social need for shelter by accepting the system of discrimination imposed by management. Her acceptance of that system would be enlightened self-interest, if the self is taken as a one-sided being that belongs to no group. But in fact she does belong to the group of women and part of what she is is determined by that fact. Thus her cooperation in the system of discrimination for the sake of a better salary would go against the realization of what she is as a woman. This would, nonetheless, be an act of enlightened self-interest since cooperation with management would help insure the satisfaction of the pre-social needs making up the pre-social person. The principle of enlightened self-interest fails, though, to accord with ethical naturalism since it leads to behaviour that is not in accord with the social nature of humans.

The defect of the principle of *selflessness* comes from an entirely different direction. It too violates the second postulate of ethical naturalism. It does so by leading to a denial of the person altogether, whereas the principles of selfishness and enlightened self-interest violated the second postulate by denying only the social part of human nature. How, though, can the social part of the person be denied if the goal of the overarching group is to be realized? For this the group goal has to become the goal of an entity of which persons are mere aspects. Its goal is not then simply the set of goals of the persons in it. The Nazis in Germany justified their imperialist ambitions by attributing to a nation a spatial drive. Frontiers were not lines but limits on the national organism's 'geo-political force'.[6] Even the goals persons pursue as a result of being aspects of the group may have to be sacrificed as this mysterious geopolitical force pushes to the national goal. There is then no part of the person—pre-social or social—that is sacred in relation to the group goal.

We are then left with the principle of *group interest*. Since the person is formed in a group some of his or her needs will be formed by the group and their realization will be promoted by the group. Even the degree to which needs common to all persons, irrespective of group, can be satisfied will be raised by being a member of a group. A policy of ignoring interests characteristic of the group will, then, be one that goes against the grain for the persons in it. There are two reasons for this. First, an adequate realization of these *common* needs—the ones had irrespective of group—generally becomes more difficult when group interests are widely ignored. Not all poor kids are Horatio Algers, who can make it rich. Not even all workers can be supervisors, who avoid exploitation. For most people in lower classes or oppressed groups, solidarity with their group is the means by which they can improve the degree to which both they and the group are able to realize the common needs. Second, the realization of the *special* needs for cooperative behaviour and mutual understanding that result from growing up inside the group would be frustrated if people in the group took to ignoring its distinctive interests. The group would thereby be weakened and would be less able to promote the realization of these special needs. The ethical naturalist must, then, insist that, when interests characteristic of the group are in conflict with other needs of a member of the group, the conflict is to be resolved in favour of group interests. Otherwise, human nature is blocked.

Is this not a tyranny of the group over the private individual? It is often represented as such. But nothing is farther from the truth; there is nothing that corresponds to what would have to be meant here by the private individual. The private individual would have, on its own in isolation from social influences, certain urgent needs that would pit the individual against the group. Wilt Chamberlain would as a private individual want to play basketball at Madison Square Garden precisely when American blacks were making a crucial push toward liberation. But this desire has to be seen in the context of gate-paying crowds, profit-making team owners and gymnasium owners, and sports-writers' ballyhoo. These factors are important in Chamberlain's desire to make the performance at the Garden. They belong to a system of marketing entertainment and have little to do with being black. So the conflict between Chamberlain's need to play and his group's interests in liberation is not in any way a conflict between a private individual and the group. The needs that conflict with groups—though often appearing as purely personal—have their source in the standards and conditions created by yet other groups.

This puts the conflict between the woman employee's need for better housing and her group's interest in non-discriminatory hiring into perspective. Her need for housing is genuine and thus she has a genuine need for the larger salary she would get by helping the company continue sexual discrimination. If we say that she should take the job, apologizing for her on the grounds that a single individual cannot fight for women's rights, then any woman can be excused from entering the fight on the grounds that her presence will not make the difference needed for victory. Beginning the fight by saying NO to co-optation is as good a place as any to start. There is the additional fact that her very need for better housing has its source in the system of discrimination that allows women in the US to earn only 60 per cent of what men earn when both are employed full-time. Helping management discriminate would perpetuate the conditions from which she herself has suffered.

Saying NO to co-optation is not in this case adequately described as denying oneself personal satisfaction. For, by entering the struggle for women's liberation, one is taking a step toward ending those conditions that deny one adequate housing. The important difference here is the one between immediate and deferred satisfaction. By deferring the satisfaction one remains true to one's nature as formed by the group of women, and one can expect the support of other women over common problems. By choosing the immediate satisfaction of getting better housing, one is at odds with oneself as a social person formed by one's sex, and the support of other women over common problems will become more elusive.

Notes

1   Thomas Hobbes, *Leviathan* (1651), Bobbs-Merrill, Indianapolis, 1958, Pt. I,
    Ch. XV, p. 125 (italics mine).
2   John Locke, *Second Treatise of Government*, Sec. 95.
3   'But the human essence is no abstraction inherent in each single individual. In
    its reality it is the ensemble of social relations' (Karl Marx, *Theses on
    Feuerbach VI* (1845) in *The German Ideology*, International Publishers, New
    York, 1970, p. 122).
4   John Dewey, *Reconstruction in Philosophy*, Henry Holt, New York, 1920,
    p. 118.
5   David Hume, *An Inquiry Concerning the Principles of Morals* (1751), Sec. V,
    Pt. II, in David Hume, *Enquiries*, 2nd ed., ed. L. A. Selby-Bigge, Clarendon
    Press, Oxford, 1902.
6   Franz Neumann, *Behemoth : The Structure and Practice of National Socialism :
    1933–44* (1944), Harper & Row, New York, 1966, Pt. I, Ch. V, Sec. 2.

III

Are there Ethical Absolutes?

So far it has been claimed that the validity of ethical principles is to be determined from the point of view of ethical naturalism. From this point of view, valid ethical principles are ones that accord with human nature. The question to be asked now is whether the validity of ethical principles is absolute or relative. The themes developed in the last two chapters will be sufficient to yield an answer to this question. For, from the fact that persons have a social nature and that ethics is naturalistic, it follows that the validity of ethical principles is relative rather than absolute.

1 What are absolutes? Claims about velocity are relative claims. To say that I am walking at a rate of four miles per hour is to make a relative claim. It is relative to a system in reference to which the velocity is measured. Suppose I make the claim about myself while walking along the deck of a boat, taking measurements on the basis of the deck as the system of reference. The distance I move on the deck, *per* unit of time, is my velocity relative to the deck. But the claim about me might have been made by someone on the bank as I passed by on the moving boat, with measurements taken in reference to the bank. The distance I move in front of and away from the bank, *per* unit of time, is my velocity relative to the bank. These facts are summed up by saying that velocity is not absolute but relative to a frame of reference.

This analogy will help us in formulating ethical relativity. Still, ethical relativity involves some special complications. In ethics there are many kinds of reference systems, whereas in the case of velocity only physical objects are reference systems. Ethical claims might be relative to individual persons; we would then have 'individual' relativism. They might be relative only to groups of persons; we would then have 'social' relativism. They might be relative only to historical epochs, each of which would contain many social groups; in this case we would have 'epochal' relativism. If ethical principles are absolute, they are not relative in these or any other ways. If they are absolute, there is no individual person, no special group, and not even a particular epoch that can be a reference system for the validity of the principles.

Just what sort of reference system is an individual, a group, or an epoch? The deck is a reference system for my walking in that I measure the distance I move by starting from some point on the deck. But for ethical purposes the reference system includes a characteristic set of tendencies. It is drives, desires, interests, needs, aversions, inhibitions and the like that are the tendencies important for ethics. This accords with ethical naturalism, since such tendencies are aspects of what people are. An individual person's characteristic tendencies to behave in certain ways would, then, be an indispensable basis for assessing ethical principles relative to that person. In the context of social relativism, the tendencies characteristic of members of a given group are an indispensable basis for assessing ethical principles relative to that group.

There is nothing mysterious about tendencies. We not only attribute them to people but also to all other physical entities. Trees tend to get moss on the north side of their trunks; unpainted nails tend to stain with rust the wood they are driven into; foxes tend to dig their holes on slopes. When we say that there is a tendency we usually mean a bit more than when we say there is merely a capacity. Surely foxes have a capacity to dig their holes in a lot of places, but you find their holes more often on slopes. So a tendency is a capacity *plus* a conditional likelihood. Since foxes have a tendency to dig their holes on slopes, they not only have the capacity to do so, but given the presence of slopes it is likely they will have dug holes on some slopes. The presence of slopes is here the condition for the likelihood.

It is an easy step to apply this explanation to tendencies characteristic of members of a group, or in short 'group tenden-cies'. The only new idea in the case of a tendency important for ethics is the idea of the tendency being 'characteristic' of some-thing, in this case a group. To say that the tendency is characteris-tic of a group is to say that the tendency is to be explained on the basis of what being a member of the group implies about its members. Being a member of a family normally implies being a member of a system of mutual enrichment that is cooperative to the extent that age and ability allow. This relation of cooperative enrichment is the explanatory base for tendencies characteristic of members of the family. It explains the tendency of parents to feel a bond with their children they do not feel with the children of others. It explains the tendency not to grant affection strictly on a basis of deserts. Group tendencies are then capacities characteris-tic of members of the group that are likely to be actualized given certain circumstances. The circumstances are often exceptional rather than familiar, since dominant groups attempt to block the realization of tendencies of the groups they dominate.[1]

What then is an ethical absolute? It is an ethical principle that is valid in respect to a set of tendencies that is itself absolute. In other words, this set of tendencies is not one characteristic merely of a single individual, a single group, or a single epoch. It is to be found in any individual in any group in any epoch. Not just any such set will do. For no ethical absolute can be valid just on the basis of a one-sided view of what humans are. The set of tendencies on which absolute principles are based can be nothing short of a set of tendencies that together manifest *all* of what it is to be a human. So an ethical absolute can be valid only in respect to a total human nature that is both trans-social and trans-historical.

Why must it be total? The mere fact that some set of tendencies, say the set composed of the needs for food and sex, is typical of humans generally does not make this set a sufficient basis for ethical absolutes. Humans are more than such a partial set of needs. Their other needs will interact with those in the partial set. Restrictions will have to be put on the realization of needs in the partial set to make it more possible to realize the remaining needs. These restrictions are essential if human nature as a more or less coherent structure is to be realized. Yet ethical naturalism requires that the coherent structure not be blocked. The formulation of ethical absolutes must, then, depend on reference to a *total* human nature.

It is doubtful, though, that human nature is absolute. Having a trans-historical human nature would be like having a unique spatial reference system—an absolute space—which is 'really' at rest. Since people are social in the way indicated in Chapter I, Section 4, there is no trans-social and trans-historical human nature. For, many of the tendencies manifesting the natures of such social persons are ones they have as a result of belonging to certain groups in certain epochs. It is as fruitless to pursue an absolute human nature—one any human in any group in any epoch has—in anthropology as it has been to pursue an absolute space in physics.

Ethical absolutism has been the dominant theme among philosophers who have developed an ethical theory. Immanuel Kant, for example, adopted an absolutism that led him to propose a requirement of universality. He expressed this requirement by saying that no action should be taken except on the basis of a principle that the agent is prepared to have everyone act on.[2] Suppose the principle of the businessperson who invests in ventures in less developed countries is that, if personal gain requires it, people can be subjected to violence. The people on whom the violence will descend are, in this case, the natives in the less developed countries where this businessperson has invested. By Kant's test—which he called the 'categorical imperative'—the foreign investor should not act unless he or she is prepared to have the natives, and indeed anyone else, act on this same principle that sanctions the use of violence for personal gain. He or she must, then, be prepared to be subjected to violence from any side for the sake of someone else's gain. In these circumstances, everyone risks losing and, Kant would hope, once the investor recognizes this he or she should then give up this principle of action.

Of course our foreign investor will be no Kantian universalist, at least not where his or her interests and those of his or her class are better served by a relativism incompatible with universalism. Our investor will think that the principle that violence can be used if needed to protect personal gain is true relative to the nature of foreign investors and is not universally valid. Natives, for example, have no right to protect themselves by guerrilla violence since they have a different nature.

Is there not a way of making this relativism compatible with the Kantian requirement of universality? The principle that foreign investors in less developed countries have a right to protect their gains by organized violence is formally universal since it applies to everyone who happens to be a foreign investor in less developed countries. Still, those who accept this principle are not willing to allow everyone, without restriction, to use violence to protect personal gain. Though formally universal, the principle is not universal in content since it does not apply to all persons. The Kantian would rightly reject this principle since the investors who hold it would not be willing to extend its application to literally everyone, including natives.

The Kantian requirement of universality is not compatible with this relativism; it is, as we shall see in the next paragraph, an expression of absolutism. The principle that violence can be used to protect personal gain is, for the foreign investor, valid relative to the tendencies of a particular group, the group of foreign investors. This principle does not hold relative to the tendencies of the opposed group, the natives. This relativity, espoused implicitly or explicitly by the foreign investor who wants to be righteous, conflicts with Kantian universality. Is it possible to defend Kantian universalism against the investor relativist?

To answer, we must ask what is behind Kant's test of universality. Kant thought rational tendencies fully constituted the nature of humans as they are in themselves and not just as they appear to be. Thus these tendencies were sufficient for assessing ethical principles. Moreover, he thought we were *all* equal as rational beings, however the appearances of rationality might differ. This view of human nature is absolutist: human nature is the same in all groups and epochs. This absolutism committed Kant to his requirement of universality for ethical principles by the following line of thought. Whatever the social and historical context, we all have the same human nature. An ethical principle valid for some of us that is not valid for others would not be based on what we are in ourselves, our human nature. So a single human nature requires that a principle valid for one of us be equally valid for all of us. Such a conception of a single rational nature for all humans will be impossible to square with the social conception of the person. The defence of the social conception of the person in Part Three, will, thus, undercut the foundations of Kantian absolutism and hence of his universalism.

2   The ethical as the final arbiter   It is easier to criticize a defence of another position than it is to build a defence of one's own. So we start here with a criticism of the central defence of absolutism, before turning to the more difficult job of defending relativism in the next section. Both the criticism and the defence are preliminary, and will be greatly extended in the rest of the book.

The central defence of absolutism comes from a common conception of ethical life itself. Defences of absolutism by appeal to principles existing in some spiritual dimension or to a trans-historical conception of the person, such as Kant's, are so many rationalizations built out around this central defence. If human life has an ethical dimension, it should be possible—according to the central defence—to resolve *all* conflicts by appeal to ethical principles. It should be possible to tell everyone how to resolve their conflicts in no matter what situation. Why is this important? If the parties to conflicts are responsive at all to ethical principles and authority, there is no need for a resort to force to settle conflicts. It is this grand conception of the ethical, rather than force, as the final arbiter that has inspired so many philosophers. But if this grand conception is to be any more than an illusion, there must be absolute ethical principles. For if the parties locked in conflict cannot discover a norm that transcends their differences, they will abide by the relative standards that led them into conflict, and a resort to force will be inevitable.

Is ethics in fact a final arbiter? Is this conception of ethical life the correct one? The answer to be given here is NO. To say ethics is not a final arbiter is to say more than that there will always be conflicts terminated by the threat or the use of force. The resort to force may imply only that ethics is ignored as a final arbiter. Though not *actually* the final arbiter, ethics *could be* the final arbiter. Yet the view of ethical life advanced in this book implies that ethics *could not* play the role of final arbiter at all.

Reinhold Niebuhr held that relations between groups would always be 'predominantly political rather than ethical'. Still, he believed that there were absolutes, such as equality, that could function as the final arbiter. These absolutes do not actually play the role of final arbiter because of what he took to be the unavoidability of 'human selfishness'.[3] The important things is that for Niebuhr ethical life itself implies the possibility that ethics is a final arbiter.

Sometimes abstractions run away with us, and this is what has happened in the absolutist's argument. It is true we said that the ethical concerns conflicts between persons and their groups and hence that ethical principles are designed to cope with such conflicts. At the time one might have thought that the groups involved could be any groups, even the most far-reaching. Since then enough has been said to make clear the necessity for certain restrictions on what the relevant groups are. The absolutist wants to ignore those restrictions and thus treat a provisional abstraction as though it were a final truth.

The restrictions derive from the social conception of the person, which claims that at least part of what a person is is fixed by groups to which the person belongs. Conflicts between a person and a group, and hence between that person and other persons in the group, are not to be resolved in a way that undercuts that part of the person's nature resulting from membership in some other group. This is just a consequence of sticking with ethical naturalism. A worker and an owner are both members of that far-reaching group called capitalist society. A conflict between the two is one that is not to be resolved by denying the worker, say, some aspect of his or her nature that results from being a member of the working class. This is a serious restriction since, due to the antagonistic relation of classes to one another, many such conflicts between worker and owner cannot be resolved without curtailing the realization of the nature of one or the other. To insist at this point that ethics is still a final arbiter would be to insist that ethics resolve conflicts in ways that undercut what people are.

Ethics concerns conflicts between persons and only certain of their groups. Some groups are too broad to be reference groups for ethics since resolving conflicts in them would undercut aspects of human nature derived from narrower groups. The absolutist, for whom ethics is a final arbiter, claims there is an ethical resolution of conflicts even in reference to the broadest group, the human race. Such a resolution will, on the one hand, be in terms of ethical principles held to be valid on the basis of only an abstract and hence one-sided view of what humans are. It will, on the other hand, violate any more adequate conceptions of what humans are by undercutting aspects of their natures derived from membership in narrower groups.

In opposition to this abstraction, the view supported here is that the relevant groups are ones within which common purpose runs deeper than systematic opposition. Ethical life arises from conflicts between persons and these groups. Ethical principles, which guide us in resolving these conflicts, are relative to these groups. The human race or even the totality of capitalist society is so far-reaching a group that it contains systematically opposed groups. This systematic opposition of groups implies that the resolution of some conflicts will thwart the development of people in one or more of those groups. Ethics in such a case becomes a pretension of universality to cover pleading for special interests. While this pretension lasts, any resort to force can be blamed on 'human weakness'.

Thus, we can recognize that our life has an ethical dimension without requiring that our ethical view of things be 'complete', or even in principle completeable. It is incomplete so long as there are broad groupings that contain systematically opposed groups. For ethics cannot resolve all conflicts within such broad groupings. The absolutist tells us that we could have an ethics that is complete in the sense of resolving all conceivable conflicts. In telling us this the absolutist abstracts from the fact that our ethical principles serve the limited purpose of resolving conflicts within groups where common purpose rather than systematic opposition is the distinctive feature.

3   Ethical relativism   At bottom, relativism is the view that there are many instances of social conflict which it is not fruitful to treat in terms of right and wrong valid for both sides. Bringing right and wrong to a bargaining table at which there are repre-sentatives of groups cast by society in unalterable opposition is not only a waste of time but is often harmful for the side that moralizes. Right and wrong belong *inside* a group in which opposition runs less deep than common purpose. Between such a group and those outside it, there is a competition of opposed interests with little more than procedural rules and compromise to resolve inevitable conflicts. What these rules are and who wins from the compromises depends on the relative power of the groups. The rules acceptable to the more powerful group are often elevated to the status of laws. Laws then become one means beyond the ethical of resolving conflict in a society composed of conflicting groups.[4]

This is not to say that there is no ethics at all, but only that too often the absolutist abstraction has blinded us to its limited role. There is conflict in our lives that ethics does handle, conflict within a group in which opposition does not run as deep as common purpose. Ethics builds the strength of such a group through increasing internal harmony.

It is a mistake to say that ethics has little importance since it has only this harmonizing role. Because it cannot solve all conflicts gives no license to ignore the fact that it solves some. That there are and will be conflicts which can only be settled by procedural rules backed by power or by naked power itself in no way reduces the significance of the fact that there are conflicts that are settled within more limited groups on an ethical basis.

Within the limited groups it is the common purpose or group interest that provides the basis for the relativist conceptions of good, obligation, and right. These conceptions can only be sketched here in preparation for more detailed subsequent discussion. First, how does relativization to a group restrict the *form* of a moral claim? Since good is relative, the claim that an action is good is incomplete without a clause indicating what it is relative to. The appropriate complete form is 'Action x is good relative to group A'. Similarly the appropriate complete forms for claims of obligation and right are 'Action x is obligatory for person a relative to a's group A' and 'Person a has a right relative to group A to perform action x'.

Second, how does relativization to a group restrict the *content* of a moral claim? An action is a *good* one relative to a given group provided it is one that in some way advances the interests characteristic of that group (see Chapter XII, Section 2). An action is *obligatory* for a person relative to the person's group if that action is necessary in order to avoid a setback to the interests characteristic of that person's group (see Chapter X, Section 3). Finally, a person has a *right* relative to some group to perform an action when putting obstacles in the way of that person's doing that action would set back the interests characteristic of that group (see Chapter XVI, Section 2).

We must now examine, not the reasons for these particular explanations, but the reasons behind the general view that good, duty, and right are relative to groups. The fundamental reason is the social nature of the person. In judging ethical validity, one never gets away from the nature of the person. An ethics that led to the consistent frustration of natural tendencies of persons would be suspect. The denial of the person in certain respects is right only when it permits the realization of the person in others. The absolutist can accept this while being sceptical of the social conception of the person, with its implication that the nature of the person changes as society changes. But there is little to be said for the allegedly trans-social and trans-historical conceptions of the person defended by the absolutist. They have rarely been more than time-bound conceptions of the person treated as though they were valid for all time. That is, the absolutist tends to project into the past and the future, as constituting a total and immutable human nature, features persons have due to the distinctive nature of the absolutist's own contemporary society.[5]

The social conception of the person allows that some of the features of any person are common to all others. As noted in Section 1, this is not enough, though, to yield ethical absolutes. People typically tend to arrange things so that they deliberate and carry out their decisions on matters of significance to them. Is it not, then, an ethical absolute that all should be allowed to deliberate? A set of tendencies common to all humans is a necessary but not a sufficient condition for an ethical absolute. In the social conception of the person, the common tendencies of the person are joined with tendencies that are limited to certain epochs and groups. Since the common tendencies are not more natural just by being common, they are not to be advanced at the expense of the historically limited tendencies. The difficulty is, though, that to give everyone the right to satisfy the common tendencies, insures undercutting someone's historically limited tendencies. Thus the right to satisfy the common tendencies can be valid only if ethical naturalism is wrong.

By allowing everyone the right to deliberate—in the above sense which presupposes taking action on the basis of the decision reached—one would seriously threaten the realization of certain socially derived tendencies. In the capitalist context, the need to deliberate about things of significance for managers is exercised by making plans for the organization of labour in the production of profit. As a consequence, the worker becomes an instrument for the making of profits in an environment over which he or she has only minimal control. Yet this absence of control is regarded as significant, for a recent US Department of Health, Education, and Welfare report says, 'What the workers want most, as more than 100 studies in the past 20 years show, is to become masters of their immediate environment . . .'[6] Deliberation for the manager is compatible with deliberation for the worker on the condition that one or the other sacrifices socially derived tendencies to control specific areas. The manager can give up the control of labour and deliberate about something else, or the worker can cease to regard control of the workplace as important and be satisfied with deliberation about something else. From the point of view of the common tendency to deliberate, these substitutions are irrelevant. But from the point of view of the social person they are a denial of human nature. The general fulfilment of common needs is then incompatible with the realization of human nature, at least in a context of systematically opposed groups.

We must be clear that it is only if the common set of tendencies is a *total* human nature that such a set of tendencies could be the basis for ethical absolutes. Only then would allowing everyone the right to realize such a set of tendencies not require that anyone sacrifice any natural tendencies. If, though, the common set is only *part* of human nature, one side of human nature in one group would have to be sacrificed to another side of human nature in another group, with no good reason as to which group should sacrifice.

From the two premises that the person is social in nature and that ethics must cohere with the nature of the person, that is, that ethics is naturalistic, a form of ethical relativism is easily seen to follow. The first premise indicates that we are dealing with persons of different natures, which, according to the second premise, will have to have different ethical principles appropriate to them.

The validity of principles for workers is determined by reference to the fact that their core persons are affected by their being members of a group that must sell their labour for someone else's profit. Tendencies characteristic of persons of that group will validate principles that do not hold for owners. A case could be made for claiming that the worker has a perfect right to try to limit the length of the working day and the owner has a perfect right to try to lengthen it. The range of conflict between the two groups is not one over which there stands a set of ethical principles that both groups should recognize and that will resolve all conflicts between them. To insist otherwise can only result in imposing on one of these groups an ethics that is designed to serve the interests of the other. There will indeed be some ethical principles shared by opposing groups. The justification for a shared principle will, though, not go beyond groups. The shared principle will be justified relative to either group by the tendencies of people in that group.

Are not the premises of the social conception of the person and ethical naturalism compatible with individual relativism? Why does the form of relativism accepted here have to be a group relativism? Different persons in one and the same group can have different core tendencies. A naturalistic ethics cannot reject those differences. Does it handle them by delivering a different ethics for each person?

As argued in Chapter I, conflicts that are strictly within the self are not ones that raise ethical issues. It is only when there is conflict with a group to which one belongs that an ethical issue is raised. Relativizing an ethics to an individual would suppose that the individual needed ethical guidance in coping with conflicts within his or herself that had no counterpart in group conflicts. This, of course, is nonsense, for so long as the group is left out, there is no moral imperative to sacrifice some needs for others one might feel. In short, individual relativism is excluded since ethics is social.

There is, though, a more serious issue hidden here. Two members of the same group may have different core tendencies because, independent of membership in this group, one is a member of another group that the other is not a member of. Here there is need for a postulate of coherence. A person is subject to ethical principles only if, through the groups to which he or she independently belongs, a coherent human nature is developed. If, however, these groups conflict and thus generate conflicting forces within human nature, no comprehensive ethics compatible with ethical naturalism can be applied to such a person. The postulate says that we are dealing, unless otherwise indicated, with persons who independently belong to groups that together form a coherent human nature. And so when we speak of ethical principles valid for a group, reference is made to those in the group who are not independently members of other groups for which the principles fail.

4   Objectivity   When Einstein set physics on a footing of relativity, he did not make physics a 'subjective' science, one that deals with our consciousness rather than with the world independent of us. Of course, there were those who tried to say he had introduced the observer into physics and had thereby made physics subjective. But in fact he had only said that the magnitude of the spatial or temporal distance between two events is relative to a specified physical reference system. Similarly, relativity in ethics does not make ethics subjective. Ethical claims are relative to groups. They are not relative to what we *think* our group's interests are.

If it is right to work for the liberation of a colony, then this is an objective fact in respect to some—the natives. On the basis of the tendencies of that group, it can be determined whether or not they should work for liberation. Do the tendencies of the natives to realize their national identity, to seek a way out of military oppression, to obtain control of the natural wealth of their country fit with the opening of a national liberation struggle? That there is such a fit is an objective fact on which the socially relative ethical claim can be based. It is not enough that the natives have certain opinions and feelings; these might be things they have been led to have by colonialist propaganda. Their struggle must be a viable one for the realization of tendencies that flow from their role as natives and not for the realization of goals they accept as a result of propaganda. Without an objective examination of the group and its circumstances, it is impossible to determine whether the struggle would be a viable one and whether these tendencies are in fact the natural ones for natives to have. Thus without objective study, it is impossible to determine the correctness of the relative ethical claim that opening a national liberation struggle is the right thing to do.

For the colonialist, the question whether the liberation struggle should be opposed with full military might or whether a compromise should be sought while only token opposition is mounted is equally an objective one. It does not hang simply on the subjective feelings or the opinions of the colonialists but on the tendencies of the groups benefitting from colonialism and on the objective possibilities of success of various strategies. The abstract moralizing of the intellectuals in the metropolitan country has little more than subjective worth; it expresses, for example, the outrage of these intellectuals over the brutal tactics of the colonialists. But for the colonialists themselves, the question of a response involves an assessment of their interests. That their ethical response turns out to be opposed to that of the natives is an indication that ethics is a means of obtaining solidarity only inside groups united by a common purpose. It is not an indication that either the colonialists or the natives or both are so blinded by their selfishness that an ethical absolute that would resolve the conflict is hidden from them.[7]

Even so it must be understood that taking an objective attitude—that is, being open to the findings of a thorough study of one's group and its circumstances—does not exclude partisanship. An investigation of the facts is always in a context of purpose. Our purpose guides our investigation and limits the fullness with which the facts are reported. It is absurd to suggest that outside concrete purpose there is such a thing as the search for truth itself: if one were involved in a detached search for truth, one would never get beyond describing the irregularities of every square inch of one's wall, for there indeed the truth is easily discernible and in endless supply. The truth we seek is, however, always sought as important for something. The native is objective when carefully examining the situation to see whether a liberation struggle will be fruitful, but certainly the facts are sifted for a partisan aim and many facts are properly ignored. Deliberate falsification within the partisan group rarely if ever serves partisan interests. Thus objectivity, guided by group purpose, is a characteristic of any genuine justification of a group-relative ethical claim.

Notes

1   On tendencies *versus* facts see Georg Lukács, *History and Class Consciousness*, (1922), trans. R. Livingstone, Merlin, London, 1972, pp. 181–5.

2   Immanuel Kant, *Groundwork of the Metaphysic of Morals* (1785), trans. H. J. Paton, Harper Torchbooks, New York, 1964, pp. 88–90.

3   Reinhold Niebuhr, *Moral Man and Immoral Society*, Scribner, New York, 1932, p. xxiii. This conception of humans as naturally selfish will be rejected in Chapter VIII, Section 1.

4   For further discussion of the relation of law and ethics, see H. L. A. Hart, *The Concept of Law*, Clarendon Press, Oxford, 1961, Ch. IX, Sec. 3. The assumptions are widely different from those here, but the distinction of law from ethics is maintained.

5   C. B. Macpherson interprets John Locke's absolute conception of human nature as just such a projection of time-bound features into all time, in his *The Political Theory of Possessive Individualism*, Oxford University Press, New York, 1962, pp. 246–7.

6   *Work in America*, Report of a Special Task Force to the Secretary of Health, Education and Welfare, MIT Press, Cambridge, Mass., 1973, p. 13.

7   For a discussion of the opposed values of French colonialists and Algerian natives, see Franz Fanon, *The Wretched of the Earth*, trans. C. Farrington, Grove Press, New York, 1968, pp. 44–5.

IV

The Role of Values in History

ETHICAL life undergoes changes in form. For the nature of the person is a factor in determining both the origin and the validity of ethical principles. And the nature of the person varies as his or her social context varies. When the possibilities that it is natural for the person to try to realize vary, goods, obligations, and rights vary. History is not then laid out under a single valid ethical code. It contains within it a development of the ethical side of life corresponding to the development of social and hence material conditions. The purpose of this chapter is to isolate some of those factors influencing the nature of the person that make it necessary to view ethics as internal to history rather than as a final arbiter outside history.

Showing the importance of these factors will confirm the general view of historical materialism. Historical materialism implies, among other things, that the social existence of people is the framework determining how ethical principles originate, what content they have, and which of them are valid. Since social existence changes through history from one form to another, historical materialism would predict that ethical life undergoes changes in form.

1 Stability and change One important feature of groups has thus far not been sufficiently emphasized—*domination*. Some groups dominate others, and generally they do so not just by accident but in virtue of the kinds of groups they are. The domination takes different forms corresponding to the natures of the groups in the relation of domination, which is a relation between a dominant and a dominated or lower group. The domination of one group by another can take place in several dimensions, such as the economic, national, and cultural dimensions. The domination relation between groups generally requires a larger group. Even when one nation dominates another, the two are part of an imperialist system that serves to get representatives of the dominated nation to cooperate with the domination of their nation. Where one class dominates another, there is a social system that likewise serves to draw members from the dominated class into cooperation with the domination of their class. There will, of course, be cases of domination through naked aggression where an overarching group has no immediate relevance and is thus not formed until domination by force is replaced with domination by other means. Then an overarching group becomes a useful means of perpetuating domination between two of its sub-groups. The overarching group plays this role through setting up institutions that supposedly act in the interest of all groups in the whole but in fact serve to perpetuate domination. A larger group that serves to perpetuate the relation of domination within one or more pairs of sub-groups shall be called simply a 'sum group'. There will be a sum group when the dominant group needs support for its domination by means that do not typically follow from its own characteristic features.[1]

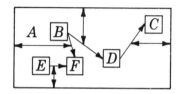

Figure 1.   A domination structure

The structure implied by these ideas is illustrated in Figure 1. The sum group, A, is the whole rectangle. The sum group and its institutions do of course dominate lower sub-groups, but this is, from the point of view of explanation, a derivative fact. The primary fact is the domination of one sub-group by another, which a sum group perpetuates through the development of institutions and ideologies. A class society has it police and its patriotism that dominate the movements and thoughts of its lower classes, but this domination serves to continue the domination of these classes by a ruling class, which is itself a sub-group within the class society. The sub-groups B, C, D, E, and F are the squares within the rectangle. The arrows between the squares represent primary domination relations. A dominant group in one relation can be a lower group in another. So D is both a lower group in respect to B and a dominant group in respect to C. F is dominated by both B and E. The double arrows from the periphery to the single arrows represent the perpetuation of domination relations by the sum group A. B need not dominate C just because it dominates D and D dominates C.

The American Indians are a lower group in respect to the

dominant group that is made up of American whites within the context of the sum group that is US society. The domination is itself a historical phenomenon, since its dimensions now have their roots in earlier relations of violence between Native Americans and an expanding white frontier. There is the present *economic* domination of the Native American in the form of the many violations of treaty rights concerning the use of reservation land and resources, the degrading living conditions, and the inevitable control of the Native American market by white corporations. There is *national* domination because of the fact that the various Indian nations are forced to live within the framework of the Bureau of Indian Affairs which, as an arm of the US government, serves Native Americans within the constraints of white interests. There is, mainly as a consequence of all this, *cultural* domination which has brought in various alien institutions. It has brought to the Native Americans a school system organized in terms of the values of whites and the distortion of Native American history. It has brought religion that came from the forces that conquered the Native American, and was used by these forces to quell opposition. It has brought territorial restrictions that destroyed the tribal patterns of life based on a system of hunting and fishing areas. Consciousness of these aspects of being a lower group led to the militant actions in the early 1970s of the American Indian Movement (AIM). The members of AIM have been face to face with the military of US society—the sum group. Even the most liberal members of the political establishment of the sum group saw AIM as a fuse that could ignite a whole powderkeg beneath white domination of Native Americans.[2]

Let us now look at the differences between the ethical principles of the various groups involved in a relation of domination. A group's position in regard to domination is the key to the ethics valid for it.

(1) Within a *lower group*, such as the Native Americans, those ethical principles are valid that serve the role indicated in the last chapter, the role of harmonizing and stabilizing the lower group itself so that the group is in a better position to realize its interests. These principles call for solidarity, that is, for pulling together against the inroads of the dominant group. They direct members of the Indian group not to be bought off by the officials who serve the interests of the white majority. Unless everyone in the lower group pulls together, bitterness and defeat will be widespread.

Solidarity is not only important in day-to-day actions but it is also important for realizing the long-term end of an oppressed people. The interest people in the lower group have in casting off domination defines this end. This end becomes the main basis for the validity of the ethical principles of an oppressed people. The struggle of an oppressed people aims at, not just making an unbearable condition incrementally better, but advancing to a genuine victory over domination. As an African liberationist put it, 'Rather independence with poverty than affluence with slavery.' A victory over domination is central in the ethics of a lower group.

The principles of the liberationist are viewed as principles of rebellion by the institutions set up to harmonize and stabilize the sum group. A sum group exists as a structure of domination. Any challenge to the relations of domination within it is, then, a challenge to the sum group. It responds with the threat of and, often enough, with the actual use of violence in order to keep the structure of domination intact. It sets up and employs its courts so that challenges to the relations of domination are treated as criminal acts. Relative to the sum group, the ethical principles that, from a naturalistic point of view, are valid for the lower group are not only invalid but are even expressions of selfishness. It is selfishness only for one who sees the common good as the preservation of a system of domination. It is not selfishness for one who sees the common good as the elimination of domination over a lower group.

(2) What about the ethics of a *dominant group*? The ethical principles of a dominant group will be ones that call for solidarity within this group in maintaining the domination it enjoys. To the extent that these principles do this, they will not come into conflict with the aims of the sum group, which serves to perpetuate the existing relations of domination. Of course, a dominant group may try to push its own advantage so far that the whole structure of domination becomes unstable. At this point, the ethical code of the dominant group would call for restraints that would stabilize the structure of domination, since the dominant group benefits from this structure. Whereas the ethics of a lower group points in the direction of eliminating existing domination, the ethics of a dominant group points in the direction of preserving it.

(3) Is there also an ethics of the *sum group* itself? There is and it can only be understood as a function of the relations of domination that exist within the sum group. The ethics of a sum group is *ostensibly* valid for all groups within the sum group. Like the ethics of each of the sub-groups, it is an instrument of harmonization and stabilization within the sum group itself. But the difference is that the ethics of the sum group calls for people from a group dominated by another to live in harmony with those who dominate them. The relations of domination are, for the sum-group ethics,

to recede into the background as a spirit of mutual toleration and, indeed, even of brotherhood and sisterhood comes to prevail throughout the sum group. The ethics of a sum group is advanced by the schools, the churches, the press, and the political parties. These institutions attempt to impose a common ethical code within the sum group, which is a means toward the stability and the harmony of the sum group. It is the ethics of the sum group that is being challenged by AIM and that has penetrated the Native American community through the schools, the churches, and the officials that the government appoints to control the community.

Can the ethics of a sum group be valid? The ethics of a sum group will be in conflict with the natures of people in at least some of its sub-groups. People in the sub-groups are what they are partly because of their membership in those sub-groups. Conflicts between the sub-groups will, then, be reflected in oppositions between the natures of people in those sub-groups. People in a dominant group will, on the whole, act to continue the existing domination relation. Yet the long-term interest of people in a lower group is doing away with domination. Thus since the ethics of a sum group is a means for continuing the existing domination relation, it does not pass the naturalistic test for validity.

A person is pulled in one direction by his or her dominated sub-group and in another direction by the sum group. Two questions arise here. First, does the principle of coherence tell us that such a person can have no ethics? It does not. The reason is that, as was noted, a member of a dominated group is not independently a member of the sum group. For in general being a member of a dominated group implies that there will be a sum group to which one will also belong. Second, given then that one can have an ethics, will it be that of the sum group or that of the dominated group? The direction the sum group pulls in is derived from the dominant group's need to perpetuate its domination. Hence that direction is derived from a group to which a member of a dominated group would not belong. As derived from such an outside group, this direction does not have the priority for the member of the dominated group that the direction the dominated sub-group pulls in has. Thus the ethics of such a person is based on his or her dominated group and not on the sum group.

The ethics of a sum group is, since it fails the naturalistic test, part of the 'ideology' of the sum group. An ideology is a set of claims that serve more or less well to perpetuate the domination within a sum group. Those claims are in general neither valid nor true whether considered relative to that sum group or as absolute claims. They are made to seem valid or true by representing what might well be true in the absence of domination as though it were true in the real world, where there is domination. As noted in the Preface, the critical aim of this book is to show that the ethics of contemporary capitalistic society is in large part ideology.[3]

2   Imposed and latent consciousness   Values are changing the world. They give momentum to movements of lower groups. They help to cast off given forms of domination, thereby changing the sum groups themselves. This change takes place not because people look to values that are outside the process of change, but because they are guided by values that represent their possibilities within history. A dominant group wants to hold in check the process of changing the domination relation. Thus it is in the interest of a dominant group to have the values of a lower group replaced in the consciousness of the lower group with the values of a sum group, which serve to insure a stable domination relation. This is not to say that the dominant group conspires to replace the values of a lower-class group. The process of replacement is better understood as involving in large part an automatic encouragement of values stabilizing domination.

Any doubts about the importance of a set of values—an ethics—should be dispelled by this fact. Dominant groups sense the destabilizing potential of the ethics valid for a lower group. They then tend to encourage blocking the recognition of this ethics by principles that advance the stability of the sum group. Valid principles are then countered with ideology.

When is a principle ideological? Abstractly our answer was that it must perpetuate domination within a sum group. How, though, does it do this? If people acted out the tendencies of their sub-groups, the domination relation would be challenged. The acceptance of an ideological principle must then cover up awareness of the historical possibilities of the core person. It blinds one to oneself. One of the main issues here is what is and what is not part of one's nature, one's core person. Instead of discussing that now, it will be helpful to deal concretely with the relation of ideology to human nature as it applies to race. There will be a fuller treatment of the general issue in Chapter XI.

The problem of personal identity is not distinct from the problem of the validity of values. The core person determines ethical validity. Malcolm X understood this when he said, 'My black brothers and sisters—*no* one will know *who* we are. . . until *we* know who we are! We never will be able to *go* anywhere until we know *where* we are!'[4] Malcolm's name is a permanent reminder of the problem of personal identity for an oppressed group; the 'X'

stood for the unknown African family name of Malcolm's forebearers and it replaced the name 'Little' that a US slavemaster had
given Malcolm's forebearers.

Blacks in the US were and are swamped with the culture of a
sum group that has whites as a dominant group within it. That
culture promotes stability of domination at the expense of the
black's own understanding of his or her identity. The core person
of the black is, as Malcolm points out, only half perceived due to
the position the black is forced to occupy in society, and
consequently due to the adoption of that society's values of
assimilation and personal material gain. For the core person to be
perceived, 'The black man in America has to lift up his own sense
of values.'[5] This core black person is largely a product of the black
group itself. It is not the black person described by the sum group.
That there is such a core black person is confirmed by the
enormous positive response within the black community to those
blacks who by word and deed questioned the consciousness the
blacks had had of themselves.

The acceptance by a lower group of values that serve to stabilize
domination leads to 'imposed consciousness'. It is imposed
because it originates in the interests of *another* group, which is in
fact a dominant group. Thus ideology as defined above is imposed
consciousness. The values imposed will, then, run counter to the
tendencies a person has through group membership and thus
counter to the nature of the person who accepts them. This person
has interests characteristic of a lower group. These interests would
lead to an ethics of change if they were not curbed by, among other
things, a stabilizing ethics of a sum group.

To curb these interests, the ethics of a sum group needs to be
accepted, and this does not come about just by indoctrination.
There must be something that makes the indoctrination stick. The
objective conditions in the society frustrate the needs characteristic of the lower group. In their place, substitute needs are
constructed. Racism, for example, is a substitute need that grows
in face of job insecurity and low pay. It is a need to act and think in
ways that are supposed to show racial superiority. The desire for
the satisfaction of substitute needs gives a basis for the acceptance
by the person of the imposed ethics. Relative to the need for these
substitute satisfactions, the imposed ethics has the semblance of a
valid code. Racism as a substitute need bolsters the ideological
principles that not everyone has a right to a job and that large pay
differentials are justified.[6]

The ethics of a sub-group remains at the level of 'latent
consciousness' so long as the ethics of the sum group is actually

adopted. This is not to suggest that one is somehow conscious of something one is not really conscious of. Rather, it means that, when one's consciousness is imposed, something out of the ordinary, a jolt, is needed for one to become aware of what one ought to do as a member of one's sub-group. It is not regular happenings that touch off the capacity to recognize the sub-group principles. By contrast, an effectively imposed sum-group ethics is one we think in terms of in the normal course of events. It takes extraordinary discipline and preceptiveness to break through imposed consciousness altogether. Most of us shuffle along finding it too inconvenient to do what indeed our group requires. We thus allow strands of an imposed set of values to enter constantly into our deliberations.

Once one is aware of the fact that one is a member of a sub-group, and that stabilizing the domination relations of the sum group cannot advance and will in fact block the interests of one's sub-group, there is little practical difficulty in recognizing what is and what is not in accord with the coherent development of one's core person. In advocating black capitalism,[7] Richard M. Nixon said in a campaign address on 25 April 1968, for his first term as president, that 'in order to *have* human rights, people need property rights'. Blacks, as members of a largely dispossessed group, could easily see this for what it was. First, it implied that blacks are undeserving of the protection of their rights until they have become an owning class. Second, it implied that blacks are attacking the very basis of human rights when they destroy that property in the ghettos that is used to exploit them. There is little in Nixon's moralizing that is in accord with what blacks are. Though the sum group purveys these principles that tie human rights to property, they correspond to nothing in the core person of members of a dispossessed group. Once the requisite awareness of group membership and domination relations has arisen, even the substitute satisfactions that the sum group grants an oppressed people can be seen to be empty. They help keep the lid on while the needs deriving from the person as a member of a lower group are frustrated. Also, the need for these substitute satisfactions is, as noted, the basis in the self for imposed consciousness, including the acceptance of the ethics of a sum group.

3 Class and domination   The notion of domination is incomplete without the notion of class. The two polar classes in US society and in capitalist society as a whole are an owning class and a working class. Other classes—the managerial-professional and the marginally employed—are derivative from these polar classes.

These polar classes are *not* defined by high and low income, but by something more basic, by the fact that the role of a member of the owning class is to expand through investment what is already owned and that the role of a member of the working class is to produce so that someone else's holdings can be expanded.

In other words, class is a matter of what people do in the production process characteristic of the society they live in. As Marx and Engels put it, the modern working class is 'a class of labourers, who live only as long as they find work, and who find work only so long as their labour increases capital'.[8] Whether they ride bikes or Cadillacs to work, whether they live in a ghetto or relax by a swimming pool on returning home from work, the significant thing is that productive workers (a) live by selling their labour to someone else and (b) sell their labour only when there is the prospect that those to whom they sell it will be able to expand their holdings through making a profit from utilizing that labour. It is these aspects of the role of workers in the capitalist process of production that place them in conflict with industrial and financial capitalists. Whether they meet their friends at decorous clubs or at hippie bars, whether they profess a philosophy of rugged individualism or sponsor benefits for children with sickle-cell anemia, the significant thing is that those who own the mines, the factories, the warehouses, and the trucks, used in production for the market—the capitalists—own these things in order, through profits, to expand their holdings. Conflict arises through the fact that it is only by means of someone else's labour that the private holdings of these owners can grow.

Domination in a class society is organized around such a polar structure of classes. The kind of domination illustrated so far was racial, not class, domination. Still, the domination of one race by another involves the factor of class. It is the interests of the dominant *class* within the sum group that are the reason for having a domination among races.

Here are some of the factors that play an important role in linking racial to class domination. The low costs of black labour, both during and after the period of slavery and up to the present, have been an effective means of keeping the wages of many white workers lower than they would have been had there not been a layer of intensely exploited workers below them.[9] This has been a financial boon to the owning class. Profiteering by legal and illegal means in the black ghettos of large cities is an important factor in keeping up the rate of profit for white businesses. The ideology of racism itself does not persist independently of the efforts by the owning class to promote profits. Rather the doctrine of black racial inferiority has been taught as a doctrine that will separate and hence weaken the working class. Such a doctrine—whether advocated by Professor William Shockley in genetics or by US Nazi leader Frank Collin—is an important undercurrent in the ideology of the sum group that is capitalist society.

Other forms of domination in a class society show similar links to class domination. The reason for having those forms of domination is their reinforcement of class domination. There are several mistakes this formulation is meant to avoid. It does not claim that the only reason there could ever have been for, say, the oppression of women is class domination. It does not, then, claim that the origin of the oppression of women in history must have been class domination. Women are oppressed in primitive societies, like the Yanomamo in Brazil, where there is nothing that can literally be called a class structure. And it does not claim that, if there had not previously been some form of non-class domination, class domination in any class society would immediately generate it. We cannot say that capitalist domination would have created women's oppression had it somehow not existed. Capitalist domination can find plenty of reason to carry on and transform the domination of women which it inherited from the feudal epoch, without having to be able to generate women's oppression on its own. Capitalist domination can then be the reason there is women's oppression under capitalism even though it is not the cause, or even potentially the cause, of such oppression just from within itself.

Despite all this the above formulation is strong enough to be controversial. The centrality of class polarity does not mean merely that class domination is *a* reason, but that it is *the* reason, for other forms of domination. Hence, the sexist attitudes of men are not themselves sufficient to sustain women's oppression. Attitudes exist and change only in relation to a social context. Thus in the capitalist context, sexist attitudes are intermediate factors in getting at the reason for women's oppression. Likewise, an appeal to the family as sufficient of itself to sustain women's oppression in an industrial society fails because there the family exists and changes only in relation to the broader structure of such a society. In some primitive societies family structure did play the central role.[10] But in a capitalist society, family is an intermediate factor in getting at the reason for women's oppression. The family becomes a means of literally reproducing capitalist society.

Despite the centrality of class domination, appearances are often misleading.[11] Sometimes it appears that racial, sexual, national, or religious factors are themselves a fully adequate explanation of some pattern of domination. In fact, the explanation is one-sided without due recognition that these factors act as they do only in the context of an overarching class domination.

The domination of one nation-state by another is sustained by the interests of the dominant class in the dominating nation-state. Historical US domination of Guatemala cannot be understood independently of the interests of the fruit companies. The domination of men over women, cannot be passed off as a result either of an inherent brutishness of men or of an inherent weakness of women. In the present epoch, the domination of men over women, which of course originated much earlier, is perpetuated so as to provide men with the satisfaction of knowing that though they do not control their lives as workers they at least control a family. It is, of course, perpetuated for other reasons, among them to provide a source of cheaper labour, since in a male dominated family a woman's income is treated as merely a 'second' income.

If class domination is central to all these forms of domination, then the ethical principles that arise to stabilize class domination will be ones that will automatically tend to stabilize these other forms of domination. These other forms of domination buttress class domination so that the ethics of a sum group characterized by class domination will legitimate these other forms of domination. Marx and Engels put this idea in these words, 'The class which has the means of material production at its disposal, has control at the same time over the means of mental production, so that thereby, generally speaking, the ideas of those who lack the means of mental production are subject to it.'[12]

4 Sex and class The centrality of class domination has important implications for a problem that ethical relativism must face. Everyone is a member of several groups. If there is no guarantee that the obligations resulting from membership in these groups will be consistent, which obligations are to be selected? Is there a need to go beyond groups altogether to an absolute standard of selection in order to resolve any possible conflict? If so, either ethical naturalism or the social conception of the self is wrong, since together these led to ethical relativism.

The answer is to be found in the centrality of class domination. The supposition that there will be ethical inconsistency resulting from membership in more than one lower group does not stand up. The reason for this is the way the groups are tied together for their liberation. Class domination is the linchpin of the entire present system of domination. Implicit in the aim of liberation of any non-class group must then be the aim of doing away with the current form of class domination. The ethical codes valid relative to non-class oppressed groups will be consistent with the interests of those groups themselves only if they are consistent with the interests, and hence the ethical codes, of dominated classes. Without implying that there is a genuine conflict, one can then say that in ethics class has precedence over other groups.

It is of course true, conversely, that lower classes cannot ignore the legitimate aims of oppressed groups. So there seems to be a symmetry that undercuts the priority of class morality. On the one hand, the fight against the domination of women can win only reforms while ignoring the centrality of class in the system of domination. The right to vote, equal pay for equal work, and free abortion might be won this way. But this process would be like cutting off the heads of a hydra. Women's oppression would remain in some form so long as class domination finds it useful. On the other hand, the fight against the domination of the working class cannot ignore the interest of women in liberation. Ignoring it produces a wider separation of working men from working women, weakening the unity of the working class in the struggle to overcome class domination.[13] This symmetry that requires a mutual respect between lower classes and oppressed groups is actually to be expected. For if class domination is central then other forms of domination are used to weaken the strength of the lower classes. Lower class respect for the aims of oppressed groups is a response to this fact. Because class domination is central, the interests of lower classes require that consideration be given to the legitimate aims of oppressed groups. The priority of class morality is then maintained.

In asserting this priority, it needs to be kept in mind that there is no denial of the validity of the morality of oppressed groups. The priority derives simply from the fact that oppressed groups have their interests partly determined by the fact that class domination is the reason for other forms of domination. Only if one were to consider an oppressed group in artificial isolation would it seem possible to derive a code for it that conflicted with a code for a lower class. Then indeed a person belonging to such an oppressed group and to a lower class might seem to have the problem of an incoherent nature. The principle of coherence would rule out an ethics for such a person. An oppressed group—a sex, a race, a nation—does not, though, exist in isolation; it exists in a system in which class domination is the reason for its domination.

Consider an example of apparent conflict between an oppressed group and a class. Preferential hiring for women is in the interests of women in so far as it ends the pattern of discriminatory hiring. It might seem to conflict with working-class interests by intensifying conflict between men and women workers. It would be absurd to reject preferential hiring on the ground that it fails to satisfy an abstract principle of equal deserts for equal merit. We are not dealing with abstractions but with the concrete struggle of women to overcome age-old domination. It is also unconvincing to approach the matter solely on the grounds that in the short run male workers would be embittered by the preferential hiring of women. The question is really whether this bitterness can be turned around into a sense of unity within the workforce. This sense of unity would arise from the realization that greater sex equality improves the prospect of doing something about class domination. If there were some other means of ending sex inequality, insisting on preferential hiring might intensify the bitterness. In that case, the likelihood of deepening the split between men and women in the working class would require that the other means be employed. Otherwise, only an apparent victory would be won for women since class domination would be strengthened. It seems unlikely now, though, that means other than preferential hiring represent anything but stalling tactics.

The same nice reinforcement between the goals resulting from a lower class and those from oppressed groups breaks down when we look at a dominant class. A woman from the owning class is faced with a contradiction between the aims characteristic of being a member of a dominated group—women—and the aims of being a member of a dominant class—the owning class. Ethics is not a final arbiter; so there need be no valid ethical principles to which one can appeal to resolve such a conflict due to groups to which a person belongs independently. This of course does not mean that in agonizing over such a contradiction people from the owning class do not think they are being highly moral. But such moralizing expresses more than anything else the sense such people have of being caught in a contradiction and the need educated people generally feel of being able to give an account of what they do when they are unsure of themselves. The principle of coherence tells us there is no ethics for such people. That the pull of the power of domination is great for members of the owning class is evidenced by the fact that they rarely ever effectively challenge the relations of domination, even of sorts that do not directly involve class, but at best propose palliatives.

Notes

1 Since the character of the sub-groups is what makes a sum group necessary, a member of a sub-group is not independently a member of the sum group. This affects the way the postulate of coherence (Chapter III, Section 3) applies to people in sum groups; they can still have an ethics even though the tendencies of a sub-group conflict with tendencies generated by the sum group.

2 For an account of the domination of the American Indian, see Robert Burnette and John Koster, *The Road to Wounded Knee*, Bantam, New York, 1974.

3 An attempt to show that much of contemporary social science is ideology can be found in Robin Blackburn's 'A brief guide to bourgeois ideology', in *Student Power*, ed. A. Cockburn and R. Blackburn, Penguin, Baltimore, 1969, pp. 163–213.

4 *The Autobiography of Malcolm X*, with Alex Haley, Grove Press, New York, 1964, p. 252.

5 *The Autobiography of Malcolm X*, p. 276.

6 Ironically, these ideological principles are unsupportable even by reference to the overall needs of the white worker. For example, when black income is reduced relative to white, white workers end up making less in absolute terms as well as less relative to white capitalists. See Michael Reich, 'The economics of racism', in *The Capitalist System*, 2nd ed., pp. 381–8.

7 For a full-blown critique of the policy of black capitalism, see Robert L. Allen, *Black Awakening in Capitalist America*, Anchor, Garden City, New York, 1970, Ch. V.

8 Karl Marx and Frederick Engels, *The Communist Manifesto* (1848), Foreign Language Press, Peking, 1968, Pt. I. See Harry Braverman, *Labor and Monopoly Capital*, Monthly Review Press, New York, 1974, for an account of changes in the working class resulting from monopolization.

9 For a record of discriminatory inequality in the steel industry, to take only one case, see 'Consent decrees on equal opportunity in steel industry', *Bureau of National Affairs, Inc., Daily Labor Report*, Sec. 73, Washington D. C., 15 April 1974.

10 Gayle Rubin, 'The traffic in women', in *Feminist Frameworks*, eds. A. M. Jaggar and P. R. Struhl, McGraw-Hill, New York, 1978, pp. 154–67.

11 And they have misled a sociologist like Ralf Dahrendorf who rightly sees that there are groups in pairs that are related by domination but wrongly assumes there are no systematic connections between such pairs. His uncritical acceptance of the pluralist view of society (see Chapter VII, Section 3 below) is the basis for his error. See Ralf Dahrendorf, *Class and Class Conflict in Industrial Society*, Stanford University Press, Stanford, Calif., 1957, pp. 213–15.

12 Karl Marx and Frederick Engels, *The German Ideology*, p. 64.

13 Marilyn Power Goldberg, 'The economic exploitation of women', *Review of Radical Political Economy*, Vol. II, Sec. 1, 1970.

PART TWO

A Critique of Ethical Absolutism

V
Reason and Utility

SOMETHING must have gone fundamentally awry for us to have been led to the depressing conclusion that morality is no more than ideology when it is used to resolve conflicts between classes. However effective ideology may be in practice, the same ethical principles will in general not be valid for members of opposing classes. This conclusion goes against everything we have been taught about the necessity of pulling together despite differences of group interests. It seems too quick to dismiss such a necessity as sheer ideology—as a concoction by institutions of the sum group to perpetuate the existing relations of domination.

If it does seem too quick, then let us try to get around this depressing conclusion by an appeal to reason. Our class-relative ethics of Chapter IV resulted from taking seriously the needs formed by group membership. But by taking them seriously have we not left our highest capacity out of the picture—the capacity to reason? By calling reason to the rescue, we may be able to unscramble the conflict of classes and stand above the relations of domination between them. Reason promises to advance us from the cauldron of class warfare to an honourable truce and from there to universal brotherhood and sisterhood.

This chapter discusses the potentialities of reason to advance us beyond group conflict when reason is used in the calculation of utilities. The next chapter discusses the potentialities of reason to advance us beyond group conflict when it is used in drawing up a social contract. It turns out that in each of these roles reason itself is a partisan force. It conceals but does not overcome the relativity of ethical life to group position.

1 Utilitarianism in outline Utilitarianism was not just a doctrine of the learned. Through the Benthamites—so-named after the great utilitarian Jeremy Bentham[1]—it influenced the movement that led to the passage of the Reform Bill of 1832 in England. This bill gave greater electoral representation to the emerging manufacturing interests. Utilitarianism was a critical doctrine, requiring that 'sacred' principles be made to stand the test of their consequences. It was thus a doctrine of reason against authority, romantic inspiration, superstition, and hardened custom. But, of course, it was a doctrine of a calculative and empirical reason rather than of a reason that all on its own pretended to have an inward vision of moral truths.

Suppose we are faced with the question of reforming the laws governing the operation of the penal system. It might be proposed that the reforms be guided by the principle that crime, being an evil, must be counteracted with another evil, punishment, that is equal to the first. The two evils thereby destroy one another and the universe is then back in its original position. What guarantee is there, though, that the theory of evils negating one another is correct?

For the utilitarian, the only question is whether punishment improves palpably the condition of society. The utilitarian forgets about evils meeting and negating one another in some abstract way; after all a life sentence for a murder does not resurrect the victim. What is important is the effect on society down the road. If, in fact, meeting evil with equal evil leads to an increase in the incidence of crime, society can take little satisfaction from the fact that through the penal system evils that occur are always negated. In sum, the use of reason prompts us to drop the moral mythology about balancing evils and to look to the social good.

This is utilitarianism in practice; for its theory we must delve into the notion of the social good. First, each person is viewed as having a set of desires. It is immaterial how these have been formed. Satisfying these desires is a matter of central importance for the utilitarian. Actions are viewed as having 'utility', that is, as being able to yield in the given circumstances a certain amount of satisfaction. The same actions will not have the same utility for different persons, for different selves will have different desires. For the utilitarian, though, satisfactions in distinct people can be quantitatively compared. This is necessary since, as we shall see, there is to be a *sum total* of satisfaction produced in a number of distinct persons by a certain action. Moreover, the satisfactions of two different desires in the same person can be compared. This is necessary since, as we shall see, there is to be a *ranking* of actions in regard to greater or lesser utility. If fulfilling one of the desires yields greater satisfaction than does fulfilling the other, then an action that fulfils the former is one with greater utility than one that fulfils the latter.

Second, each action is to be judged in terms of its utility. Among a set of alternative actions, it is 'right' to choose the action that yields a greater amount of satisfaction than any of the others. If one acts, one 'ought' to choose the action with the greatest utility. Here the satisfaction is the sum of the satisfaction of all the individuals affected in any way by the action. After all, there is no rational basis for considering only my own satisfaction, so in putting ethics on a rational basis no discrimination is made between persons. Maximizing the satisfaction of humans becomes the aim of the person who wishes to do what is right. As Bentham's disciple, John Stuart Mill, put it, 'actions are right in proportion as they tend to promote happiness; wrong as they tend to produce the reverse of happiness'.[2]

Reason comes into the picture *both* for the purpose of calculating the utilities of the actions open to one to choose and for the purpose of guiding one toward an impartial view, one that encompasses not only one's own satisfaction but that of everyone else as well. This rational impartiality also gives the utilities of my group no greater weight than those of another group. It is clear, though, that the possibility of calculating the most useful action depends on the two assumptions made earlier: satisfactions of different desires and of different persons must be such that they can be compared. Otherwise they cannot be added together in order to decide which action has maximum utility.

2 Satisfaction Has this rational system of ethics gotten beyond the relativist conclusion arrived at earlier? Part of the problem is that the notion of satisfaction needed by utilitarianism is one that different groups apply differently. This leads straight back to the relativism that calculative and impartial reason was to avoid.

A long-standing objection to utilitarianism has been that maximum social satisfaction may well require considerable individual suffering. In a world of ten people that includes eight sadists, maximum satisfaction will clearly be at the expense of a suffering non-sadist minority. Or five explorers caught in a cave will surely all die before rescuers reach them unless they kill and eat one among themselves.[3] Killing proves to be the way to maximum satisfaction for the five. Hypothetical examples of this sort raise serious questions for utilitarianism. It is not our purpose, though, to decide whether they can be answered satisfactorily. Still it is worth noting that each example is presented on the assumption that comparisons of satisfaction can be made. It is that assumption that is to be probed here.

In a period of economic difficulty for the corporations, some of them appeal to the public for cooperation in realizing what is called 'the social good'. The United States Steel Corporation took out advertisements in 1973–74 in the major newspapers and mag-

azines pleading with people to recognize the necessity of increased labour productivity and of wage restraint in order to keep
the country internally healthy and externally secure. Behind this
display of public interest, US Steel is assuming that greater social
satisfaction is to be had if two conditions are met. The one is that
workers rededicate themselves to the 'work ethic' thereby increasing their productivity. (In 1977 it was revealed that low productivity in steel in the US was due primarily to the fact that profits
in steel were not going back into steel to modernize the industry.)
The other is that workers do not demand that their wages be
increased. (This plea for wage restraint coincided with a period of
stagnant wages; real spendable income for US workers was back to
its 1966 level in early 1974.)

How does US Steel know that the loss of satisfaction by millions
of workers due to the speed up of work and due to wage restraint is
to be offset by the gain in satisfaction resulting from higher
profits?[4] One need not doubt that there is great satisfaction
resulting from higher profits, satisfaction to owners who desire to
make profits, as well as to those who benefit indirectly from
whatever it was outside steel the profits were being invested in.
Still just how much satisfaction would be derived from a slower
work pace and from more income for the worker? Perhaps it is so
great that it offsets the loss of satisfaction due to a lower rate of
profit. Perhaps it is even so great that it would offset the loss of
satisfaction for the owners resulting from changing from a system
based on private profit to a genuine socialist one that is based on the
satisfaction of needs of workers' generally. Clearly, though, the
directors of US Steel do not regard the satisfaction of workers as
ever being this great. Just how does one of the wealthy persons who
owns a fraction of US Steel, and of other corporations too, and
whose annual income runs to six figures judge the satisfaction a
worker experiences in not being sped up and in getting a wage
increase in a period when wages have been stagnant?

The point is *not* that it is the worker rather than the owner who
should be judging the amount of his or her satisfaction. The point
is that there is something fundamentally wrong about the whole
idea of calculating the sum of satisfactions coming from several
groups without already assuming values. For it just does not seem
possible to compare these satisfactions without adopting the values
of one or another of the groups.[5] Yet utilitarianism is supposed to
rank values in terms of quantities of satisfaction, and not to
presuppose values in order to compare satisfactions. From the
perspective of workers, the commitment to advancing those
interests of workers that are characteristic of their class determines

how satisfying things are to be. From this perspective, the satisfaction from not being sped up and from being paid more will have a magnitude that is not strictly comparable to the magnitude it will have from the owner's perspective. There is simply no impartial basis for calculating a sum total of satisfactions arising out of conflicting groups.

The following objection to this reasoning has been raised by the welfare economist, Amartya Sen.[6] Sen grants that different people have different interests or desires, but he thinks this is no obstacle to an interpersonal comparison of satisfactions that assumes no set of values as a standard. The crucial thing to consider is the degree to which a person realizes his or her interests in the concrete situation he or she is in. There is greater satisfaction when a situation allows for greater realization of interest. If someone is having a hard time, I might say that I am glad I am not that person, thereby expressing an interpersonal comparison of satisfaction.

What is wrong here is the attempt to abstract from the process of realizing interests a notion of satisfaction that is neutral in regard to these interests. If this were possible then any two people could be compared in point of satisfaction. There is, though, nothing that answers to this abstract notion of satisfaction. When I find I have received a salary raise, there is indeed satisfaction, but it is not something separable—a pure utility—from the interest in getting a raise. The satisfaction just is the realization of this interest. In some cases there is something we call pleasure when an interest is realized, but this need not always be there. Many satisfactions occur without the jumpy, screamy feeling one has when one experiences pleasure. Some utilitarians, like Mill, did assume that there was a pure utility having the form of pleasure and that people aimed not at the realization of interests of various concrete sorts but at pleasure. Thus they are called hedonistic utilitarians. Sen would be right about interpersonal comparisons if pleasure were indeed a separable component constituting the element of satisfaction whenever interests are realized. It is denied here that pleasure has this role and also that anything could have this role. Satisfactions are the realizings of interests, wants, desires and cannot be scraped off them so that these satisfactions can be compared.

This indicates that either the utilitarian position is unable to be a guide to action at all or it provides a guide that is relative to previously established group values. It is unable to be a general guide to action at all if the satisfactions of people in different groups cannot be compared. That is why, in the last section, we assumed they were comparable. If satisfactions are not separable from interests, as pleasures are, how are they to be compared? To compare the satisfactions of people of different groups one has to rely on the values appropriate to one of the groups but not to both. To the directors of US Steel the satisfactions of obtaining a higher rate of profit and of perpetuating the system of private profit are considerably higher satisfactions than are those of not being sped up in a factory and of keeping up with inflation in take-home pay. The former are higher than the latter in relation to the central value of the owning class—the growth of investment.

No wonder then that the idea of greater social satisfaction is rarely used in a non-partisan way. It is not to be expected that it ever could be since any estimate of the total social satisfaction will be based on the use of the values of one group for comparing satisfactions in different groups. But such values will be expressible in the ethical principles valid for one or another of the groups.

This destroys the pretensions of utilitarianism to provide an ethics that makes conflicts between groups yield to reason. So long as it does *appear* to provide such an ethics then reason has forsaken its impartiality and become a partisan of one group or the other. What seemed so promising about utilitarianism—its appeal to the common good rather than to fixed principles to resolve disputes over what to do—turns out to be illusory. The reason is that the common good itself turns out not to be genuinely common. Rather the common good is based on a standard of satisfaction appropriate to some faction in society. Utilitarianism was unjustly treated as the morality of 'shopkeepers' by its initial critics. That criticism correctly grasped that, as a guide, utilitarianism is based on the partisan conception of satisfaction held by one of several groups. It failed to grasp that the partisan conception could equally well be that of the shopkeeper, that of the worker, or that of the corporate director.

3 Desires Utilitarianism takes the desires that give rise to these satisfactions just as they are. They are not criticized in the light of their origin. Actions that are right yield greater amounts of satisfaction on the basis of the given desires. This feature of our rational ethics merits consideration from the perspective of the distinction of Chapter IV, Section 2, between imposed and latent consciousness.

Recall that what a member of a lower group desires is in part a matter of imposed consciousness. That is, in the effort to stabilize domination, institutions of the sum group propose certain goals as desirable and people come to treat these goals as their own. They are led to make them their own because the inherent interests of the lower group are frustrated. Substitute satisfactions are allowed by the institutions of the sum group. Corresponding desires emerge to get these satisfactions. This new set of desires is characteristic of the kind of domination in question.

This poses a serious problem for the utilitarian. The problem is stated in the form of a dilemma, called here the brave-new-world dilemma:[7]

Either reason decides what affords the greatest degree of satisfaction in respect to desires as they are now felt *or* reason decides what affords the greatest degree of satisfaction in respect to those desires that one's nature would lead one to feel were it not for the stabilization of domination.

If the former is the case *then* the greatest satisfaction is compatible with the most thoroughgoing tyranny, which lulls everyone with substitute satisfactions while allowing no political self-determination.

If the latter is the case *then* the greatest satisfaction is decided by valuing the satisfaction of desires characteristic of human nature higher than that of substitute desires.

Hence *either* utilitarianism finds nothing wrong with a fool's paradise in which a tyrant lulls everyone with push-button satisfactions *or* utilitarianism values freedom for the realization of human nature independently of consideration of freedom's utility in generating the greatest satisfaction.

What, according to the brave-new-world dilemma, is the alternative to following utilitarianism all the way to a tyranny over people made passive by substitute satisfactions? It is to drop utilitarianism altogether by judging, in accord with ethical naturalism, that satisfactions of human nature are *higher* than substitute satisfactions. The impartiality of reason as between satisfactions would then have vanished. This is incompatible with utilitarianism because 'higher' here does not mean greater utility. The desires whose satisfactions are to be maximized are not, then, imposed desires but ones that are selected on a social conception of what we are.

To be fair, we must grant that the support of tyrannical domination presents no real inconsistency within utilitarianism but only an inconsistency with our common beliefs. All that can then be claimed at this point is that, if the relativism advocated in this book seems an outrage to common beliefs, then so also does this consequence of utilitarianism. This takes the wind out of the view that utilitarianism offers a rational ethics avoiding the alleged high degree of absurdity of the ethics of group-based interests.

There is another side to the issue that bears mentioning. It is that people are never fully bought off by a fool's paradise of substitute satisfactions. Reforms which are intended to perpetuate domination by providing substitute satisfactions are constantly being introduced. People remain restless even with these satisfactions. They are prone to actions that, consciously or not, are directed at the realization of the desires characteristic of the nature of the person. This does not at all mean that the reforms have failed to achieve a greater aggregate of satisfaction than revolutionary action could. Revolutionary action may be taken without believing that there will be a greater aggregate of satisfactions in the resulting new condition. In short, people change society not so much to get a greater quantity of satisfaction as to realize certain specific kinds of satisfaction, such as that resulting from self-governance.

This leads to a conclusion that is incompatible with treating utilitarianism as a guide to action. Since the person is social, people are naturally motivated to bring about or to perpetuate certain social patterns. Such a pattern would be a certain organization of work or a certain type of political representation. These patterns represent ways in which the desires of many people are organized. We are not motivated to realize the greatest sum of satisfactions taken in an unorganized and isolated fashion. Not only does the social nature of the person make the pursuit of pattern quite a natural thing, but also the social nature of the person is the basis for making the pursuit of social arrangements of certain kinds our duty. The type of arrangement that it is my duty to pursue will depend on that group, among those to which I belong, to which the system of domination gives the major role—my class. It is, then, social pattern and not unorganized totality of satisfactions that is decisive in ethics.

4 Social feelings Our first criticism was that reason is not impartial in comparing satisfactions. Our second was that reason is not impartial when it rates desires based in human nature higher than substitute desires in order to avoid the consequence that it is right to support a tyranny over contented people. Our third criticism will concern a prop of the utilitarian theory that we have yet to mention.

The theory requires that there be something more than reason to go on. According to the theory, impartial reason enables one to get beyond the consideration of one's own satisfaction and to consider everyone else's satisfaction as well. But reason alone is not sufficient for action; there must also be interest in the things reason proposes. If interests go one way and reason goes another, then the whole conception of a rational ethics is bankrupt. There must be interests, sentiments, feelings that do not cancel out the impartiality of utilitarian reason. If one's interests are selfish, what good will it do to calculate by means of reason the satisfaction to all members of society resulting from an action one is considering? The only satisfaction that will count will be one's own. Motivation to act for the social good lacks here a firm foundation in interest. John Stuart Mill says, 'This firm foundation is that of the social feelings of mankind; the desire to be in unity with our fellow-creatures, which is already a powerful principle in human nature and happily one of those which tend to become stronger, even without express inculcation, from the influences of advancing civilization.'[8] Notice that this fellow feeling or sympathy behind the ethics of utility is for Mill an inherent feature of humans only in seed. Fellow feeling must be nourished by social progress so that not only does it become more intense but also it extends to wider groups of people. Social progress leads to 'removing the sources of opposition of interest, and levelling those inequalities of legal privilege between individuals or classes' that make it practical to ignore the satisfactions of many humans.[9]

Mill does a beautiful job of skirting utopian thinking about the human person in these passages. He knows humans now inhabit antagonistic groups and that hence they do not take a sympathetic interest in all alike. Reason might tell me what will generate the greatest satisfaction for all, but my group connections lead me to take little sympathetic interest in the interests of large sections of humans. As a consequence the greatest satisfaction of all is an abstraction that does not determine my choice of an action. By skirting utopian thinking the prospects of using a rational ethics to settle conflicts between groups evaporate.

Reason does not discriminate among persons or groups; it pushes to the farthest reaches of mankind and considers the desires of everyone. It respects no boundaries; even if there were humans on Mars, or in another solar system, their satisfactions would be considered right along with those of our next-door neighbours. This universalist character of reason comes to naught in choice unless it is backed by an equally universalist fellow feeling. Mill tells us that 'political improvement' has not yet developed fellow feeling to extend it to the next class much less the next planet. Our social feelings actually lead us to advance the satisfaction of our local group, not of humanity. Ethical utilitarianism—that it is *right* to maximize satisfaction for all—is not then backed by psychological utilitarianism—that people *desire* to maximize happiness for all.

The fact that reason does not have the full support of feeling is a challenge for the utilitarian reformer. Reforms should be carried out that terminate in everyone having a stronger feeling of unity with all humans. Why? Reason tells us that satisfaction is to be increased and that one obstacle in the way of increasing it is partisanship and factionalism. If there is destructive conflict between groups, the total satisfaction will be reduced. The few enlightened utilitarians, who do have a developed sense of humanity, not only know but also feel the need to develop this sense in everyone.

The difficulty for utilitarianism is then this. There are two ways of going about social change. One way is to try to realize the possibilities that arise within a group but that are blocked by the relations of domination in which that group stands. Here social change starts with what humans tend to be but are not allowed to become in given concrete circumstances. The other way is to try to realize a goal that does not emerge from the present context as a real possibility. Such a goal is not something people mobilize themselves to struggle for. It emerges at the level of abstract reason rather than at the level of awareness in struggle. The forces needed to get social change must, then, be mobilized from above by an 'enlightened' group of reformers. These reformers attempt to persuade people that they are misguided in their present partisan struggles and that they should strive to become something which is not among the possibilities naturally opened up by the concrete conditions surrounding them.

There is, then, a built-in tendency for utilitarian reform to be reform from above. This results from the fact that its purpose is to change people from what they are. The support of the masses is needed to put the reform schemes through, but there is little or no control from below in the formulation of the schemes and in their execution. By contrast, changes based on the possibilities for human nature opened up by existing circumstances can be realized from below. This does not mean there is no leadership, for in fact leadership is necessitated by the existence of imposed consciousness and the need to overcome it. What it means is that people are not limited to the role of being a battering ram for pushing reform schemes through. In their struggles, which exist because of domination, they have the opportunity to break with imposed consciousness. This opportunity is improved with leadership. In the process of breaking with imposed consciousness, the group exerts control over the formulation of proposals for change and their execution.

In a period of antagonism among classes, the person will naturally have interests that are characteristic of his or her class.

The promotion of those and related interests *is* the task of the person. No alien norms introduced from above are needed. By contrast, the promotion of general satisfaction by the development of a sense of humanity in everyone is not, in the present context, a goal with more than a rhetorical appeal for any but the reformers themselves. Utilitarian reformers are eventually forced to recognize that building genuine brotherhood and sisterhood can only be done from below, by starting with an emphasis on solidarity within the dominated groups in which most people find themselves. Failing in their attempt to create fellow feeling from above, the reformers' schemes serve merely to entrench existing relations of domination or to create new ones. About such reformers, Eugene V. Debs, the socialist unionist and politician from Terre Haute, said that if they can lead you into the promised land of general satisfaction then they can just as easily lead you back out again.[10]

Notes

1 Jeremy Bentham, *An Introduction to the Principles of Morals and Legislation*, (1789), eds. J. H. Burns and H. L. A. Hart, University of London: The Athlone Press, London, 1970.

2 John Stuart Mill, *Utilitarianism* (1861), Bobbs-Merrill, Indianapolis, 1967, Ch. II, p. 10. For Mill's view of the relation of right, obligation and justice, see Ch. V of *Utilitarianism*.

3 Lon L. Fuller, 'The case of the speluncean explorers', *Harvard Law Review*, Vol. 62, 1949, pp. 616–19.

4 For a discussion of how social interests affect comparisons of satisfactions that comes to a conclusion different from that here, see I. M. D. Little, *A Critique of Welfare Economics*, 2nd ed., Oxford University Press, New York, 1957, Ch. IV.

5 John Rawls, *A Theory of Justice*, Harvard University Press, Cambridge, Mass., 1971, p. 324.

6 Amartya Sen, *On Economic Inequality*, Clarendon Press, Oxford, 1973, p. 14.

7 Suggested by Aldous Huxley's *Brave New World*, Doubleday, Doran, and Co., Garden City, N. Y., 1932.

8 Mill, *Utilitarianism*, Ch. III, p. 49.

9 Mill, *Utilitarianism*, Ch. III, p. 41.

10 Eugene V. Debs, 'Industrial unionism' (1905), in *Eugene V. Debs Speaks*, ed, J. Y. Tussey, Pathfinder, New York, 1970, p. 124.

VI

Contract and Self-Interest

UTILITARIANISM fails to provide a way around relativism. But there are other possibilities, one of which is called contract theory. Considerations about human nature regain importance in contract theory. The ability of contract theory to provide a way around relativism hinges on its conception of human nature. It will be shown that the contractualist view of human nature is either empty or else based on the interests of the ascendant merchant and manufacturing class of early capitalist society.

Contract theory became important before utilitarianism. The classical contract theorists were Hobbes and Locke in the seventeenth century. Utilitarianism was given its classical formulations in the eighteenth and nineteenth centuries. The reason for considering contract theory second rather than first is that it has been picked up for use again after the failure of the utilitarian reformers. Social conflict has not been eliminated either by welfare measures or by the ideology of fellow feeling. The idea of an agreement between conflicting groups to set aside differences and pursue a common purpose appears attractive again. Such an agreement is the core of contract theory.

1 Contract theory in outline Contract theory in ethics is a theory about the basis for the validity of ethical principles. Contract theory has its most obvious applications in attempts to provide a basis for the ethical validity of social policies, institutions, and laws. It shows why, for example, a certain distribution of income is just or unjust. To get a clear idea of the theory, it is well to look at how it is used to solve some concrete social problems.

In all cases, the theory bases validity on an actual or hypothetical agreement. But not just any agreement will do. The agreement must be one that satisfies two conditions. The *first* is that the parties to the agreement or contract enter it as self-interested persons. That is, they enter it in order to realize some need they have that is other than a need to advance the welfare of others. The *second* is that, in coming to the agreement, the parties consider themselves only as what they really are and not as what they have

68

become as a result of the accidents of history. Only their absolute human nature is relevant to the agreement when the agreement actually serves to establish validity.[1]

When the Labour Party took over the government in Britain in 1974 it wanted union leaders and union members to join with it and the owners in a 'social contract'. The miners had, the year before, gone on strike for significant wage increases. In getting them they forced out the Tory government. A continuation of unrestrained labour militancy would make stable government impossible and wreck efforts to put life into the sagging British economy. By joining in a social contract, workers would voluntarily agree to economic restraint in their behaviour. For their part, the owners would accede to minimum demands from labour and invest their gains to strengthen the economy. In short, saving capitalism in Britain was a goal sufficiently important to warrant asking the workers to give up their wage demands for it.[2]

Did the principle of wage restraint become valid as a result of this social contract? The answer must be in terms of the two conditions for validity. First, do the parties to the agreement enter it on a basis of self-interest? The reason for this condition is very simple. If one party is interested merely in advancing the welfare of the other, then the latter need not promise anything in return for having its welfare promoted. Without a basis in self-interest, there is no contract at all and hence no basis for validity. Where, though, was the element of self-interest in wage restraint? The British workers and their union leaders would have to have believed that wage restraint in 1974 would be responsible for a significant improvement in living conditions later on. Otherwise, wage restraint would have been a mere gift of greater profits to the owners. (This is in fact what it was: by early 1978 average income was down 12 per cent from its 1974 level.)

What, then, about the second condition? Did only the fundamental factors of human nature, from which the accidents of history had been stripped away, enter into the considerations that made the agreement on wage restraint seem rational? The contract theorist's human nature is an absolute human nature, as is clear from the requirement that historical additions to it are to be left out of these considerations. The very idea of entering into a contract of a serious sort implies stepping out of current conflicts sufficiently far to be able to judge them from above. Without this detachment, the agreement is a mere fraud, entered into to gain time. To realize this detachment it is necessary for the parties to consider one another only in their essential features when deciding the content of an agreement.

Wage restraint, though, was not arrived at by making the needed abstraction from the struggle between labour and capital. The agreement was worked out on the assumption that people have the natures they do in a capitalist society. The reason this assumption is made is that the system of private profit is integral to this contract. Preserving the system of private profit was quite clearly the goal of the contract. Wage restraint was to keep this system afloat. So it would have been inappropriate to assume that the parties to the contract have natures different than what they have in capitalist society. This means, though, that instead of stepping back from the conflict implicit between labour and capital, one assumes that people have the natures they have in this conflict when they are asked to make the social contract. The contract is, then, merely a way for the dominant class, the capitalists, to buy time, and not an agreement based on an absolute human nature.

Even if, as was not really the case, the first condition, the condition of self-interest, was satisfied, it is perfectly clear that the second condition, the condition of human nature, was not satisfied. If anyone ever did enter into Harold Wilson's social contract, the principle of wage restraint agreed to would not have become valid on the basis of that contract.

2   Free and equal persons   Looming up before us is the issue of an appropriate content for human nature. What is the absolute human nature that must be considered in agreements that yield valid principles? Whatever their other differences, contractualists are united in their claim that core persons are fully characterized as free and equal agents. Suppose we wish to determine whether one has a right to accumulate a vast fortune. In the framework of contract theory we ask whether, as self-interested individuals, we would accord this right on the basis of what we all are of ourselves, independent of the accidents of history. Or as we can now say, on the basis of the fact that by nature everyone is free and equal.

But what do this freedom and equality mean? To say that persons are *naturally free* is to say that by nature they are independent of others. This implies two quite separate things. First, that by nature persons are not subjected to the will of other persons; there are no natural born slaves, serfs, or wage earners. In history there are people who are subject to the will of others, but this is always an accidental feature of those people. Second, that by nature persons are not constrained by being concerned with the interests of others. So by nature they are self-interested. Benevolence is, then, another of the accidental features that people acquire in the course of history but do not possess by nature.

To say that persons are *naturally equal* is to say that by nature the interests of no person are ranked second to the interests of any other. The development of stratification among groups will certainly have the effect of treating the interests of different groups differently. The perpetuation of significant inequality in the distribution of income and wealth in a country like the US is, however, not a sign that there is a natural hierarchy of groups in regard to the distribution of goods. Natural equality means that, independent of the accidents of history, no one has a better claim to a share of the available goods than anyone else.[3]

Freedom and equality emerge naturally because we start with contracts. One detaches one's self from one's actual position in the struggle within society in order to make a contract with people on the other side of the struggle. One will, then, bargain without assuming that either side is dominated by the other or that one side has special rights the other does not share equally. Suppose one side belongs in a position of domination and insists on its domination in the bargaining. The final result will not be an agreement. It will be a reminder to the dominated side that its inferior position limits the scope of its action. Or suppose one side has more rights than the other and insists on these rights in the bargaining. The final result will not be an agreement. It will be a declaration of privilege. So, pushed to the limit, a contract requires that the parties to it regard each other as free and equal.

It is one thing, though, to say that in arriving at a contract there should be no assumptions of servitude or privilege among the parties. It is quite another to say that what is agreed upon in making the contract guarantees freedom and equality. In fact, we agree upon principles that tell us in what ways it is legitimate to abridge freedom and equality. The natural freedom people have 'to order their actions . . . as they think fit' does not exist for the wage earner in a factory. Yet the wage contract by which the worker agrees to restrict this natural freedom would be regarded as a basis for the right of the owner to expect the worker to work as directed. According to the usual view, the worker and the owner approach each other, and agree, on a footing of freedom and equality. The worker is not antecedently subjected to the owner, and there is no assumption, prior to the contribution each makes to the production process, that the owner has special rights to a larger share of the product.

Of course, this view is pure ideology. The worker is not free since in general the worker must subject him or herself to some employer in order to live. Moreover, it is assumed that ownership gives a right to the surplus labour produced over and above what is needed to feed, house, clothe, educate, and transport labour. But the point is that not all agreements that give rights to restrict freedom and equality need be flawed by this lack of detachment.

It is easier to arrive at the requisite detachment where the question is one of broad social policy rather than, as in the case of the wage contract, one of concrete action. Thus let us return to the case of the right to accumulate a vast fortune. We come together as equals to decide whether we wish to sanction inequality of wealth.[4] The right to unequal wealth must be grounded in an agreement that people come to after detaching themselves from their actual position as regards wealth. If a contract validates the right to great wealth, then not just the rich but also the poor must be able to agree on this right.

An argument implicit in Locke in favour of a right to inequality in wealth is that equality is inefficient. Since the parties to the contract are self-interested, this inefficiency will move them to favour inequality. Without the accumulation of wealth, there will be no one who can employ labour in large amounts and thus enterprise will remain at the level of many small shops. The production of goods of all kinds will be curtailed and those who had hoped to be better off as a result of equality find that instead they are actually worse off.[5]

This, then, is the kind of argument people might find persuasive when they detach themselves from their actual circumstances as regards wealth. If they insert into their deliberations the fact that they are, say, deprived of wealth, then, of course, they will be reluctant to agree that vast holdings of property by others are to be protected. But having made the abstraction from these circumstances, they are supposedly able to see that a system of inequality would prevent the low standard of living of a system of equality. The right of unequal wealth would then be a valid one since it comes from an agreement among people considering themselves as free and equal.

This argument for inequality supposes that wealth is a private matter. The only alternatives allowed are then inequality in the distribution of private wealth and equality in the distribution of private wealth. The possibility that public wealth might provide the basis for the production of adequate amounts of goods is ignored. Wealth would be public if those who work at any enterprise made all decisions about it, or if the citizens of a certain region controlled the enterprises in it, or if the state, whether controlled by its citizens or not, ran all enterprises. Large-scale enterprises can come about under any of these different forms of public ownership. Productivity need not remain as low as it would be in an economy of small enterprises. So the argument is inconclusive even on the assumption of human nature as free and equal. Nonetheless, it is clear how freedom and equality function in reaching an agreement on the basis of the above argument. They function to set the parties above the biases of class perspective. The right to unequal wealth agreed to from the perspective above these biases would, then, be an absolute right. It would be grounded in an absolute conception of human nature as free and equal. But is this really a way around relativism?

3 Free enterprise and freedom What is the justification of the view that humans are by nature free and equal. This section will show that there is a certain plausibility to thinking of human nature in terms of freedom and equality when we think of humans as owners in a free enterprise system. In this section, we shall show that this gives a relative conception of human nature, not the absolute conception of human nature needed by contract theory. In the next section, the emptiness of the absolute conception of human nature expressed in terms of freedom and equality will be shown. The conclusion to all of this is, then, that contract theory fails to provide an alternative to relativism since to be absolute the conception of human nature it rests on must be empty.

A critical look at contract theory provides further confirmation for the theory of historical materialism. The contractualists Hobbes and Locke were among the ablest thinkers of the period of early capitalism. They assumed the developing social and economic relations of that period and generalized them in order to provide a moral and a political outlook that would be coherent with those relations. Their efforts must be seen in the light of their assumption of these social and economic relations. The very idea of a contract as well as the ideas of freedom and equality must be brought down from the plane of empty abstractions and observed as they functioned in the seventeenth century social and economic context. Writers often hide the context in which their terms take on meaning for them in order to give their writing an appearance of timelessness. They write with one eye on the social context in which they live while eliminating from what they explicitly say all trace of that context. The relativist nature of their concepts, which historical materialism predicts, gets concealed behind a veneer of absoluteness.

Ethical ideals express the needs of a group against the obstacles put in its way. In the present case, freedom, equality, and contract expressed the aspirations of the emerging commercial class of the seventeenth century. There was a *negative* basis for these aspirations. The idea of freedom was the specific idea of not having to take into account the interests of the old ruling classes. To defer to these interests would have continued to limit the development of the free exchange of property and of a free labour market. The drive toward equality was a drive toward making feudal rank and status irrelevant in economic dealings. Merchants and usurers aspired to stand on an equal footing with the lords, princes, and kings they served. But there was also a *positive* basis for these aspirations.

People were to be viewed not in terms of their birth but as at least potential possessors of commodities. The contract then replaces the personal tie as the dominant element in relations between persons. And this is the key to the whole constellation of ideas of the age. A system that treats people as possessors of commodities—things that enter into economic exchange—is one in which people must regard one another as capable of entering the contracts by which commodities are exchanged. The labour power of workers becomes a commodity they sell for the ability to buy consumer goods. But people are capable of entering contracts only if they are free and equal. The concept of equality becomes a fundamental one only 'in a society in which products of work have the form of commodities and hence in which the chief social relation that people have to one another is that which they have as possessors of commodities'.[6]

On the one hand, in Stuart England, prosperous craftsmen were asking for the right to invest their *capital* in their trade. This was in opposition to the restrictions upon such investment by the mercantile corporations. These corporations had charters giving them control over the crafts. The traditional corporations had an interest in restricting the economic agency of the craftsmen. But to win freedom from such restrictions was not to win absolute freedom. All that was required was that an old set of interests—the interests of those corporations—no longer had to be taken into account. The agents could then be self-interested. Of course, the interests of certain others were taken into account by the new economic agent. The new freedom and self-interestedness had to be understood relative to earlier restrictions. On the other hand, the prosperous craftsmen who set up independent companies wanted to ignore traditional restrictions on the number of *labourers* they could employ. These restrictions protected the interests of less ambitious craftsmen and the interests of the mercantile corporations.[7]

The demand for freedom from the old restrictions on capital and labour, and the demand for equal status with the older corporations, was being made by men who, in relation to the traditional ways of considering the interests of others, appeared as completely self-interested. Thus they appeared as completely free, where freedom is understood primarily as not being constrained by taking an interest in the interests of others. But the new way of free enterprise introduced its own complex of interests in the interests of others. The representatives of the new wealth could overturn the old order only in a revolution which ended the reign of the Stuarts. But for this they needed the cooperative efforts of those who would benefit from the new order and cooperative effort is impossible without taking an interest in the interests of others.

The conception of human nature that stands behind contract theory is, indeed, a firmly based one. It is based on the importance of contracts for early capitalism. However, it is silent about or abstracts from important aspects of the historical setting in which contracts took on such importance. This abstraction leaves us with freedom in the sense of the absence of *any* interest in the interests of others and with equality in the sense of the absence of *any* ranking of the interests of different people. This abstraction is correct in relation to the restrictions of the old order and to the growing importance of possessing and exchanging commodities in the new order. But it ignores the restrictions of the new order. Though firmly tied to the historical setting from which it was abstracted, this conception of human nature is nonetheless one-sided.

Does this conception of human nature have today the same firm though one-sided base that could give it plausibility? The growth in size and power of a minority of the economic units of capitalism has undercut the centrality of the contract. It is a pure fiction to view the management of General Motors and one of its customers as standing on an equal footing in regard to an agreement guaranteeing parts for a new car. In this monopoly phase of capitalism, power relations dominate. Inequalities and lack of freedom have a central place thus making it impossible for the contract to be the key factor. The role of the utilitarian reformer was to try to counteract the worst effects of these inequalities. The notion of contract, with its supposition of freedom and equality, seemed unable to deal with the problem. Contract theory was in fact used to vindicate inequalities, as we saw above. Utilitarian reform has been a failure: inequalities continued to lead to wars, high levels of unemployment, and hostility between classes.

This failure has sparked a new interest in contractualism. The older contractualists, who started with equality to justify the inequality that was needed for capitalism, were less sensitive to the

social evils resulting from this inequality. The newer contractualism, elaborately systematized by John Rawls in *A Theory of
Justice*, tries to put the reforming purpose of the utilitarian on the
firmer base of the contract. The utilitarian saw success as requiring
the building of brotherhood and sisterhood. The continuation of
sharp class and race conflict indicated that this goal is as far off as
before. Contract theory requires, in place of brotherhood and
sisterhood, only the self-interestedness of the person entering a
contract. Could, then, the purposes of reform be more successfully
implemented on a new contractual rather than the old utilitarian
base?

As a programme for reform, the new contract theory will be as
big a failure as utilitarianism. The difficulty for contract theory
now is that, whereas the contract presupposes freedom and
equality, the power of vast wealth limits drastically the areas in
which human interaction is on the basis of freedom and equality.
Agreements are made for the powerless by representatives who
make a career of collaborating with the powerful. The British
social contract on wages is a fine example. The trade union leaders
could announce an agreement in the name of the workers for the
good of the society. Yet the inequalities of power affect the human
nature of both sides to the agreement. The agreement was not,
then, one that satisfied the requirement of absolute human nature.
People are aware of the inequalities and are not going to be gulled
into believing they can participate, as they are, on a footing of
equality with those who dominate them. They are then aware that
the problem they face is not the sacredness of a contract but the
difficulties of organizing themselves to change the balance of
power.

4 Human nature and the state of nature The idea of
humans as free and equal did express the aspirations of a rising
commercial class. The idea might, though, be more than that.
What is to prevent those aspirations from being the expression of
human nature as it really is? Only with early capitalism, then, did
humans aspire to be what they really are. Contractualists believed
there was an appropriate abstraction showing that *all* humans were
free and equal. This would vindicate the aspirations of the
commercial class for it would be acting as all humans should have
acted. This abstraction arrives, it needs to be noted, at an atomic
view of the person: it takes away social relations and leaves us with
a self-interested entity whose interests have not been put in a
ranking with those of others. What is to be said for such an
abstraction?

The idea of an abstraction from social contingencies to human nature as free and equal is given religious expression by Thomas Jefferson in *The Declaration of Independence* when he said, 'We hold these truths to be self-evident, that all men are created equal, that they are endowed by their Creator with certain unalienable rights, that among these are life, liberty, and the pursuit of happiness.' God gave us freedom and equality which the various forms of society have, in different degrees, taken away from us. As God-given freedom and equality constitute a trans-social and trans-historical human nature. Jefferson's conception of the legitimate powers of government deriving 'from the consent of the governed' needed the backing of this conception of humans as free and equal. Consent gives legitimacy when it is not forced and not based on the submissiveness of lower orders to higher ones. In short, Jefferson's contractualist view of government, which conceals the reality of government as an instrument of class power, needs to be rationalized by the claim that behind the lack of freedom and equality in society there is a truly human freedom and equality.

The secularist Hobbes does not speak of what the Creator endowed humans with but of 'the natural condition of mankind'.[8] And Locke speaks of 'the state of nature'. In the natural condition or the state of nature one sees what humans really are. For one constructs the natural condition or the state of nature by abstracting from all forms of society or government. Let us imagine the steps through which such an abstraction might take us.

Since we want to end up with a perfectly free agent, we must abstract from all dispositions of kindness. Kindness constrains one to take an interest in the interests of others. We must go beyond this to self-interestedness. Work relations require cooperation, which will not get very far without consideration of others. Carrying a load together requires the close attention of each person to the interests of the others in not being overloaded, squeezed against a wall, or knocked off balance. Freedom is reached only by abstracting from work relations, for work relations require a minimal regard for the well-being of others. Indeed, the same argument will show that cooperative endeavour of any kind must be abstracted from.

The consequences of this are far reaching indeed. Without cooperative endeavour, our creatures will not have a language. For language functions as a symbolic way of making cooperative endeavour more efficient. The social basis for the existence of language disappears with the disappearance of cooperation. Without language the most characteristic human traits lose their footing. How could the being we are left with at this stage of abstraction be said to be rational? The processes of human rationality are intimately tied up with our ability to formulate connections between means and ends and to review our ends in the light of our conception of ourselves as human. But the formulation of these means-ends connections and the having of that conception of human nature involve the medium of language. Blocking the development of language deprives us of our distinctively human rationality.

Pushing the abstraction through leaves nothing we could call human. The capacities for cooperation, for articulation, and for rational choice are gone. This drives home again the correctness of the social view of the person. The abstraction to free and equal atomic entities leaves us outside the domain of the human altogether. What we end with is, then, hardly the essentially human on which the validity of ethical principles could be based.

Notes

1   'The guiding idea is that the principles of justice for the basic structure of society . . . are the principles that free and rational persons concerned to further their own interests would accept in an initial position of equality as defining the fundamental terms of their association' (John Rawls, *A Theory of Justice*, p. 11).

2   Tony Cliff, *The Crisis: Social Contract or Socialism*, Pluto Press, London, 1975, Ch. III, 'The social contract—a new form of incomes policy'.

3   These are elaborations on the conceptions of freedom and equality used by John Locke, *Second Treatise of Civil Government*, Sec. 4.

4   For the classic contractualist justification of unequal wealth, see Locke, *Second Treatise of Civil Government*, Secs. 44–50.

5   A related argument from efficiency bases itself on incentives rather than on the ability to initiate large-scale enterprise. According to Rawls, 'the greater expectations allowed to the entrepreneurs encourages them to do things which raise the long-term prospects of the labouring class' (*A Theory of Justice*, p. 78).

6   Karl Marx, *Capital*, Vol. I, (1867), International Publishers, New York, 1967, Pt. I, Ch. I, Sec. 3 (A, 3). For a detailed elaboration of the economic basis for the notions of freedom and equality, see Karl Marx, *Grundrisse* (1857-58), trans. M. Nicolaus, Penguin, Harmondsworth, 1973, pp. 241-6.

7   For details, see Maurice Dobb, *Studies in the Development of Capitalism*, International Publishers, New York, 1947, Ch. IV.

8   Thomas Hobbes, *Leviathan*, Ch. XIII.

VII

The Mutable Imperative

RELATIVISM has been outlined and defended against some notable alternatives. Here a transition begins to the more systematic task of developing the philosophical background of relativism. This task will involve giving more attention—in the chapters to follow this one—to human nature on the one hand and to the nature of social entities on the other hand. Our espousal of a particular set of ethical principles is, after all, intimately connected with the particular image our conditions of existence make it appropriate for us to hold of ourselves and our groups. We cannot then grasp what goods, duties, and rights are without going beyond the kind of conceptual study that examines them in isolation. The study of ethics remains an emaciated abstraction so long as it fails to consider the broader context that includes what we are and what the social entities are in which we live.

Mid-twentieth century Anglo-American moral philosophers almost succeeded in ending ethics as a field of serious study by treating such an abstraction as though it were ethics itself.[1] These philosophers were among the intellectuals of nation-states that were sufficiently strong to ride out, without serious challenge to their social systems, a period of depression and war that shook the stability of other nation-states. During and immediately after World War II, the old social order was challenged by radical resistance movements in France, Italy, Greece, and Yugoslavia. But in Britain and the US the unrest of the depression years was not transformed into such a massive challenge to the existing social system during the war. The intellectuals of Britain and the US were not then motivated to promote a genuine critique of prevailing ethical principles. Yet if these ethical principles had been seen in the context of the social system in which people were living, a critical examination of those principles would have been inevitable. One would not have been able to separate these principles from their role in perpetuating that social system.

To begin the transition to the systematic discussion of human nature, it will be instructive to show in this chapter how relativism combines aspects of both utilitarianism and contract theory. The conflict between the emphasis on consequences—made by the

79

utilitarian—and the emphasis on the structure of humans—made by the contractualist—is one that is overcome as events unfold in history. It is not the irresoluble conflict these theories would make it appear to be.

1 **Deontology and teleology**   The utilitarian judged actions in terms of the overall satisfaction they brought about and hence in terms of their consequences. The contractualist, however, judged actions ultimately on the basis of a view of human nature. More specifically, the contractualist judged an action on its conformity with principles that are validated on a conception of human nature that applies to self-interested persons entering contracts.

Using the notion of consequences as a pivot, we can, then, regard these two views as belonging to two categories of ethical theories. Theories that determine what is right or obligatory exclusively by reference to those consequences of actions that are desired for their own sake have been called 'teleological', since *telos* in Greek meant *end*. Consequences desired for their own sake are desired as ends not as means to other things. For such theories a good is simply what humans desire for its own sake.

Those theories that appeal to something other than the desirability of consequences of actions, while not necessarily ignoring it, in specifying the good have been called 'deontological'. For theories of this second category, either the right thing to do or obligation is appealed to in specifying the good. Hence they have been called deontological, since *deon* in Greek meant the *obligatory*.[2] The right and the obligatory are not then determined by the good in a deontological theory. But this need not mean that the right or the obligatory is ultimate in a deontological theory; something else, such as human nature, may lie behind them.

Consider this example of how obligation might be more basic than goodness. Things humans aim at are not as such good. They are, we suppose, good so long as they contribute to greater equality. This is so since it is assumed that the highest duty is to create greater equality. Equality is not then a good because people aim at it but only because people are obligated to aim at it. In this hypothetical example consequences are not ignored; they are, though, selected for goodness on the basis of obligation.

The general idea behind deontology is that there is a structure which places bounds on the ends that can be regarded as goods. That structure may ultimately be a set of duties. But behind duties, human nature, a social system, or the tendencies of an emerging group might be the fundamental structure on which goodness depends. The teleologist, though, is less concerned with the *qualitative* aspect of structure than with the *quantitative* maximization of value.

Let us turn now to some simplified teleological theories. One theory is that whatever tends to increase the Gross National Product to a given extent should be done in preference to anything that would increase the GNP to a lesser extent. This would be a full teleological moral theory if a large GNP is assumed to be the only kind of thing that is really good. On this theory it does not matter what it is that increases the GNP. All we are concerned with is that the total market value of the goods and services that are generated within a year should be increased. This may mean making Yo-Yos in larger quantity, producing more elaborate containers for dry cereal, and increasing the production of copper merely for weaponry. These things should be produced since producing them has the consequence of increasing GNP more than producing other things.

In actuality, the GNP theory as to what is right to do has advocates only because it is associated with the belief that, 'What is good for the GNP is good for the country'. Even if a larger GNP means less health care and less schooling for the sake of more Yo-Yos and bombs, the overall benefits of a larger GNP are held to be greater. Hidden behind the GNP theory is, then, a more basic teleological theory. According to the more basic theory, a large GNP is not itself a good but only a means to the well-being of citizens.

Yet teleological theories need not be centred on such *social* aggregates as GNP or total satisfaction in the community. They may be centred on the individual. The theory that tells you to prefer what develops your mind to a greater extent is just such an individualist teleological theory. Mental development is assumed here to be the prime good. This is clearly a rather weak theory since if everyone followed it no one would take out the garbage or change the baby's diapers. If, however, I hold that the theory is valid just for myself and a few of my very special intellectual colleagues, whereas there are others for whom day-to-day tasks are an obligation, then, in a way different from the GNP case, a more basic teleological theory is looming in the backgroud. That more basic theory makes the development of one's ability, whether mental or not, a good. Thus it says that the right thing to do is what develops one's abilities most. This more basic theory is still an individualist one, making no direct appeal to a social good .

We end this section by elaborating further the contrast between teleology and deontology. Is it right or wrong to be intolerant of another's beliefs? The teleologist will say that the goodness or badness of the consequences of intolerance determines the matter. But the deontologist will say that the act and its consequences must be viewed in the light of duty.[3] For the deontologist, consequences are not to be ignored since there may be duties to perform whatever acts have certain specified consequences. Such duties are, for the deontologist, never derived from a prior assumption of the goodness of those consequences.

Though the right thing to do is, for the deontologist, not based on the goodness of consequences, it may still have some basis more concrete than duty. For example, contract theory provided a basis in human nature. To say the right thing to do reflects what humans are by nature is not, though, to have assumed that human nature is a good to be aimed at. Were human nature the prime good, then the teleologist would base the right thing to do on its ability to maximally realize human potential. The basis is quite different for the contractualist. It is that what we are determines what it is right for us to do which in turn determines what things are good. Similarly, the deontologist might argue that what is right springs from the social structure we live in. It is the fact that it has this structure, and not that developing this structure is assumed beforehand to be a good, that is the basis for right. The distinction between fitting with a structure and maximizing, among consequences, an assumed good is the basic one between deontology and the teleology. Following the pathways of a structure—either that of the individual or that of a society—is, for the deontologist, doing the right thing.

2 How consequences affect principles Several strands from previous discussions can be brought together at this point to make the distinction between teleology and deontology look a lot less persuasive. *First*, recall that the benevolent agent of utilitarian theory and the atomic free and equal agent of contract theory are both idealizations. In ethical life we find the social person whose interests are limited by group conflicts.

Second, the utilitarian treats all desires as equally natural in order then to calculate utility in terms of the satisfaction of these desires. Yet one must beware of taking desires of humans as natural simply because they are claimed to be natural by institutions of a sum group. The good cannot be specified without distinguishing desires that are imposed from those that are not.

Third, through social change new groups will arise and old ones will be changed. These changes will reverberate within humans, leaving them with different desires and fundamentally changing their internal structures. These changes in humans are not accidental but result from the clashes that take place between groups as a result of relations of domination.

In effect the overall picture we must adopt of the human person is one that includes, first, social feelings limited by group affiliation, second, differences in the importance of desires, and, third, changes within persons over time. Deontology and teleology both reject this picture and hence rest upon distortions of the actual situation. Neither can, then, be made compatible with naturalism.

To show this let us start with deontology. It argues that there is a single set of principles of right action. It assumes that the consequences of actions will not change the validity of these principles. But consider what happens when—in accord with the third point above—the social order or the human type on which certain principles were grounded has already served the role that gives it an importance in history. A new social order and with it a new human type has become possible in changed historical circumstances. The consequences of acting on those principles block the realization of possibilities opened up by these new circumstances. By not tying the validity of principles to such consequences, it is understandable how the deontologist, who started by defending a new order in the seventeenth century, ends as a defender of the twentieth century *status quo* against new social forms. The old principles are still defended because of a refusal to recognize that the old social forms have already made the contribution they were designed to make and that historical circumstances are ripe for new social forms. The principles are no longer valid since acting on them supports out-moded social forms, ones which thwart the realization of important new human possibilities opened up by new circumstances.

No one expressed this conservative implication of the deontologist more forthrightly than did the German philosopher Hegel when he said, ' . . . these laws and institutions are duties binding on the will of the individual, because as subjective, as inherently undetermined, or determined as particular, he (the individual) distinguishes himself from them and hence stands related to them as to the substance of his own being.'[4] Duty is, then, a matter of following the pathways set out in the structure of current society, and, since humans are social, in the structure of· human nature. A particular interest, as opposed to the common interest of the whole society, is given no validity. Class interest will be particular relative to the interest of the whole society. So class interest has no final validity. Further, a particular interest representing a drive for a new social order in opposition to given laws and institutions is not legitimate. To suggest that it could be would be to recognize that the consequences of those laws and institutions were undermining them and hence the principles of duty based on them. Yet for deontology consequences cannot undermine principles since principles alone give consequences their moral relevance.

Now take teleology. It emphasizes the consequences of an action independently of any ordering of them by an overarching structure. It is concerned only with the sum of the values of the consequences and not with any structure among them. Even if the things that are good have structure, it is not their structure that is important as regards what one ought to do, but their goodness. And it is this goodness which is to be maximized.

Since, however, people are social in essence, there is no avoiding the fact that goodness is determined by social structure. The quantitative aggregate of the value of the results of the same actions will be different from the point of view of different social structures. Moreover, norms and ideals originate in the way needs are typically organized by social existence. Of course, without the drive of needs there is nothing valued and hence nothing good. But—in accord with the second point above—among things desired and needed a selection is made, based on structure, to arrive at what is genuinely good. The results of actions are then good not just by being desired but by conforming to norms originating in the organization of needs and hence in the social group. This is not just to reaffirm what we denied in criticizing deontology. For we are now talking about an organization of needs that is not 'set in concrete'. It is a variable organization, one that—in accord with the first point above—limits desires in different ways according to group membership.

The conclusion to all this is that there is a 'dialectical' relation between principles and goods, between structure and results. That is, in time, each is seen to modify the other. The deontologist is wrong to isolate principles from historical changes that lead to conflicts with the consequences of acting on those principles. The teleologist is wrong to postulate a dependence of right and duty on good while denying the converse dependence due to the limits imposed on what is good by social structure. Each theory sees only one side of the relation. Both end up making false claims that result from taking an incomplete view to be complete. Our relativist view accepts the importance of consequences in evaluating principles and the importance of principles in selecting genuine goods from among desired consequences. It thereby avoids falling into the one-sidedness of either teleology or deontology.

Results without structure among them would be the concern of beings that, unlike humans, are not social. Structure apart from results would guide beings that, unlike humans, have an unchanging social existence and hence an unchanging human nature. To claim that rights and duties are founded on something that is timeless is to abandon the first postulate of naturalism enunciated in Chapter II. According to that postulate, any factor relevant to the ethical life belongs to the space-time universe. Yet everything relevant in that universe is changing, including the human and social structures on which rights and duties are based.

It is because of change that it is consistent to hold both that principles are to be judged by consequences and that consequences are to be judged by principles. The principles of one time are to be judged by whether their consequences block the possibility of a new social order opened up by changed historical circumstances. The consequences are not relevant of themselves but only through their bearing on a possible social order. There is then no conflict with the view that consequences are judged by principles. What is important, from the perspective of dominated groups, is that the principles used for judging consequences are no longer those of an old social order. They are the principles of a social order that, under new historical circumstances, has greater potential for advancing the interests of those dominated groups.

There is, then, no immutable, categorical imperative, as Kant thought, but only a mutable, social imperative. As against te-leology, human and social structures, and not just consequences, determine the principles of ethics; but as against deontology it is the consequences of upholding these structures and hence these principles in new historical circumstances that determine whether they will remain valid or be replaced by new structures and principles.

3   Toleration and pluralism   Many people will go a long way with this relativist criticism of immutable principles but pull up short at the very end. Sure, they will say, most principles are not immutable; they hold only for certain social positions at certain times. The apparent immutability of these principles results from the fact that when we are taught them we are not given the reasons that make them valid in the given circumstances. But it is equally sure, they will say, that way at the back of our ethical life, obscured by all kinds of concerns of the moment, is a principle that when pulled out for examination will shine forth as an immutable imperative. This principle will in turn point to some feature of the human self that gives it a basis, a feature that, though difficult to observe in unmixed form, is present in all classes and in all epochs. This principle would seem to vindicate deontology against relativism. The principle that holds greatest promise of playing this role is the principle of toleration.

Groups may well have conflicting interests. But does that give any of them the right to declare 'war' on the others? Those conflicting interests may ground quite different sets of values and duties. To that extent relativism is correct. But the principle of toleration stands above this diversity as an absolute in order to prevent diversity from leading to conflict. According to the principle of toleration not only individuals but also groups should recognize the diversity of values and duties in society and learn to live with this diversity in a peaceable manner. While one need not actively work for the interests of those in other groups, one should nonetheless tolerate those interests. The principle of toleration seems to admit of justification in a manner agreeable to the deontologist. Such a justification could be framed as follows:

Humans are by nature social in the sense of being fashioned in a manner characteristic of their most important groups; and society is by nature a plurality of groups; hence the nature of humans would be violated if some groups made it impossible for members of other groups to realize their characteristic interests.[5]

The argument here is in the spirit of the second postulate of ethical naturalism: human nature is the basis for toleration. Moreover, no absolute is recognized in understanding human nature, since human nature is held to vary within the plurality of groups. The surprise element in the argument is that it leads by way of relativistic naturalism to an absolute. The absolute is to be the toleration of this relativist diversity.

On this justification of the principle of toleration we can erect a whole theory of politics. A plurality of groups and hence of interests is presupposed. Thus pluralism in the merely *descriptive* sense of there being multiple groups with diverse interests is presupposed. Now, however, we come to a *normative* pluralism. According to the normative theory of pluralism, the institutions of the sum group are not to neglect the interests of the member groups in a society with a plurality of groups. This serves the aim of pluralist politics which is to prevent violations of the principle of toleration. The interests of all the major groups are to be taken into consideration in making decisions that affect them all. A felicitous balancing of conflicting interests is to be sought. Governmental institutions are not to be the tools of any one interest group; big manufacturing, big unions, big banking, and big agriculture are all to be considered. In education, pluralism is at work in allowing spokespersons for all these interests groups to present their points of view; this consequence of the principle of toleration is, then, called academic freedom.

The above justification of the principle of toleration, and through it of normative pluralism, is lacking in one important respect. If we add the fact that presently groups are bound together in a net of domination, then the justification falls apart.[6] The justification depended on our acceptance of the claim that it would be wrong to deny people the possibility of being as their groups have shaped them. What is the consequence of this for members of dominated groups? They are, by continued domination, being denied the realization of their natural impulse to escape domination. Thus by the very principle the justification employs we get, once we have added the fact of domination, that domination is *not to be tolerated*, at least not forever.

It is obvious what happens when circumstances arise in which it is no longer appropriate to tolerate domination. Conflict breaks out with a dominating group; the interests of the dominating group in continuing its domination are no longer tolerated. All the hopes of a reconciliation of interests in a harmonious totality are dashed. The normative pluralist cannot protest this turn of events, since it has to be admitted that where there is a structure of domination the human natures of the various groups cannot be jointly realized. The dominant group must dominate and the lower groups must attempt to throw off domination.

It is now possible to say precisely what was wrong with the justification of the principle of toleration. It rested on a wholesale application of the second postulate of ethical naturalism. In effect, it was argued that since human nature is inviolable, every human should be allowed to realize his or her human nature. Then the contradiction arises that some people can realize what they are only if other people do not realize what they are. To avoid this contradiction the naturalist postulate must be applied more carefully. It applies only when there is a coherence among the natures of the humans to which it applies. There is a lack of coherence between the natures of people in dominating and lower groups since some of these people can realize themselves only at the expense of the rest. The pluralist goes wrong in supposing such a coherence, whereas in fact the existence of domination rules it out.

The requirement of coherence leads to a relativity of toleration. It is no longer the absolute it is pretended to be by the deontologist. The needed coherence is more fully realized in individual sub-groups of a sum group than in the sum group. Yet this does not mean that lack of toleration is to be the typical stance of groups toward their conflicting counterparts. Domination will have to be tolerated by a lower group when there is no practical way of throwing it off. Circumstances do arise in which it is fruitful to begin a struggle that ends the period of toleration and aims at liberation. Toleration, far from being absolute, is not only relative to groups but also to times.

4 Fascism and intolerance These last remarks suggest the mutability of the imperative of toleration, its variability in regard to its validity in different social contexts. The owning class in Germany in the mid-1920s tolerated the existence of trade unions and of parties whose support came from the working class. This was a period of stabilization after the years of turmoil in the wake of World War I. There was a large Social Democratic Party and a large Communist Party, both drawing much of their support from the working class. The economic stabilization not only made possible but also was advanced by the toleration by the owning class of these bodies. A pluralistic harmony was approached during the period. However, in Germany the increased investment and monopolization of the period did not lead to a stable rate of return on capital; with more invested, the costs of production became larger and there was a downswing in profit rates. The problem was intensified by the US depression. The benefits the working class had derived from the period of stabilization were ending. Unemployment increased and unemployment insurance payments were cut back. The resultant restiveness in the working class could threaten the existence of the profit system, a development that, it was thought, might even engage the intervention of the USSR on behalf of the working class.

The polarization of social forces was growing. By 1930, the fascist Nazi party showed enormous electoral gains on the basis of significant middle-class support. The economic crisis threatened middle-class citizens with the loss of advantages they had gained over the workers. Soon the leading capitalists were prepared to support the Nazis, and their large unofficial army, as the battering ram they needed to crush the working class.[7] With unemployment soaring the Communist Party also improved its electoral position dramatically in 1930. While the Communist Party and the Social Democrats vacillated, attacks were made by the Nazi Storm Troopers on union headquarters and the head-quarters of the workers' parties; the courts offered no relief. With the backing of the big owners, Hitler finally took power in 1933 and soon thereafter independent unions and the workers' parties became extinct.

Toleration had been a duty for the owners in the mid-twenties; the prospect in that period of growth through cooperation justified it. But after the world-wide depression began in the late-twenties, Germany entered a quite different period, one in which the task of the owners was not economic growth but salvaging the system. To salvage it, the working class would have to be disciplined with wage cuts and increased productivity.[8] Such an attack on the working class would be dangerous if workers were effectively organized for economic and political action. Efforts to destroy potential sources of such organization were called for. The brutal and bloody crushing of unions and working-class parties by the Nazi regime insured the perpetuation of the German capitalist system.

Was it right not to tolerate the working-class organizations? Must we not say that steel baron Thyssen, munitions baron Krupp, electronics baron Siemens, and the dictator, Hitler, were wrong? Of course we must. We say it, though, from the point of view of those who suffered the crushing blows of the Storm Troopers. Perhaps this was not what was meant. Perhaps one wanted to know if we were not going to say they were *absolutely* wrong.

There were a lot of Social Democrats who—following their theoretician Eduard Bernstein in believing in absolute morality—thought Thyssen, Krupp, Siemens, and Hitler were absolutely wrong. That did not make them take serious steps to stop Hitler. By supporting Hitler's right to rule on constitutional grounds, they hoped to convince him of the absolute rightness of tolerating their continued participation in politics.[9] Yet only months after he became chancellor, Hitler confiscated the party's property and dissolved the party itself. This is some indication of the limits of the ethical, of the fact that it is not a final arbiter but something that is valid only in bringing harmony to groups no more comprehensive than classes and races. Ethics is limited to the realm in which it can guide action, and the ethics of toleration that the Social Democrats still held in the early thirties stood no chance of guiding the action of an owning class that saw itself threatened. Hopefully the mistake of tolerating the rise of the Nazis in Germany will not be repeated—again in the name of absolute toleration—in Chicago and London a half century later by allowing fascists to march in the streets while they systematically brutalize blacks.

Notes

1   For example, J. L. Austin, 'A plea for excuses', in his *Philosophical Papers*, Clarendon Press, Oxford, 1961; R. M. Hare, *The Language of Morals*, Clarendon Press, Oxford, 1952; and C. L. Stevenson, *Ethics and Language*, Yale University Press, New Haven, 1944.

2   For a survey of various kinds of deontology, see Richard T. Garner and Bernard Rosen, *Moral Philosophy*, Macmillan, New York, 1967, Ch. V.

3   Kant maintained not only that the rightness of an act was derived from duty but also that the moral worth of the agent performing it required that the act be motivated by duty (*Groundwork of the Metaphysic of Morals*, Ch. I).

4   G. W. F. Hegel, *The Philosophy of Right* (1821), trans. T. M. Knox, Clarendon Press, Oxford, 1952, Sec. 148.

5   This justification of the principle of toleration is based on that set up by Robert Paul Wolff, *The Poverty of Liberalism*, Beacon Press, Boston, 1968, p. 134.

6   See the critique of the view that in the US behaviour is guided by normative pluralism by William Domhoff, *Higher Circles*, Vintage, New York, 1971, Ch. VII.

7   Daniel Guerin, *Fascism and Big Business* (1936), trans. F. and M. Merrill, Pathfinder Press, New York, 1973, Ch. I.

8   In the decade 1929–38, worker income as a percentage of national income dropped 3 per cent and the volume of production increased 24 per cent even though the number of employed increased only 9 per cent (Neumann, *Behemoth*, p. 435).

9   To prevent Hitler from taking full power, leaders of divisions of the Social Democrats' anti-fascist militia, the numerically strong *Reichsbanner*, went to Berlin from the principal cities by motorcycle on 5 March 1933, and begged for orders to fight. Their party could only reply, 'Be calm! Above all, no bloodshed' (Guerin, *Fascism and Big Business*, p. 127).

PART THREE

A Social Conception of Human Nature

VIII
Morals and Universal Natures

ONE of the two pillars on which the claim that imperatives are mutable is supported is the social theory of the person. The other is the two postulates of naturalism. Against the social theory of the person stands the old metaphysical doctrine of universal natures. According to this doctrine each member of a kind—such as human-kind—must have a nature that is just like that of any other member of the kind. However, this is not the doctrine that will be adopted here. The view adopted here is the more modest metaphysical claim that within a given kind there is room for a variety of natures.

This detour through metaphysics will not lead us out of ethics. Admittedly, there is in practice considerable compartmentalization in philosophy. But much of this has resulted from falsifying efforts to treat different fields in philosophy as though they are independent. In particular, it is impossible to treat fields like ethics and metaphysics as independent without destroying philosophy altogether.

1 Laws and natures As Aristotle observed, children tend to regard other people as they do their parents. But this tendency is part of a broader one. Even as adults, we read what we find in ourselves and those closest to us into the rest of human-kind. This is a help in getting adjusted to the unfamiliar; until we learn by wider experience how different unfamiliar people are, some of the routines that we developed at our point of origin just might be of use among strange groups. If we did not project what we find in familiar persons onto others, the world would be a lonely place. We would feel we had little control over our interactions with unfamiliar people.

Putting non-human things in kinds—categorizing them—is a further extension of this same need to feel at home in the world. We put them into kinds so that we can project onto even the most distant things the patterns we have observed in things close at hand. We feel more at home in the universe once we categorize both pendulum bobs and planets as bodies with mass. For, then, laws of bodies with mass can be extended from pendulums to the planetary system.

There are some big assumptions behind using categorization for the purpose of carving out a realm in which the same laws apply. The one we want to focus on here is the assumption that, in carving out the realm, we have grouped together things that are *exactly* similar in nature. The categorization is, thus, not intended as an arbitrary act of putting things together. It cannot be and still serve the purpose we want it to serve. We want it to carve out a realm where the same laws apply, and one will not get such a realm just by picking here and there, where it pleases one. Indeed if the same laws do apply, this will not be due to the accident of our picking the things out together but by virtue of what the things are of themselves. It will be by the very being of the things in the kind that together they constitute a realm for common laws.[1] To say that the things in a kind have exactly similar natures is just to say that what the things in the kind are is a basis for there being one set of laws that holds for them, a set of laws that defines a single overall pattern of behaviour. The basis for their being in one kind is not the set of laws since laws are merely an expression of what things are of themselves, their natures. It is, then, a common nature that is the basis both for the common laws and for the kind.

Categorizing, like other human activities, is not, though, limited to a single purpose. Instead of being for the purpose of carving out a realm where there is only a *single pattern* of behaviour, categorizing can still be useful as carving out a realm within which there are *numerous patterns* of behaviour with certain clear connections between them. Such a realm with numerous patterns, which will be incompatible with one another, can be called a 'weak' kind in contrast with the single-pattern 'strong' kind described above.[2] The connections might be evolutionary ones, as when the pattern of feudal behaviour evolves into that of modern capitalist behaviour. Or they might be connections of mutual determination, as when the patterns of behaviour of complementary classes—such as owners and workers—determine one another. We can then speak of members of human-kind in these different epochs and classes despite variations in human nature among them. The picture is more complicated than it was in the case of categorization for the purpose of defining a realm with only a single pattern of behaviour. And the satisfaction of knowing that one is at home in the world as a result of this more complicated categorization is neither as immediate nor as intense. The purpose of putting things with different but connected natures into a single kind is the more sophisticated one of finding one's way in the world by means of revealing contrasts rather than by means of exact similarity.

How does this discussion of kinds relate to ethics? *First,* consider the application to ethics of the idea of a strong kind, which involves only one pattern of behaviour for all its members. A strong kind like human-kind is useful in thought for the purpose of separating off not just a realm of entities that we can assume *will* all behave in a certain way but also a realm of entities that we can assume *ought to* behave all in a certain way. We project not only physical but also moral laws onto all members of the strong kind. And again the categorization is not intended as an arbitrary one: if entities do belong to this kind then they are, of their natures, such that both the physical and moral laws in question do in fact apply to them. So human nature guarantees not only the truth of some physical laws but the validity of some moral laws.

It is disconcerting enough not to know whether an entity one encounters obeys certain familiar physical laws. But what if one encountered a deliberating entity about which one could not assume that it ought to behave in familiar ways? One could not even assuage one's worst fears as to what it might decide to do by attempting to persuade it that it ought to behave in a standard way. There is then a tendency to feel at sea in a world in which moral patterns cannot be assumed constant across human-kind. That is why there is an initial tendency to categorize all humans as belonging within a single strong kind.

Second, consider what happens when a kind encompasses several patterns of behaviour, each appropriate for a different group of its members. Here we are dealing with a weak kind. Evolutionary sciences, such as biology and astronomy, have taught us to think of kinds as encompassing entities of a variety of natures. These various natures are, nonetheless, connected through the evolutionary process. Moreover, within recorded history, there is data most fruitfully interpreted by thinking of human nature itself as variable. This entails thinking of different patterns, including moral ones, as reflecting differences of human nature. The data anthropology has accumulated on differences among peoples becomes, in the context of the methodology of evolutionary science, evidence for differences in the natures of those peoples rather than evidence for differences of a purely accidental sort.

Why do people resist giving up the notion of a universal human nature, a nature that is the same throughout human-kind? Why do people insist on treating human-kind as a strong kind? By keeping this notion of human nature, one can be reconciled to the most disconcerting human realities. One thereby avoids feeling at sea when dealing with others. One can reconcile onself to hostility between persons, classes, races, and states. The realities are bad and perhaps may never change, but everything is all right since one knows that there is a moral law that would lead to a better outcome.

By contrast the message of the theory of the social person is that there is no such reconciliation of oneself to reality through seeing how things should have been. For there is no single set of moral laws that could have prevailed on all sides of the conflict. Comforting oneself with the thought that the conflict ought not to be is not real reconciliation but flagrant self-deception. The theory of the social person implies that there is a variety of human natures and thus, by the principles of naturalism, that there is a variety of moral laws. Doubtless, this view does not make one feel quite as at home in the world but this is no argument against its truth. It can make one feel at home only to the extent one is willing to learn by moral contrasts rather than by projecting moral uniformity.

2 **The devil theory** Rejecting the view of a universal human nature cuts two ways. It cuts against the basis for the belief that humans are inevitably wicked. This belief is usually appealed to by conservative thinkers, who use it to say that changing the *status quo* is an exercise in futility, humans being what they are. Because of the human penchant for wickedness, there are limits to what social change can accomplish. It also cuts against the basis for the belief that humans are fundamentally good. This belief is appealed to by some reformers and revolutionaries. They think they have a stronger case for social change if they can show that by changing social circumstances humans will be able to manifest their natural goodness. As we shall see, though, the true revolutionary does not need this crutch.

Before showing, in Section 3, how rejecting a universal human nature undermines the basis for a 'devil' theory of humans, there are two things that need to be done. In this section these shall be done only for the devil theory, the 'angel' theory being saved for Section 4. First, we shall look at the devil theory in use. Second, we shall show how wickedness can be derived from tendencies that are in no sense wicked taken together with special social circumstances.

Aristotle provides us with a good example of how the devil theory gets put to use. People can all too easily be induced to think, he says, that private property is the root of their troubles.[3] In fact, though, it is 'the wickedness of human nature'. A community is united, he says, not by possessing things in common, but by education, which passes on to the new generation the customs and laws of the society. Besides, he concludes, if there were anything to communism, it would have come into practice, and our customs would have been different.

It is existing customs and practices that are given a boost by this argument. According to Aristotle, we achieve unity and reduce conflict by making the citizen respect the norms that city-states like Athens and Sparta have taken centuries to develop. One is playing with fire in Aristotle's opinion if, in the face of all of this experience, one wants a new order of things: one will succeed only in unleashing the human beast from the control of virtues that the traditional education of the citizen has painstakingly produced.

You will have detected another implication of this position, one that relates to the theme of domination. If there is a universal but wicked human nature, then we are always so close to the precipice that hangs over chaos that social arrangements cannot be left to chance. There must be a strong hand that sets limits to human interaction and undertakes the education that will generate virtues, that is, patterns of behaviour that stay within those limits. Indeed, any degree of order in human interaction is preferable to the chaos that would result if the Old Adam in humans were allowed free rein. Thus the conservative Burke wrote,

History consists, for the greater part, of the miseries brought upon the world by pride, ambition, avarice, revenge, lust, sedition, hypocrisy, ungoverned zeal, and all the train of disorderly appetites . . . . Society requires not only that the passions of individuals should be subjected, but that . . . the inclinations of men should frequently be thwarted, their will controlled, and their passions brought under subjection. This can only be done *by a power out of themselves*.[4]

You will now see that this theory has enormous implications for us as social beings. It is important that such a theory be challenged. This is not so much because, if it were successfully challenged, those who support domination would stop using the theory. It is mainly because successfully challenging the theory can change the self-image of people who suffer from domination. So long as they have been led to think even of members of their own group as naturally selfish and aggressive, their motivation for attempting to overthrow the domination that stands in the way of possibilities they cherish is seriously weakened.

To challenge the devil theory, consider an imaginary case regarding iron. Every time a piece of iron is made in the mills it has to pass through a powerful electro-magnet. This turns the piece into a magnetic substance. When iron bars so produced lose their magnetism they are immediately collected as scrap. And so magnetism is a feature of all the iron bars we have a chance to observe. We might be tempted to say, if we are ignorant of this procedure in the mills, that magnetism is part of a universal nature of iron. In fact, we who know the procedure in the mills know that an iron bar becomes a magnet only after being placed in a magnetic field.

How are we to think of the selfishness, the cruelty, and the aggressiveness of humans? There are drives aplenty of a perfectly neutral sort, in respect to goodness or wickedness, on the basis of which these supposedly wicked drives can be given their explanation. (These drives are, to be sure, not neutral, wicked, or good of themselves but only in reference to the group goals of advocates of devil and angel theories.) Of course, the neutral drives alone do not explain the bad drives; for that a context, like the electromagnet, is needed. Still such neutral drives or needs would be 'basic' in respect to the rest, which can then be called 'derived' drives or needs. In the same way, the magnetism an iron bar acquires is accounted for by basic features of the bar. The atoms in it are surrounded by electrons. In the presence of an external magnetic field these electrons line up their orbits. The result of this lining up is that the bar as a whole becomes the source of a magnetic field.

The best place to look for neutral basic needs will be among the needs that must be satisfied for survival. They tend to be found throughout the kind, though there will, of course, be atypical instances. These are 'survival' needs. They are the needs for food, sex, support, and deliberation. Under the heading of the need for food, it is to be understood that other needs for physical maintenance are to be included. The needs for shelter and air come under this heading. The other headings are also to be understood as standing for rather broad groups of needs. Though these survival needs are typical and to that extent universal for human kind, they do not constitute a full human nature, which includes social and hence non-universal features as well. Still, even this meagre list picks out something distinctively human. It does this by including the needs for support and deliberation. Under the heading of support there is the need for cooperation in practical activity. This is the fundamental context of support, without which there is no support in the sense of sympathetic understanding. Yet in the absence of deliberation, cooperative activity is not itself distinctively human. The need for deliberation places human activity beyond the level of the instinctual and introduces into it the element of reflection involved in choice. Deliberative beings have as a component in the determination of their behaviour their own reflective activity; as such their choice is free. The list of survival needs gives humans the distinctive character of being reflective, and hence free, social agents.[5] With this as their character, it is understandable how they have a variable nature.

They deliberate cooperatively on how through their action they are to change their own environment to satisfy their needs; the resulting changes affect what they are themselves. So the universal traits making up the survival needs, though not themselves a full human nature, provide humans with the distinctive character that they change the world in deliberative cooperation and thereby consciously change themselves. At this point we need to ask whether these survival needs are indeed basic: do they explain, in different contexts, the existence of other needs, in particular, do they explain the 'wicked' drives?

In different epochs, different methods of distributing and producing what humans need are adopted. This is not a matter of arbitrary experimentation. These methods fit more or less well the means available at the time and place for applying these methods. In turn, these methods affect human nature. According as the methods of distribution and production change, there will be certain important changes in essential human dispositions. This is just what historical materialism would predict.

In the communal economy of certain primitive peoples, the distribution is egalitarian and there is not a division within production between the role of owners and that of working non-owners. Inside the community at least, selfishness as pertaining to material goods had almost no place.[6] Nonetheless, in some primitive communities it is possible to find extreme forms of aggressiveness. Again, this is not an inherent trait, but seems to be tied to the fact that it is difficult for such communities to provide enough food to sustain population growth. Female infanticide is practised to limit the number of child bearers. As a result, villages attack one another for the possession of women. The aggressive traits cultivated for this purpose are then manifested in a brutal system of male domination.[7]

The distribution in an egalitarian primitive community contrasts sharply with that in a modern capitalist society. This is based on the fact that the division of roles in production in a primitive community is far different from that within capitalist production between those whose role is to work so others can reap profits and those whose role it is to reap and to invest profits. Given this division of roles and the inequality in distribution resulting from it, there is not unexpectedly a high incidence of acts of selfishness in regard to material goods, as well as of outright cruelty and aggression. The dominant class aggressively protects its privilege with violence, as it did in the Ludlow, Colorado, massacre of 1914 and in the Attica, New York, massacre of 1971. The inequities in distribution give those who are deprived an impulse to take what they are not given for the satisfaction of survival needs, an impulse thousands acted on in the looting in New York City during the electrical power failure in July 1977.

None of these facts about capitalist society require that we treat selfishness, aggression, and cruelty as part of a universal human nature, any more than under the above method of producing iron bars is there any call to say that magnetism is part of a universal nature of iron. The existence of selfishness, aggression, and cruelty in capitalist society can be accounted for on the basis of neutral survival needs *in the context of particular methods of distribution and production*. It is possible to make a similar remark about these traits in other societies. Thus the survival needs have the role of basic needs in humans.

The strongest support alleged for the devil theory of human nature is not empirical but political support. For the devil theory implies the view that existing domination is safer than what might result from trying to change it. This political support will persuade only those who already defend existing domination. Nonetheless, what has been suggested above in an attempt to explain selfishness, cruelty, and aggression—without having to say that human nature is pervasively wicked—must be taken as at best a very sketchy hypothesis for further empirical investigation. All the details have to be filled in, as no one has yet done. Still, this hypothesis explains data taken from various forms of non-selfish and non-aggressive communitarian life that are not compatible with the devil theory.

3   Basic survival needs   A theory of a universal human nature is the final resort for the advocate of inevitable wickedness. The above argument weakens the devil theory. But its supporters think they can salvage the theory by basing themselves on universal human nature. Their argument is admirably simple.

The *first premise* to the argument is that human nature is universal. That is, human nature is common to all members of human-kind. The *second premise* is that, in at least some humans, wickedness is a feature of their nature. This feature is not just an environmentally conditioned trait of the autocrats who have ruled their nations, of the criminals who have taken lives for personal gain, and of the egoists who have abused the feelings of others. It is something these people have as a basic inner drive. From these two premises the *conclusion* follows that wickedness is to be found as part of the nature of every member of human-kind. For if human nature is common to all members of the kind, any feature that is part of the nature of any individual is part of the nature all humans have.

The social theory of human persons is in direct conflict with the first premise. It denies a universal human nature. The social theory is a special instance of the idea that human-kind is a weak, not a strong, kind. In a weak kind there are several different but connected natures, and hence no one nature common to all members of the kind. Once, though, the premise of a universal human nature is rejected, in favour of the social theory of the person, the above argument collapses.

The social theory of the person can reinterpret in an acceptable way the second premise, that wickedness is a feature of the natures of at least some persons. For all that needs to be allowed is that social circumstances can be responsible for features that make people what they are. There is this much truth, then, to the claim that some people are by their nature wicked. The flaw in the theory that human nature is universal is the supposition that, if certain circumstances bring out a feature that is part of what some people are, no other circumstances can make a conflicting feature part of what other people are.

The collapse of the above argument does not put in doubt the universal character of the survival needs. Still, one might wonder, how the survival needs can be universal and indeed natural features of humans if this status is denied to wickedness? The source of the puzzlement is quite understandable. The basis for the view that wickedness is natural to humans was the view that there is only one human nature throughout human kind. Having emphatically denied this view of human nature, how is it possible to claim that survival needs are universal, natural features of humans? To clarify this we need to reiterate the point that just because a feature is natural does not mean it amounts to a full blown human nature.

As was emphasized in Chapter III, Section 1, the nature of an entity is the basis in it for *all* the ways that are natural for it to behave. It is not a basis for merely one side of what is characteristic of that entity. We cannot then say that a Detroit autoworker and an Indian peasant have a common nature because the four survival needs are common to them. Each of the survival needs is indeed a natural feature of most humans. But these needs for food, sex, support, and deliberation are, even together, only one side of the nature of anyone. This allows for the fact that the Detroit autoworker and the Indian peasant have different natures. The one has some features natural to him or her that are not even to be found in the other. Being prepared to join a walkout when the assembly line is sped up twenty per cent might be natural to the autoworker, but it is not among the tendencies of the peasant, who may not have considered the problems of industrial labour. There is then a distinction between having a common feature naturally and having a common nature. Humans have the universal needs naurally without thereby having a common nature.

Having made this clarification, we now summarize our two positive reasons for making the survival needs universal natural needs. First, they account for the emergence of other needs in the presence of certain contexts. In an analogous way, electrons account for magnetism. Thus as basic needs, the survival needs have an initial claim to universality. The important derived needs do not, since contextual features enter their derivation. Some authors, of course, postulate selfishness, cruelty, or aggression as basic without, it seems, having gone through all the possibilities of derivation. For example, Lorenz postulates feeding, reproduction, flight, and *aggression* as the four 'big drives'.[8] But much of his evidence seems to admit of reinterpretation as evidence for the derivative character of aggression.

Likewise, the sociobiologist Edward O. Wilson thinks that humans are strongly predisposed to aggressive responses. He admits that the forms aggression takes have been conditioned by human culture and can become much less brutal. But he alleges that genetic factors make it unlikely that humans can become less prone to aggression. Though for Wilson aggression does not well up spontaneously in people as it does for Lorenz, he too can be viewed as treating aggression as a basic rather than a derived feature of humans. He gives no serious consideration to the possibility that with changed methods of distribution and production the predisposition toward aggression can be markedly reduced. Rather, his view seems to imply that the predisposition toward aggression follows from traits that are basic enough to make such a change in distribution and production impossible. But he offers no evidence genuinely supporting the view that there are fixed features of humans which make reliance on aggressive responses inevitable.[9]

Our second reason for postulating universal natural survival needs is that a common backdrop is needed for the connections between the diversity of natures in human-kind. The evolutionary connections arise because through support and deliberation changes are brought about in the way all the survival needs are satisfied. Different methods of distribution and production are both brought about by the survival needs and generate different methods for realizing survival needs. Human nature changes through the agency of survival needs and as methods for satisfying survival needs change. The complementary connections between human nature in different classes are likewise based on the diversity of roles new methods of production bring in. So these connections too have their explanation in the way survival needs are satisfied.

In short, survival needs common to human kind do not rest on a common human nature. But as we saw, the devil theory does appeal, in the last resort, to a common human nature in order to have a basis for saying wickedness is universal. Since survival needs are basic in respect to other needs and since they explain changes in human nature there is a good warrant for saying they extend through the kind as part of human nature. In some social circumstances, the survival needs will generate a penchant for wickedness. But the possibility remains of a method of distribution and production that satisfies survival needs while minimizing the incidence of wickedness. In the contemporary world—both East and West—the struggle for such a method is the struggle for socialism.

4 Human nature as freedom   Few people would maintain that, as things are, humans actually behave as though they had the nature of angels. So in order to get a contrast for the devil theory, one needs to hold that there are powerful forces that block the natural development of humans. By blocking this development, these forces conceal how good we really are. Conversely, the devil theory contends that through the force of education and custom the wickedness of humans is mitigated, much to their collective good fortune.

The angel theory claims that the penchant for goodness will be manifested only under a better social system. Since human nature is assumed to be common to all humans, the penchant for goodness must be seen as a thwarted part of human nature in social systems that are less good. However, on the social theory of human nature, there is no reason to make the penchant for goodness universal.

One version of the view that humans have a basically good nature holds that humans are beings who realize what they are only in the free, that is, unconstrained, exercise of their basic drives, whatever these may be. What is important is that their free exercise will be good. Throughout history these drives have been forced into patterns that limit realization. These patterns are the constraints society has imposed on individual gratification, initially because of acute scarcity and then because of the desire to preserve forms of domination long after these forms have served their purpose of overcoming the problems of scarcity that gave rise to them. One can even view the development of constraints on free gratification as having their origin in the system of basic desires. For the frustrations these desires ultimately experience as a result of lack of constraint conditions them to operate according to certain routines of constraint. When and if the means of gratification become less scarce, the constraints can be loosened and human nature will begin to be realized. The free development of the basic drives is precisely the realization of human nature. This view has been advocated by the influential German social critic Herbert Marcuse.[10]

The devil theory goes with the view that moral laws maintain social order to prevent the destructive consequences of human nature left to itself. The angel theory goes with the view that valid moral laws defend freedom against the repression of human nature by social order. These respective views of what makes up a universal human nature support either order or freedom as the aim of moral laws. These laws will then be absolutes, being based on the requirement of the coherent realization of a universal human nature. And so the sides line up in an interminable and intensely abstract debate over whether order or freedom is prior.[11]

There is something radically wrong with the framework within which this debate takes place. The framework is that of a universal human nature, on which absolute moral laws can be based. The social view of the person rejects the general idea of a universal human nature. In particular, there is no universal human nature which has the unconstrained exercise of its basic drives as one of its features. Indeed the historical struggle for freedom provides no evidence for such a universal human nature, as the following makes clear.

We certainly observe humans struggling to overcome the respressive mechanisms of social order. It is correct to say that in doing so they are motivated by a desire for freedom. They develop, or have had, needs that the particular form of social order they live in does little to satisfy. A new order is developed that relieves this particular frustration to a greater or lesser degree, though of course it may introduce other frustrations. This new order is free relative to the old. It is not legitimate to conclude, though, that there is still a higher kind of freedom, one that is not realized by these transitions from one way of constraining needs to another way. This higher freedom is supposed to be a freedom from *all* social mechanisms that would in any way hinder the 'free play' of the instincts. The limited freedom realized by changing a particular form of social order into a less repressive one is certainly understandable without the possibility of an absolute freedom to realize drives apart from the constraints of any order. Accordingly, the theory that there is a universal human nature which can be realized only in the free play of the instincts has no basis whatsoever in the evidence of the multiple struggles of humans to overcome repression.

Notes

1　Aristotle, *Physics* (fourth century B. C.), trans. R. Hope, University of Nebraska Press, Lincoln, 1961, Bk. II, Ch. I, 192b23.

2　For an elaboration of the idea of a kind that contains different natures, see Fisk, *Nature and Necessity*, Ch. III, Sec. 3; Ch. V, Sec. 2.

3　Aristotle, *Politics* (fourth century B. C.), trans. B. Jowett, Clarendon Press, Oxford, 1905, 1263b11–1264a3.

4　Edmund Burke, *Reflections on the Revolution in France* (1790), Regnery, Chicago, 1955, pp. 201, 90.

5　This is the way Marx characterizes humans in 'Alienated labour' (1844), *Karl Marx : Selected Writings*, ed. D. McLellan, Oxford University Press, Oxford, 1977, p. 82.

6　For a classic statement of the communitarian character of certain primitive societies, see Frederick Engels, *The Origin of the Family, Private Property, and the State* (1884), trans. A. West, ed. E. B. Leacock, International Publishers, New York, 1972, Ch. III.

7　Marvin Harris, *Cows, Pigs, Wars, and Witches*, Vintage, New York, 1974, pp. 83–107.

8　Konrad Lorenz, *On Aggression*, trans. M. K. Wilson, Bantam, New York, 1967, p. 85. See Bernard Gendron's critique of the view that aggression is a basic drive in his *Technology and the Human Condition*, St Matin's Press, New York, 1977, Ch. V.

9　Edward O. Wilson, *On Human Nature*, Harvard University Press, Cambridge, Mass., 1978, Ch. 5.

10　Herbert Marcuse, *Eros and Civilization*, Vintage, New York, 1962, Ch. II.

11　Jean-Jacques Rousseau states the polarity as between 'peace' and 'freedom' and his philosophy reflects the pulls from both sides, see *The Social Contract* (1762), trans. W. Kendall, Regnery, Chicago, 1954, Bk. III, Ch. IX, P. 131.

IX

How Groups Change Individuals

In the last chapter, reference was made to the interaction between a given social order and an individual's basic needs, which were identified with the survival needs. The view that it is possible for basic needs to emerge from under social organization and develop themselves freely was rejected. It is important to explain how society interacts with basic needs, since, as was pointed out in discussing deontology, the validity of ethical principles rests on patterns found in society and reflected within the structure of the person. Deontology—as opposed to teleology—correctly held that ethical principles rest their validity on such patterns rather than on an unorganized aggregate of goods. To prepare for this explanation, something has to be said about the nature of social groups. Thinking of groups in different ways is likely to lead to different ideas as to how, or indeed whether, they work changes on individuals.

1 Groups as concrete particulars Suppose atoms are endowed with consciousness. An atom in a fibre in a large tree in the forest notices other atoms around it in the tree. In fact, everything that it is most directly aware of belongs at the atomic level. The atom begins to wonder whether indeed a tree, or even a fibre, is an entity like it is, that is, another concrete particular. The tree and its fibres are less forcefully present to it than its neighbouring atoms. All the talk that goes on among these atoms about their tree is, perhaps, but a manner of referring collectively to themselves. The tree seems but a collection of atoms constricted—except for the atoms in the sap and in the leaves—to places inside the tree-like volume. A collection is not changeable; it either is some one thing or is not that thing but it is never in the process of becoming something. Moreover, a collection is not a source of changes in other entities. It is then not a concrete particular, but an abstract one, since it can be conceived to exist only by abstracting from concrete existence all the conditions of change. As a mere collection, the tree is not a basis for dispositions in its constituent atoms. Rather it is dispositions the individual atoms have on their own that make them eligible to belong to the tree.

When humans begin to reflect philosophically they often go through something like the same reasoning about those entities we have been bandying about so freely from the start—societies, classes, sexes, nation-states.[1] They conclude that groups are mere collections of people. Yet if this reasoning is correct it becomes doubtful whether there is such a thing as ethical life. Human life has an ethical dimension only because there is conflict between the person and groups.

This conflict cannot be understood merely by building groups as collections of antecedently given persons. For it depends on people having tendencies that they have only as a result of being in groups. Such tendencies represent the interests of the group in the person-group conflict. If groups are simply collections, there will be no such group-based tendencies. This will be the first thing to be shown. It leaves only conflict between persons formed independently of groups. But perhaps a mistake was made earlier. Perhaps this person-person conflict can give an ethical dimension to human life, even though up to now the ethical dimension was tied to the person-group conflict. That this is not possible is the second thing to be shown.

First, what happens to group tendencies? Consider whether groups as mere collections of particulars can provide the dispositions needed for person-group conflict to be the locus of the ethical. In Chapter I, Section 4, we found that membership in a group results in dispositions whose realization would advance the aims of the group. If the group were not a concrete particular but a mere collection of particulars, these dispositions would be anomalous. For, on the one hand, these dispositions presuppose that there is a group by their being based on its aim. They cannot then be used as the features which define the membership of the group. Otherwise, defining features would already be based on what they define. On the other hand, these dispositions could not be explained by saying that people have them because they are in certain groups. For here being in a group means merely being one among others in a collection. A collection, as an abstract entity, does not affect other entities and hence is not the source of dispositions in them. So we must reject the idea of a group as a mere collection if we are to account for those dispositions which are bridges from the person to the group.[2]

Second, suppose we stick to the collection view of groups and adjust the notion of the ethical accordingly. If groups are not concrete particulars but are mere collections, then person-person conflict must replace person-group conflict as the mark of the ethical. What, then, will the bridge be once we are down to person-

person conflict? That is, what dispositions will lead to curbing interests that conflict with those of another person? We need to assume that, for whatever reason, other individuals in conditions like our own will tend to support those interests of ours that we have developed in the same conditions. We will, then, be disposed to advance the aims of these individuals for at least the reason that they support our interests. Being so disposed is the bridge needed to make it natural for us to be obligated to other persons. What could be simpler? And yet we dispense with reliance on groups.

There is a flaw in this. Seeing it makes clear why morality has its roots in groups. The flaw is the assumption that other individuals in conditions like ours will indeed tend to support our interests. If individuals are not formed by groups but groups are just collections of them, then supporting the interests of others is far from guaranteed. More often than not, it is individuals as members of one's own or an allied group, and hence individuals as formed by that group, who tend to be genuinely supportive. On the collection view, though, appeal to individuals as formed by groups is ruled out. We can only appeal to individuals by themselves. Individuals-by-themselves are just atomic persons. Since what they are is given independently of their group membership, there can be no presumption that they would support other people in the same conditions.

The atomic person allowed by the collection view of groups can be approximated by an imaginative experiment. Doing this shows us, though, how strong the social forces must be to overcome the bond created by groups as concrete particulars. To approximate the individual-by-itself one needs to introduce the forces of domination. These forces weaken group-dependent dispositions. Consider, for example, the fragmentation of working people by discriminatory practices. The tendency to pursue the aims of the working class is weakened. Wages, hiring practices, and working conditions that are racially and sexually discriminatory lead to a weaker bargaining position for workers, to scabbing, and to speed up. As the tendency to pursue working-class aims is weakened, the individual's bonds to the class are loosened. If we imagine this weakening pushed for each of the individual's groups, the individual approximates the individual-by-itself. As a result, the expectation that one individual will curb his or her interests for those of another ceases to be significant. Weakening group-dependent tendencies, and hence supportiveness, tends in this way to destroy ethical life.

Two possibilities have been ignored in reaching this negative conclusion. They correspond to the utilitarian and to the contractarian positions. The utilitarian claims benevolence is a natural sentiment. Despite the weakening of group-dependent tendencies for purposes of domination, will there not still be benevolence? Will not people curb their interests for those of others because of benevolence? A closer look at the above imaginative approximation shows that benevolence is weakened too. Weakening the tendency to cooperate to realize interests shared by people of the same class and weakening the tendency to pursue overarching ends that will benefit people of one's class are precisely the ways to undermine benevolence in the class.

The field seems left to the contractualist, who starts from the self-interested individual whose concern is to guarantee some satisfactions when everyone is competing for the means to satisfactions. The contractualist is, then, on congenial territory when groups have been fragmented by weakening group-dependent dispositions. The difficulties are still insurmountable. For I am supposed to agree to curb my interests in favour of yours so that I might in the long run be assured some satisfactions. But what guarantee have I that you will take this agreement seriously? All my concessions, like those of the Social Democrats under Hitler, may lead only to my deeper misery. In real life we cannot afford the luxury of assuming the myth that agreements among individuals of whatever groups can be entered on a basis of freedom and equality and can thus be secure. Apart from the bonds of a class or a race or some other group, bonds that are based on some perception of the direction of the group, there is no bridge for taking us to obligation to others.

So within ethics itself there is a reason for believing that groups are concrete particulars rather than collections of particulars. Otherwise there could be no ethical life. For there could not be the group-dependent dispositions providing the bridge from the person to some other entity. Without this bridge the conflict between the person and either other persons or groups would be one between such alien entities that this conflict would not be relevant to ethical life.

2 **Patterning needs** We are now ready to talk about the role of groups in generating a social person out of the materials provided by the survival needs. The four survival needs are plausible candidates for basic needs. Basic needs are those universal needs from which other needs can be derived, either by combining basic needs or combining circumstances with basic needs.

With the advent of the chemical approach to psychology and biology, it might seem very old-fashioned to talk about needs at all.

Doubtless needs do have a physical base in chemical molecules. But there is no reason to say that there are no needs because needs have a chemical base. Not everything literally reduces to its physical base. And needs are among the entities that do not.

The needs for food, for sex, for the support of others, and for deliberation, that is, for rationally considering and deciding among future possibilities, were already listed as the survival needs. They are also claimed to be basic needs. Each of these basic needs becomes present to awareness in the form of a characteristic emotion. Thus there are feelings of hunger, sexual longing, rejection, and powerlessness. None of the needs, then, is a blind physical drive. Rather than calling them needs, they could be called desires, because attributing them to us also attributes to us capacities for emotions, which are crucial in motivating actions. In speaking about the patterning of needs, we shall, then, implicitly be speaking about a patterning of emotions.[3]

In choosing candidates for basic needs one looks for needs that in no obvious way *make up* one another and that are not themselves made up by any need outside the list of basic needs. (Being made up by another need is one way a need has of being derivative from it.) The need for food would, for example, partly make up the need for potatoes. For the need for potatoes is just the need for food so modified by circumstances as to have a specific direction. One might not deliberate if there were not needs for specific kinds of satisfaction, such as that provided by food. Nonetheless, the need for food does not make up the need to deliberate, even though the need to deliberate is felt only when other needs, like that for food, press on us. When there is no need to deliberate, as in the case of a permanently dependent individual *all* of whose other needs are taken care of by other persons, there is little basis for talking about human agency at all. In fact, no one of the four survival needs makes up any of the others. And the permanent absence of any of them might call into question the humanness of the agent.

Consider now what effect the family, as an example of a group, has on such basic needs. To avoid being too general let us take the contemporary western nuclear family, rather than any of the various forms of family that make a broader community of it.[4] The family provides a special organization of the needs we have mentioned. The need for food has its realization in at least some meals at which everyone sits down together. Typically the woman has charge over the preparation of meals. The sexual drive and the drive for food are tied together in that in the family adults eat with their sexual partners. There is a division of labour as regards deliberation, with the man typically deciding the location of the family to fit the location of his job and the woman typically deciding on the details of home management. The children are regarded as apprentices in deliberation. They may be asked to settle their own disputes but rarely to decide whether they will matriculate in the schools. Generally the need to deliberate is realized within the context of the assumption that the man is the economic provider and the woman, at best, the source of supplemental income. The need for support is integrated with all these other needs: children are given tangible signs of parental affection and material support, whereas support between the adults extends not just to their individual tasks in the family division of labour but also, in the ideal case, to their mutual task of building an exclusive union through sharing feelings. Within the family, then, there is a distinctive patterning of needs. That is, the basic needs are tied in special ways to one another and thereby given special forms of realization. And this patterning alters the persons in the family. Of course, since this form of family is not without alternatives, the person that is formed by it is not the only kind of person.

One does not capture the basic needs all naked but only as organized together, in the presence of some social structure, for realization in certain special ways. One can do away with the special organization that the nuclear family gives basic needs. But this would not mean they could exist without organization. There would be some group or groups that would do the job. It makes no sense then to speak of a proper or natural realization of these desires. The activities we engage in are as much the result of groups as of the basic needs we have postulated. Dewey puts it this way:

Like Greek slavery or feudal serfdom, war and the existing economic regime are social patterns woven out of the stuff of instinctive activities. Native human nature supplies the raw materials, but custom furnishes the machinery and the designs. . . . The important thing morally is the way these native tendencies interact, for their interaction may give a chemical transformation not a mechanical combination.[5]

Though one does not capture a basic need outside a social patterning of needs, basic needs nonetheless persist through various patterns. History stops short of altering the basic human constitution so radically. A need is a capacity to endeavour to do something. And a capacity is grounded in the constitution of the entity with it. For example, it is the crystalline structure of salt that determines its solubility. Similarly, the need for food is grounded in our physiology. That need is simply the capacity to endeavour to acquire food, a capacity realized under appropriate conditions of deprivation. However cultural changes may affect the way food is prepared and how it is eaten, this physiological ground remains relatively unchanged. Since the ground of the capacity is stable, the capacity to endeavour to acquire food and hence the need for food remain roughly the same. It is right then to speak of one need under a variety of patterns.

To say that the basic needs are only the raw materials in respect to the activity in any given epoch or class is not to say that all patterns of such activity are equally satisfying. Realizing the desire for the support of others is achieved in large part through the family in present society. Realizing the desire in this way may still leave one with a feeling of being isolated, even though it assures one's acceptance by a spouse or parents. Since we are dealing with a survival need, this much support must be given, yet the way it is given by this patterning leaves one with a sense of isolation. Likewise, when the need to deliberate is realized by parcelling out—as in the family described above—narrow areas of competence to different individuals, they may all be left with the feeling that they lack involvement in deciding the things that really count.

Thus the way basic needs are patterned by groups will generate conflicts. The conflicts are between the way these needs are satisfied within such a pattern and other needs that are not basic needs. For example, the way support is given in present society tends to make members of the family the main, and indeed almost exclusive, sources of support a person gets. This has the effect of isolating many people from the world outside the family. A need then develops to overcome this isolation, a need that has its basis in the way the need for support is satisfied. But this non-basic need to overcome isolation cannot be satisfied so long as the need for support is realized as it is in the family. Thus one faces a conflict between the patterning of basic needs and the non-basic needs arising out of it. These conflicts are important as regards social change. They are the energy behind the effort to build a new form of society that will not generate the same conflicts. But the new society should not be expected to be one in which the needs realize themselves freely without the mediation of any patterning at all.

3 Classes and roles The social person is the joint product of the basic needs and the groups which organize these needs. The influence of groups is quite real. At least in Section 1 it was established that if there is ethical life there must be such an influence. Moreover, when we describe the organization that takes place among the needs, we cannot suppose that it is an organization that exists apart from groups. It will be interesting now to note the effects of classes on individuals. After all, classes are important to us since domination among groups has its roots in class domination (Chapter IV, Section 3).

The classes of a given society cannot be treated in isolation from one another. Masters go with slaves, lords with serfs, capitalists with proletarians. If the economic roles of the various classes do not interlock, they do not form a unitary economic system. Yet it is the economic system that gives a society its distinctive classification as capitalist or as feudal. The society so classified functions as a sum group for a distinctive set of classes. Classes are conflicting aspects of one sum group, a society.[6] Feudal society had as aspects of it the various feudal classes, such as serfs and lords, journeymen and guild masters. Since classes do not exist alone but only as joined together within a society, they are limited to the status of aspects. Those classes that are essential aspects of a given society correspond to economic roles without which the society could not continue. The organization of basic needs comes through aspects of society, such as class, race, family. Society itself provides no patterning except through its aspects. One is not socialized just as a member of capitalist society but as, say, an urban black male worker in capitalist society. It is from this general perspective that we will look at the way classes pattern desires.

In contemporary capitalist society, there are a number of essential roles, each corresponding to a major class. The society could still be capitalist without, say, jet pilots but not without productive workers in general. It is in the very nature of such a society that there are people whose role is to make their living only under conditions in which they create the surplus at least part of which can be turned into a profit for those who hire them. Such people are *productive workers*. The society is built on the fact that profits are made from work and are invested in a form that can put further labour to work in order to make further profits. Hence in this society there must be productive workers in the above sense. If there were only people who worked for themselves, we would have an altogether different society. There could then be 'profits' in the sense of the production of more than one could use oneself. But there could be no investment of these profits in land, materials, and machinery in order to realize further profits through putting other people than oneself to work on those things.

Our description of capitalist society also includes reference to another role, that played by *the capitalist*. One plays this role by controlling a certain aggregate from the production of labour for the sake of increasing the aggregate over which one has control.

Many restrictions can be placed on what people who play this role can do with the products they control—their property—but they continue to play their role despite these restrictions as long as they can hope to increase that property. This increase requires the application of labour. This owning or capitalist class is quite clearly, then, interlocked with the class of productive workers.[7]

In addition to these two roles, there are others that, with the growth of capitalist society, have become essential to it. These roles too are associated with classes. For example, in addition to productive workers there is another class of workers. Its members are not directly involved anywhere in the process beginning with getting materials and food from the mines and fields and ending at the point at which commodities are delivered to the places they are sold. These are *unproductive workers* in the rather technical sense that they do not produce a surplus from which the owning class can add to its wealth. Nonetheless, most unproductive workers are indispensable for perpetuating the capitalist system and hence for perpetuating the production of surplus. Without the back-up work they do the system would be weakened. It would be weakened for want of an educated work force provided by public school-teachers, or for want of the stimulus to demand provided by advertisers, or for want of foremen and employment relations officers who insure that the pace of work and the size of the labour force is appropriate to a desired rate of profit. Public school-teachers, advertisers, and foremen are not front-line workers. They are among the back-up workers, whose special role in this regard lumps them in a different class. Without them the surplus produced by the system may be less, but this does not mean that they produce the difference. Though these people are workers, I shall, for brevity, speak simply of the working class when I mean only the class of productive workers, and of the worker when I mean only the productive worker.[8]

Let us look now at the way basic needs are organized by membership in the productive working class. This organization is not superimposed on an organization of these needs by capitalist society—the sum group for the various classes. Rather, the organization by class, which is an aspect of society, is one of the kinds of organization characteristic of capitalist society. In this way we avoid thinking of the society as though it were in some important way homogeneous in make up.

The worker in capitalist society satisfies the need for food and other physical necessities not by producing on a private plot or with personal machines but by working for another who controls the means of production and also the product. Working for General

Motors on an assembly line, for Dow in a laboratory, for Roadway by driving a semi becomes part of the process of feeding and otherwise providing for the family of the worker. Necessities are provided through work whose product has little significance for the worker since it is disposed of by the owner. The need for deliberation is realized, then, not in making decisions in regard to what one makes and how one makes it. Those decisions are made by management. Deciding on what one is going to consume is how the need for deliberation is realized. Reading newspaper features on home improvement, sporting goods, and vacations becomes a surrogate for deliberation over the conditions one is in forty hours a week on the job.[9] The need for support from others is satisfied only sporadically by other workers on the job. The union bureaucracy or a paternalistic boss preempts the role of being the support of the working person on the job. Institutionalized support replaces support at the level of the rank and file. Support given in this manner undermines cooperative work relations and leads to a lack of interest in work. The desire for sexual gratification reflects all of these modifications of the ways the other needs are realized. The sexual partner is expected, knowingly or not, to compensate for the limited ways these other survival needs are realized. The sexual partner is thereby put under pressures that strain the relationship.

The conflicts generated by the patterning of the basic needs within the productive working class are, then, undeniably great. They are largely similar for the unproductive working class. Nonetheless, the basic needs are somehow satisfied, despite the conflicts between the pattern that organizes them and non-basic needs arising, at least in part, because of this patterning. The need to make work significant conflicts with getting necessities by working for someone else's profit; limiting deliberation to consumer choice conflicts with the need to break management's monopoly on decision-making at the workplace; and the need to work as little as possible in defiance of authority conflicts with the attempt to satisfy the need for support by institutional relations with union and company officials. These conflicts become part of the dynamic for social change leading to doing away with the class structure that gave rise to them.

The organization of basic needs and of the ways these needs can be realized is then due, at least in part, to class, family, and other aspects of society. Some care is required in saying exactly what this means. It does not mean that humans are clay in the hands of the aspects of society. If this were the case, there could be definite societies and definite classes even when humans are socially unformed. This is patently absurd, even though it seems to be implied by so-called structuralist views, which treat classes and other social entities as agencies that bear down upon individuals and determine their paths.[10] This is not the model we want to use in speaking of the social organization of basic needs.

In place of the model that posits either a one-way forming of human material by social entities or a one-way forming of social behaviour by human genetic material,[11] we need a model with a two-way connection. Certain human tendencies exist only because there are the appropriate social entities. Conversely, though, those social entities exist only because there are the corresponding human tendencies. Groups do not lead a life of their own independent of human practice.

With human tendencies and social entities bound to one another in this mutual way changes in social entities are more easily understandable. Changes in social entities—the disappearance of a certain class, say—run parallel to changes in human tendencies. Change cannot so easily be understood on the view that social entities form undetermined human material. For, without a two-way connection, once humans have been formed by social entities they cannot change those entities.

Can the socialization of children be understood without resorting to the structuralist model of a one-way forming of human material by an aspect of a society, such as a class? It certainly can, if we are clear about a simple distinction. The tendencies of the socialized person exist only because there is the class; yet that class need not be the agent whereby those tendencies were formed. It is the behaviour of other humans who have already acquired those tendencies that is the agent. All these things need to be kept in mind when we speak about the social organization of needs.

4 Satisfaction without conflict   At the end of Section 2, it was noted that there is no pre-social realization of the basic needs since they are always organized by groups. There is then no unique pre-social realization of basic needs on which ethical absolutes might be based.

There might, though, still be room for absolutes. Their basis would be a society in which there is an organization of the basic needs out of which no conflict arises. We saw in Sections 2 and 3 how family and class organizations of needs produce conflicts of needs. The need for deliberation would not be satisfied in such a way as to create an unsatisfied need to control one's work place. The need for support would not be satisfied in such a way as to create a sense of isolation and a need to resist cooperative relations.

Societies could then be criticized against this conflict-free ideal. Ethical codes would be more or less adequate depending on the degree to which they promote the coming into being of such a society. Assume there is only one such society that will accomplish this trick. The social person in that society would be the full flowering of human nature, whereas the social persons in all previous history are distortions of it.

There is a great temptation to get around the limitations that relativism puts on the usefulness of ethics in this way. It opens up the prospect that ethics can indeed be a final arbiter. Those human drones—the owners—who are hampering progress toward such an ideal society do not have the moral excuse that their class recognizes no imperative to move to this ideal society. They would bear full moral responsibility for impeding the growth of humanity.

Reformers and revolutionaries like to be able to lean on such verbal crutches in appealing to their constituencies for action. But there is a flaw in their appeal, even when their actions can be justified on more solid ground. The flaw is that the appeal supposes the only thing worthwhile is satisfying basic needs in a way that does not generate conflict. In the abstract such conflict-free satisfaction sounds fine. However, humans have become more than a particular organization of their basic needs. They are also characterized by a vision of the future. Their vision of the future includes the realization of the basic needs in the context of certain new institutions whose aims are also being realized. These new institutions eliminate old conflicts without necessarily avoiding new ones.

Taken by itself the realization of basic needs in a pattern that involves no conflict is compatible with existence in a land where necessities are provided simply by pushing buttons. The only important matters of life would be ones over which only the briefest and simplest deliberations are required. In this utopia there is no production to be controlled, there are no institutions of governance, and there are no challenges, intellectual, aesthetic, or moral, to be faced. To see what this utopia lacks one has to look at what one's present vision of the future contains. That vision answers the present restrictions on deliberation by expanding the areas of deliberation. A conflict-free life with even narrower scope for deliberation is not, then, a present ideal.

It is not satisfactory to reply that under the conditions of abundance in the push-button utopia the need for more deliberation would not arise. Lacking the means to satisfy the need for deliberation would be, the reply runs, no drawback. This reply is not satisfactory since in present non-utopian society we do in fact have the need for controlling production and our institutions of governance. Our goal is to satisfy this need and not to mutilate our present natures by destroying this need which makes up present natures. In short, from the perspective of present possibilities, a situation that satisfies basic needs without creating conflicting needs is not of itself ideal. Since it is not a basis for ethics now, such a situation does not provide an absolute basis for ethics.

Even a society without classes is an ideal not because it organizes basic needs so that absolutely no conflict arises but because it overcomes the conflicts peculiar to class societies. Thus the way humans are in a classless society is not an ideal when considered absolutely, that is, without reference to the way humans are in class societies. The needs generated by the patternings of basic needs in class societies require for their realization that class societies be gotten beyond. Classless society is called for by the historical development and frustration of these needs. It has no absolute justification.

Notes

1   For a general discussion of the status of groups, see Ernest Nagel, *The Structure of Science*, Harcourt, Brace, and World, New York, 1961, p. 537.

2   For an argument that many familiar dispositions cannot be accounted for without assuming social entities, see Maurice Mandelbaum, 'Societal facts', *British Journal of Sociology*, Vol. VI, 1955, pp. 305–17.

3   Aristotle, *Nicomachean Ethics* (fourth century B. C.), trans. H. Rackham, Loeb Classical Library, Harvard University Press, Cambridge, Mass., 1926, 1105b20–29.

4   For a detailed discussion, see Sheila Rowbotham, *Woman's Consciousness; Man's World*, Penguin Books, Baltimore, 1973, Part, II.

5   John Dewey, *Human Nature and Conduct* (1922), Modern Library, New York, 1930, pp. 10–11.

6   For a general metaphysical discussion of classes as 'aspects' of societies, see Milton Fisk, 'Society, class, and the individual', *Radical Philosophers' Newsjournal*, No. 2, March 1974, pp. 7–22.

7   Recent literature in sociology indicates that a critical reappraisal of the view that classes are not preeminent among groups is well underway. A rebuttal of some simple underestimations of the importance of class is given in T. B. Bottomore, *Classes in Modern Society*, Vintage, New York, 1966. For basic data on the importance of the working class in US society, see Andrew Levison, *The Working Class Majority*, Penguin, New York, 1975, Chaps. I–II. Theoretically the most successful treatment is Braverman's *Labor and Monopoly Capital*.

8 For differences in class consciousness between productive and unproductive workers, see Robert Cherry, 'Class struggle and the nature of the working class', *Review of Radical Political Economy*, Vol. V, No. 2, 1973, Sec. V.

9 Andre Gorz, *A Strategy for Labor*, trans. M. A. Nicolaus and V. Ortiz, Beacon, Boston, 1967, pp. 69–75.

10 Lucien Goldmann, 'Genetic-structuralist method in history of literature', in *Marxism and Art*, eds. B. Lang and E. Williams, David McKay Company, New York, 1972, p. 247.

11 Sociobiology emphasizes the genetic material at the basis of social behavior to such an extent that it lacks a theory as to how the possibilities opened up by the genetic base are patterned by institutions and groups. As a result we get the kind of one-sided account of humans that sociobiologist Edward O. Wilson gives in his *On Human Nature*.

X

Alienation and Obligation

ETHICAL principles were shown to be valid relative to tendencies that individuals have as members of groups. Now we can say more about these tendencies. They are not basic needs common to all humans but rather tendencies that arise as a result of the way survival needs are patterned in a given group. They are then derivative from the survival needs, which were held to be basic. We shall call these tendencies 'historical' since, rather than being common to human-kind, they are formed in response to particular human circumstances.

These historically formed tendencies will, nonetheless, meet resistance to their realization even in the circumstances in which they were formed. Their meeting resistance gives rise to the phenomenon widely referred to as 'alienation'. This phenomenon is then very closely associated with the ethical dimension of human life. For, if followed, ethical principles would tend to eliminate the alienation characteristic of a given group within a given society. This, of course, does not mean that following such principles tends to overcome alienation altogether.

1 Historical needs We saw how class membership organizes the basic needs in a distinctive way. Now we shall show how an organization of the basic needs creates historical needs. Then we shall be in a position to talk about alienation. Everything here is grounded in the patterning of basic needs by class roles discussed in the last chapter.

Within capitalism, the productive worker has his or her desire for food and other necessities put within the context of working to increase the wealth of someone else. The need to deliberate leads people to uncover the key factors on which their welfare depends. Thus the need to deliberate leads the worker to recognize that the satisfaction of the desire to have food and other necessities is contingent upon the owner's being made to sacrifice enough from the product of labour to provide the necessities for workers. The worker also recognizes that this satisfaction is contingent upon its being profitable for owners to hire workers. If it is not profitable there will be unemployment. Yet the worker wants employment whether or not it profits the owner. It is easy to see, then, how deliberation leads to the recognition that the organization of workers for collective strength is desirable. Without organization there is no assurance of adequate wages or of protection against unemployment.[1]

Thus the very patterning of basic needs that is characteristic of working people gives rise to further needs. The need for food and other necessities is so bound up with relations to owners that, together with the need to deliberate, it creates a further need. This is a need for independent working-class organizations—unions, political parties, factory committees—that will provide protection for the realization of basic needs. This need is not itself common to human-kind: it is tied to the relations of workers to owners in the capitalist epoch. It is historical in the sense that it does not arise in all epochs or in all groups. Further, unlike the basic needs, it is not a survival need since unorganized workers do in fact survive. However, in overcoming a lower standard of living and in combatting the worst effects of unemployment, the political and trade-union organizations of working people have been of considerable effect.

The need for an organization, unlike a need such as that for food, can only be satisfied collectively. This is an important fact when we come to talk about satisfying the needs characteristic of a class. For satisfying these needs is not just a matter of giving *similar* but *distinct* goods to all the individuals of the class. It is often a matter of developing an institution that is the same for all who are involved in it. When an institution satisfies a need for organization there is no problem, as there was for the utilitarian, of how to distribute it fairly among many individuals. Only one institution is in question and it cannot be distributed.

There is a fundamental limitation in capitalist society on the above mechanism for workers' security. The organizations needed for security will be pitted against the power of the owners. When there is not a lot of fat on the economic system, the other side—the owners—will try to destroy the effects of earlier victories. There will be erosions across the whole area where security had previously been won. Workers' organizations do not eliminate a basic insecurity resulting from the fact that the state is willing to help the owners drive down wages and increase unemployment in periods of crisis. For example, the explicit aim of President Nixon's wage–price controls of 1971–74 was to slow down wage increases and allow an upturn in the corporations' rate of profit. According to the first director of the Cost of Living Council, Arnold Weber, 'The idea of the freeze and Phase II was to zap labour, and we did.'[2] Independent workers' organizations within capitalism are not of themselves sufficient bulwarks against such an erosion of workers' benefits.

These workers' organizations must be provided with features that will make them effective. But under what conditions will they be effective in providing security from want? The protection afforded by these organizations even when provided with all sorts of strengthening features can easily be destroyed. All that is required is a lower rate of profit that does not bring out enough new investment to put everyone to work at an acceptable wage. The guaranteed level of effectiveness of workers' organizations is, then, doomed to remain low under conditions of the ownership of the means of production by a minority. The workers' organizations of a country like Sweden are no exception. They were effective while the world's economy prospered. But beginning in 1977, with a large drop in Swedish exports, they have not been able to prevent a decline in living standards. So the need to have workers' organizations leads directly to the need for a new economic system within which opportunities exist for making workers' organizations consistently effective.

What kind of system would this new one be? It would be one of workers' democracy. It would have a patterning of basic desires reflecting such a democracy. For example, the need for deliberation would be realized in deliberating about productive work and overall governance and not primarily about consumption. The need for this system is the second historical need within this chain of development. Though such a need arises for workers under the capitalist system, it cannot be realized without destroying capitalism. The conflict between the need for effective working-class organizations and the capitalist system leads to this need to develop socialism. Like the need for a workers' organization the need for a socialist economy is a need for a social entity and is then collectively satisfied.

These two historical needs arise in people out of the patterning of survival needs by their class. There are other historical needs, ones that arise in people out of the domination of their own class by another class. These needs are the basis for imposed consciousness, discussed in Chapter IV, Section 2. For example, the need to support the capitalist system arises from the conditions of domination. Workers are dominated by the pattern of profit taking; when there is a higher rate of profit the system prospers and there are plenty of well paying jobs, yet when there is a lower rate of profit the system is in crisis and there is a declining standard of living and high unemployment. Having their fortunes dominated in this way gives rise to the need to support the system. This need is the basis for imposed consciousness about the system. It opens peoples' minds to the belief that without owners who make profits there would be no employment. This is of course true within the capitalist system, but it is certainly not true in general.

Moreover, economic analysis would show that worker support for the system will not prevent the crises that periodically follow prosperity. These crises are a response to the large accumulations of investment that take place during periods of prosperity. With so much invested, it is difficult to keep the rate of return on investment up to the same level. Prosperity tends to be followed by a period when the rate of profit is lower and hence unemployment higher. Thus the need to support capitalism commits workers to the loss of their gains in periodic crises. Such a need, arising from domination by the pattern of profits, is clearly an imposed need.

This need to support capitalism conflicts with the need coming from within the working class for the change of the economic system to a workers' democracy, that is, to socialism. One will not consciously support capitalism and at the same time a system incompatible with it. As a result, the need for a workers' democracy will often be latent under the domination of the profit pattern. Imposed needs and consciousness about capitalism will yield to consciousness about the need for socialism only in the context of the struggles that inevitably arise over less global goals.

2 Alienation This prepares us to give a general characterization of alienation. There are many elements within this characterization. Most of these elements have been elaborated previously. *First,* alienation concerns the blocking of historical needs, not of basic needs. One is being destroyed, not alienated, if one is denied the realization of basic needs. *Second,* the historical needs blocked are those that arise from the special patterning of basic needs characteristic of one's group. (By one's group we shall not mean one's sum group.) Hence the blocked historical needs in question are not needs imposed from outside one's group. The conscious desire to satisfy such needs is not part of imposed consciousness since these needs are not imposed. We shall call them 'internal' historical needs. *Third,* though these needs arise internally to a group they are blocked precisely because of the limitations on that group resulting from the kind of society it is in.[3] And so a change in the overall society appears as the only remedy for this kind of blockage of internal historical needs. Since one's group will be an aspect of the encompassing society, it too will be changed by a change in the encompassing society. The important thing, though, is that one would be mistaken to locate the blockage simply in one's group and then try to change this group without changing the encompassing society.

Putting these elements into a tidy formula yields the following:

Alienation arises when a given society restricts the realization of some of the internal historical needs of groups within that society.

This formula tells us only how it arises, not what it is. In itself alienation is a condition of persons. It is a tendency to be *aware* that the realization of one's needs is being blocked due to the established institutions of one's society. If it is to be alienation and not some other form of frustration, then clearly two conditions must be satisfied. First, these needs, whether one is aware of the fact or not, must be internal historical needs of one's group. Second, these needs, whether one is aware of the fact or not, must be blocked because the kind of society one is in fashions its institutions so that it blocks them. Thus the awareness associated with alienation need not include an analysis of its sources. Moreover despondency need not be associated with alienation. In fact, a fighting attitude may equally well accompany this tendency to be aware that within the given society internal historical needs are being blocked.

As the word suggests, alienation is a separation from oneself. The internal historical needs are part of the social person, and when the social structure places restrictions on their realization, one is separated from oneself. This separation from oneself is not a separation from a universal human nature. It is at most a separation from aspects of the nature one has as a member of a group at a particular time. Thus the task of overcoming alienation is always a *limited task*. It is the task of removing obstacles placed by a given form of society in front of needs formed within that society.

Since the society both originates and blocks these needs, the society is internally contradictory. The process of resolving this contradiction is, then, dialectical. For, first, the process results from the conflict between the poles of an *internal* contradiction. The conflict is not between society and a trans-social human nature. And, second, the process of resolution changes fundamentally the *nature* of the society encompassing the contradiction. It does more than do away with one of the poles of the conflict.

The dialectical task of overcoming the contradictions of alienation is *not* the absolute task of building an ideal society in which a universal human nature is fully realized. It is only survival needs that are common to humans, and the realization of these needs takes place in all epochs. This is not to say there is not starvation, mass murder, and psychological destruction going on in all epochs. Famine is still a grim reality around the world; for a decade the US used advanced technology to kill inhabitants of Vietnam; and insecurity and neglect have turned major US cities into production lines for human pathology. But unless there were also the realization of survival needs, human history would long since have ceased. This realization is then presupposed by the phenomenon of alienation.

A salient form of alienation within capitalism is felt right at the workplace. It comes from blocking the need to break management's monopoly on decision making. The patterning of the need for deliberation under capitalism results for most workers in limiting the realization of this need to consumer choice. Due to this limited realization, the historical need to break management's monopoly on decision making arises. But without this monopoly neither private nor public enterprises would assuredly serve the goal of perpetuating the dominance of the capitalist class. If workers were to make the decisions guiding enterprises, why should they make them to accord with the interests of another class, the capitalist one? The same system that gives rise to the worker's need for decision making about production also blocks the realization of this need.

Unions themselves are another source of a familiar form of worker alienation. The need for independent workers' organizations, such as unions, was seen in Section 1 to be an internal historical need of working people generally, and of the class of productive workers in particular. It was also noted that it is not enough simply to have such organizations; they must be made effective. However, their effectiveness is very limited within the context of capitalist society. Capitalist society gives rise to the need for such organizations and insures their limited effectiveness. The tendency to be aware of this limitation is a form of alienation which is common among working people. Workers are, then, alienated by the ineffectiveness of their own unions.

The effectiveness of unions is limited not just by the power of the class of owners but also by the role of union leaders. Union leaders derive at least part of their power from the assurances they give to the owners that they accept the capitalist system and can be relied on to discipline workers when there is a threat of crisis in the system. That there are such leaders is not a phenomenon to be explained by the devil theory of human nature.[4] It is a phenomenon to be explained by the fact that in a capitalist sum group every institution will come within the relations of domination of the dominant class. Unions come under the domination of the class of owners by being used to perpetuate this domination. This limits the ability of a workers' organization to realize workers' needs. Worker alienation is then the result of that domination.

Since all forms of domination now have their reason in class domination, and since it is through domination that internal historical needs are frustrated, class is a fundamental factor in explaining alienation. Alienation among minorities and women have their reason for being today in class domination. Marx was right when he explained alienation in capitalism by tracing it back to the fundamental fact that workers are dominated by having to relinquish part of the product of their labour to owners.[5] Here we have the origin both of internal working-class needs and of the necessity for their being blocked.

3 Obligation   It is now time to tie alienation to morality. But first a little spade work.

The validity of ethical principles is relative to the tendencies characteristic of groups. Taking this group relativity of ethics together with the primacy of classes yields the class relativity of ethics. This class relativity can now be formulated as the claim that ethical principles are valid relative to the internal historical needs of classes.

To illustrate, consider the matter of ethical obligation. Do I have an obligation to perform military service? The question is not to be answered simply by reference to my convenience. Nor is it to be answered by reference to abstract principles which happen to have the support of authority. I must first inquire about the political goals of the government that would draft me.[6] What policies do its military ventures implement? I must then inquire what class is likely to benefit from those policies.[7] Are those policies such that pursuing them by military means will advance or retard the tendencies characteristic of my class?

The institutions used to spread ideas that aid the sum group have a single point of view on the matter of military service. That point of view is expressed as follows. The group of which we are all a part—no matter what our class may be—is the nation-state. Our welfare is tied to that of this nation-state. If we do not do our share, we cannot expect to share in the benefits resulting from the victories of this nation-state over its enemies. And, if we do not do our share, we can be blamed for the general ill resulting from its defeats.

As we have seen, a nation-state is a sum group within which

there are relations of domination. The agencies of the nation-state, including the military, perpetuate these relations of domination by perpetuating the nation-state. In particular, in a capitalist nation-state, the military serves to perpetuate the domination of the ruling class of owners.

Two things must be decided. Are the benefits coming to all citizens from the military victory of their nation-state worth the strengthening of domination by the ruling class that results from this victory? Are the benefits coming to all citizens from the military victory of their nation-state worth the damage done to dominated groups within foreign lands by this victory? After all, a class is not held within the bounds of a nation-state. It is genuinely international; what benefits one segment of it within one nation-state might be a setback for the class as a whole.

The question of military service brings up numerous empirical issues. If I am a worker, then I should not serve if there is a clear prospect that the policies of my nation-state will, when pursued by military means, lead to a setback for the international working class. In 1920, Eugene V. Debs ran for the presidency of the US from the penitentiary in Atlanta where he was serving time for speaking against the US war effort in World War I. He had asked why members of the lower classes should die in France to help the powerful Morgan Bank. The House of Morgan would lose billions in loans to France and Britain if Germany should win. Understandably then it put pressure on Woodrow Wilson to commit the US to military action in France.

The problem is one of estimating empirically what the prospects are for one's class. World War II presented greater difficulties in this regard. The immediate defeat of fascism in Germany and Italy, and of militarism in Japan, would be a victory for workers in those countries and in the countries overrun by them. Yet for the ruling class in the US, the war opened up a tempting prospect. During the war huge profits could be made by disciplining labour with high productivity and low wages. After the war, the US could take over the economic influence, around the world, of Japan, Britain, Germany, and other imperialist countries.[8] And indeed the US emerged from the war as the unquestioned economic leader of the capitalist world.[9] The defeat of US labour during the war and the prosperity enhanced by an economic empire kept the US working class relatively quiet in the 1950s and 1960s. Militant traditions were forgotten and bureaucracies gained control of all the unions. Fighting fascism in a way that allowed labour to be defeated and an empire to be built was not, then, a winning strategy for the working class. When prosperity ended in the

1970s, the working class had been disarmed and had no strategy for fighting against the erosion of its gains.

This example shows the importance of internal historical needs in deciding obligations. The characteristic interests of a group, on which obligation is based, are the internal historical needs of its members. The indispensability of an obligatory act is, then, its indispensability for realizing internal historical needs. Military service is not obligatory unless, without it, it becomes more difficult to realize the internal historical needs of members of one's group. In sum:

Action x is obligatory for person a relative to a's group A when, in the given circumstances, a's not doing x would be likely to make the realization of the internal historical needs of members of A more difficult.

In view of the coherence of interests between lower classes and oppressed groups, lower class obligations will become the obligations of oppressed groups and, conversely, the obligations of oppressed groups will become the obligations of the lower classes. In a society in which a ruling class is the primary agent of domination there is a coherence of interests among groups seeking liberation and hence a lack of conflict of obligations among different dominated groups. In fact since there is not even a difference of obligations among dominated groups, the above formula could have been used to explain group obligation in terms of class needs provided only dominated groups are considered.

However, people in a group that conflicts with some other group do not have obligations to do things that would advance the internal historical needs of that other group. An owner has no obligation to make work conditions safer, nor does a worker have an obligation to work faster so that the owners can maintain their luxurious style of life. But rights are different, since they are relative to groups but not necessarily just to groups whose interests cohere with the groups of those who have the rights. The owner has, in certain circumstances, a right to free speech even relative to the working class.

(This contrast gives rise to a peculiar problem. A person does not belong to all groups. So it might seem that after all a person's obligations are not relative to groups. We cannot say what a worker's obligation is relative to the class of peasants or owners. The reason is simply that the worker does not belong to either of those groups. Is obligation then relative to persons, not groups? Certainly obligations vary with persons since each person is a member of a specific set of groups. But just saying that obligations are relative to person leaves undetermined what it is about different persons that determines different obligations. For this a return to groups is needed, not a return to just those groups to which a given person actually belongs, but a return to the groups to which a given person might conceivably belong. Then even if Jones is a worker, it can be said what Jones' obligation *would be* relative to the class of peasants or to the class of owners if Jones had been in one of these classes. The relativity of obligations to groups thus depends on considering not just the groups to which a person actually belongs but also the groups to which a person might conceivably belong. The absolutist would, though, allow no fundamental change in the basis for obligation as a result of these hypothetical group changes.)

Overcoming alienation is not altruism but duty. This is clear from the above account of obligation. Alienation exists because a given society restricts the internal historical needs of a group. If members of that group do not respond with efforts to eliminate these restrictions, it may be more difficult than it would be if there were such efforts for members of the group to realize their internal historical needs. In this case, members of the group would have an obligation to perform acts that have a chance of changing the society. The changes aimed at are ones that would tend to eliminate the restrictions on internal historical needs. A certain change that would eliminate restrictions might be unrealizable without preparation through other changes. Failure to try to realize that change immediately would not set things back for the group and thus would not be obligatory in the circumstances. The plea of inability to change things is, though, often an unjustifiable cover-up for unwillingness to take responsibility for the losses of the group in the face of attacks by alien groups. This unwillingness is a failure to carry out obligation. Not all such failures are failures to perform acts that have dealienating consequences, since the group losses in question may be losses in respect to basic rather than internal historical needs. Overcoming alienation is, though, a major area of obligation.

4 Survival needs and absolute morality   Since there are survival needs common to all humans, why is a group morality needed? Why should tendencies of groups, rather than these fundamental features of persons, be the basis for morality? If we start with the fundamental features of persons—with the survival needs, which are basic needs—, then our ethical obligations will be grounded in what all persons are, not in special roles defining groups. Group morality seems to make the elementary mistake of putting the historical and hence 'contingent' features of humans before the eternal and hence necessary features of them.[10]

After all, is not the reason we are supportive of oppressed people, whoever they might be, that supporting them makes it possible to satisfy their survival needs? A true ethical naturalism would respect survival needs and not group tendencies. If people are obliged to advance only the tendencies of the groups to which they belong, then there is no obligation to help those whose survival is irrelevant to or incompatible with the welfare of one's groups. A group morality posits no obligation to respect the survival needs of all persons.

Earlier, in Chapter III, Section 3, it was pointed out that survival needs alone could not be the basis for an ethics consistent with naturalism. For survival needs are only part of the social person, and the rest of the social person may not be compatible with a general imperative to realize survival needs in everyone. But now the objection just raised must be answered in a less abstract way. It is important in answering this objection to consider two cases. First, there is the case of class or group conflict. Persons who are involved in placing obstacles in the way of the class or group to which I belong for the benefit of some alien class or group have no right to my efforts to satisfy their survival needs. The Rockefellers, who had the families of striking miners in Ludlow machine-gunned, who, through their oil empire, fueled the jets that napalmed Vietnamese, and who allowed the police to kill the inmates of Attica Prison, have no moral claims against miners, peasants, and political prisoners.

Second, there is the case of 'gaps' in class or group conflict. In my day-to-day life I inevitably play a class role and hence I am, however indirectly, in interaction with members of opposing classes. But there are gaps in my existence in a class role, for I find myself in situations that can be analyzed without reference to class conflict. (The same thing holds for non-class group conflict.) I sit down next to someone on a bus and a conversation gets started on the scenery; or I am driving along a deserted street and come across the victim of a hit-and-run incident who needs immediate medical care; or I am playing baseball with my son in the park and the play expands into a game as we are joined by a group of strangers. Each of these cases represents a gap in my class existence. Each provides a foretaste of life apart from the conflict resulting from the relations of domination within class society. The class identities of the people I encounter are not unambiguously revealed for the duration of such gaps. Without their class identity, I cannot connect them with potentially antagonistic behaviour outside the gap. The rights and obligations of people during such gaps are different than they are elsewhere. Though Rockefeller of Exxon is owed nothing by me, Rockefeller the unidentified hit-and-run victim or the unidentified second baseman is.

The basis for this difference is as follows. The internal historical needs of a class have a restricted realization because of the presence of antagonistic classes. So one of the goals of a class is to eliminate the antagonism associated with existing classes. With the antagonism removed, there is the possibility of cooperative effort toward common goals. Of course, the cooperation need not be between the old classes, for their elimination may have been the price of overcoming antagonism. These new common goals then become the basis for a new morality, one not based on the old antagonism. The owning class and the lower classes will have rather different conceptions of the society that will result from eliminating the antagonism. Owners will conceive of it in terms of docile workers who still produce for private profit, but with a smile. Depending on their level of class consciousness, workers will conceive of it either in terms of cooperative control of production without owners at all or in terms of production involving owners but with a drastically reduced role. In any event, gaps in the existing class struggle are situations that prefigure the absence of antagonism. In a gap, the morality that will become appropriate in the future society already holds. Should one refuse to follow that morality when a gap occurs, one would indicate one's intention to put the needs of the person ahead of cooperative effort in the new society. Where there is no antagonism between groups, it would be selfish to reject a morality of universal cooperation.

This answers the objection raised at the beginning of this section. To answer it, the special social context called a gap was needed. It was not necessary to capitulate to the absolutists by admitting that there is an obligation to satisfy survival needs independently of any social considerations. As it turned out, the obligation to help unidentified victims of accidents and to be civil to strangers rests on a solid social basis. That basis is the cooperative tendencies of a society without the present antagonism between existing classes. In a gap in the present class conflict, there is a similar lack of antagonism. Our acceptance as an ideal of a society without the current antagonism, becomes the basis for our obligations in the gap in the current class situation.

Notes

1   The recognition of this necessity in the union organizing upsurge in the US
     in the early 1930s is documented in Irving Bernstein, *Turbulent Years: A
     History of the American Worker, 1933–1941*, Houghton Mifflin, New York,
     1967, Ch. II–IV.
2   *Business Week*, 27 April, 1974.
3   This three-part characterization is closely related to the view of alienation
     proposed by Samuel Bowles and Herbert Gintis, 'Capitalism and alienation',
     in *The Capitalist System*, 2nd ed., pp. 274–8.
4   See the perceptive analysis of union leadership by Farrell Dobbs, *Teamster
     Rebellion*, Monad Press, New York, 1972, pp. 36–46.
5   Marx, 'Alienated labour' (1844), in *Karl Marx: Selected Writings*, ed. D.
     McLellan, pp. 78–9.
6   John Rawls, *A Theory of Justice*, p. 381.
7   V. I. Lenin, 'War and socialism' (1914), *V. I. Lenin: Collected Works*,
     Vol. XXI, Progress Publishers, Moscow, 1964, pp. 299–316.
8   Anti-war socialists saw the issue as follows during the early days of the war:
     'The Second World War, then, is a war among rival imperialisms for a new
     division of the world, a war for the rights of exploitation of the masses of the
     world. The issue of the war is, simply: who is going to get the major share of
     the swag?' ('The Second World War', *The New International*, Vol. V,
     No. 10, October 1939, pp. 292–5)
9   *The Capitalism System*, 2nd ed., Ch. XIII, pp. 475–81, 'The growth of US
     private investment abroad'.
10   This argument against relativism is advanced by, among others, Kurt Baier
     The Moral Point of View, abridged edition, Random House, New York,
     1965, p. 114.

XI
Overcoming Imposed Consciousness

THE problem is not whether overcoming imposed consciousness is obligatory. It surely is since imposed consciousness stands in the way of internal historical needs. The problem is how to overcome it. This problem is aggravated by the fact that big sections of the communications and educational establishment exist primarily for the creation of imposed consciousness.

To tackle this practical problem it will be helpful to solve some theoretical puzzles first. Foremost among these is the question of how to distinguish between true and false needs, internal and external needs, true and imposed consciousness. If one's data includes merely what people actually say they want, how can one possibly distinguish between what people, as members of their class, *really* want and what they have been *made to* want by institutions of the sum group? Such a distinction would be arbitrary on this basis. It is tempting to conclude from this that there is no way to base a morality on group tendencies. This scepticism leads to the view that, if there is a morality at all, one needs to transgress naturalism to find its source.

What is needed is an adequate methodology for finding out what peoples' needs are. The verbal level, at which the pollster works, is easiest to subject to manipulation by the sum group. Clichés about social harmony can so dominate the verbal level as to make it a poor indicator as to whether there is a distinction between internal and imposed needs. In Section 3 a methodology is outlined that emphasizes struggle not words.

1 **Historical materialism** The ethical principles that come to be taught and generally obeyed do not drop into people's minds from the blue. They are a distillation of the lives those people lead in the unique circumstances in which they lead them. This hardly seems very controversial; it is assumed without question by historians and sociologists. But there is less agreement when it comes to the matter of what ethical principles are valid. According to ethical naturalism, the only factors relevant to their validity are contained within the world of people, their groups, and the things they use. In particular, it is the nature of the social person that is

the basis for the validity of ethical principles. Since the social person is partly formed by special social circumstances, those circumstances play a major role in determining validity.

Something needs to be added to naturalism in order to get historical materialism, or the materialist interpretation of history. Naturalism tells us not to go outside the familiar world in interpreting things, whereas historical materialism limits us more specifically to interpretations that give a special place to the economic relations of a society. These economic relations are the relations people have to one another in production and in terms of them the major classes at a given time are defined. (For pre-class societies, it is kinship relations that are basic.) Consequently, domination between classes has primacy in interpreting domination between other groups. There is no simple formula that the historical materialist uses to connect social and political matters with the economic relations in production.[1] There might be such a formula if that connection were one of causal determination, in which case the historical materialist could justifiably be called an economic determinist. But the connection is quite a different one.

A hard pinch will bring a scream. This is cause and effect, but there is more to it. What was pinched: a person or a stone? There is a certain kind of system present that made possible the scream as a response to the pinch. This system is what lies in the background of the many connections that exist between things done to it and its responses. Historical materialism does not say that the causes must all be economic relations, but only that the system of economic relations is the background that makes it possible for there to be connections in the social sphere between causes and effects. So it is possible to say that 'The dynamic of revolutionary events is *directly* determined by swift, intense, and passionate changes in the psychology of classes'[2] without denying historical materialism. The economic relations in the background make it possible for consciousness to cause revolutionary upheavals.

This accounts for our having said that class domination is the reason for other forms of domination (Chapter IV, Section 3). It is the reason in the way that an underlying system is the reason for connections involving it. Capitalism in South Africa was the reason apartheid was introduced in 1948. For us this means that within the system of South African capitalism there were events, in this particular case the growth of black trade-unionism, the wave of strikes among blacks, and the demand for better housing by black workers, that led to the implementation of apartheid. That these events in the wake of World War II led to apartheid, rather than to something else, depended on the kind of system they took place in. The distinctive thing about historical materialism is not, then, that it claims all causes of social events must be economic, which it does not, but that it identifies the systems in which causes, economic or otherwise, of social events have their efficacy as defined by economic and hence class relations.[3]

In sum, naturalism tells us that explanations are not to appeal to anything outside the world of people, their groups, and the things they use. Ethical naturalism is, then, a special case of naturalism. Historical materialism tells us that explanations of social and cultural matters are to be constructed against a background of the way people are organized in production. It is, then, also a special case of naturalism. And insofar as it applies to ethical life, historical materialism is a special case of ethical naturalism too. Historical materialism accounts for the validity or invalidity of ethical claims in given circumstances by locating those circumstances in the appropriate system of class domination.

Atomistic materialism is quite a different view than historical materialism. The former is a materialism since it says that all there is can be exhausted by matter in the sense of the basic entities of physical science. Historical materialism is a materialism in another sense. It accepts the premise of naturalism that in accounting for what goes on in either the social or the physical domain reference must be made to some physical, that is, spatio-temporal change. But it adds another premise, that in social explanation it is the economic system, the system that deals with the physical problem of survival, which provides the background.

Historical materialism does not require the adoption of atomistic materialism. Moreover, it is actually incompatible with atomistic materialism. For the atomistic materialist persons, say, are not concrete particulars but are collections of cells, molecules, or atoms. This puts an obstacle in the way of explanations of social matters against the background of economic systems. One can see this by starting from the fact that these systems do not exist as separate structures but exist only in mutual dependence on persons. This mutual dependence would be a mystery if persons were mere collections. Collections could have tendencies depending on economic systems only indirectly through the atoms or cells that are their members. Clearly though, the only way atoms and cells are affected by social systems is through persons.

Historical materialism is also different from any view that puts technology first. The availability of different technologies will allow for different ways of winning survival. Hence, it will allow for different classes, since different ways of winning survival will involve different economic roles. The society of ancient Athens was one with a class of slaves whereas twentieth-century US society is one with a class of paid labourers. This tells us something about technological development. It tells us at least that Athens did not win survival with giant factories. It won survival on a basis of agriculture, crafts, and trade. Still, it is not technology that is used by historical materialism to provide a basis for explaining social changes. It is the way technology is used by people that provides this basis. Mechanical development differed little between feudalism and pre-industrial capitalism. Still economic relations were different and there were things explicable by reference to the one system that would not have been explicable by reference to the other.

Many of the things already observed about ethics could have been anticipated from the perspective of historical materialism. Conversely, these things also confirm historical materialism as a general theory of social change. There is no unchanging ethics. The agency for shifts in both the content and validity of ethics has been the conflict of groups, which is based in economic relations. Still this allows individuals like Socrates, Jesus, Adam Smith, Lenin, and Gandhi to have played an important role in changing ethical views. For their teaching serves to guide their audiences to deal with new realities of group conflict. They do not so much transcend conflict as project in the boldest fashion ideas reflecting, more or less well, the tendencies of one or another of the partisan groups. A sum group develops ideas to stabilize a situation, and the antagonistic groups within it develop different internal ethical codes to strengthen their abilities to struggle against one another. There is no appeal beyond this struggle. And thus the validity of the codes rests on the goals being pursued in the different camps. None of this is surprising from the perspective of historical materialism.

2 Conflict within the person Our task was to distinguish internal from imposed needs. Imposed needs and a morality based on them are a very straightforward matter from the point of view of historical materialism. One class dominates another not just by possessing the instruments of force but also by being able to change needs and beliefs. Why are not the ethical principles based on these imposed needs as valid as the principles based on internal needs? Historical materialism can resolve this difficulty since it sees the dynamic of society in domination and conflict. By contrast, harmonistic views of society have no basis for ruling out obligations to respond to imposed needs. In a harmonistic society, imposed needs will be needs that cement and deepen an original harmony without standing in opposition to internal historical needs.

In fact, though, imposed needs do not deepen an original harmony but moderate an original conflict. They thereby transfer elements of the conflict within the society to the person. By reducing the appearances of conflict in society these imposed needs create a conflict in the person with his or her internal historical needs. This situation would be socially and personally acceptable if somehow it led to a synthesis in the person that resolved the conflict. Such a synthesis would combine 'the best' of the internal and of the imposed needs. The 'worst' of both kinds would be the real agents of conflict and would be eliminated. But there has been and there will be no such reconciliation; the conflict remains so long as the person is part of a society involving domination.[4] Ending the conflict in the person will require ending domination in society.

At this point one could throw up one's hands and exclaim that in a class society it is the nature of the person to be in equilibrium between contradictory drives. If there is conflict within the person that cannot be eliminated, ethics cannot force us to take sides in that conflict. It is one's nature not to feel pushed in one way by an internal need without feeling pushed in an opposite way with equal force by an imposed need. Alienation is not, as we said it was, a matter of having one's true nature blocked, but a matter of one's nature containing features that stand in each other's way.

This contradiction mongering is, though, only an excuse for not taking the obligations of one's group seriously. It is easier to stand on the sidelines and say that, because deep down I am just a bundle of contradictions, I do not have to take sides. But in doing this I unwittingly accept another imposed need as a basis for morality. Standing on the sidelines is not being neutral between internal and imposed needs. The imposed need in question is the need not to get involved, a need that dominant groups invest considerable effort in imposing on lower groups.

From the perspective of historical materialism, most imposed needs have a precarious existence and are thus not part of people's nature. This can be seen as follows. The economic relations used by historical materialism as a background for explanation are for the most part relations characterized by conflicting economic roles. The basic source of the conflict is the domination called for by one of the roles. Those who use others' labour and control the means of production dominate those who labour. To preserve this domination, imposed needs and consciousness are fostered. Nonetheless, the existence of domination will create conditions that will lead to open struggle between the conflicting groups. Imposed needs may limit the frequency and intensity of struggles without eliminating them altogether. The effect of struggle, though, is to make dominated people question many things they have previously accepted. This questioning undercuts numerous imposed needs, and for this reason we say they are precarious in relation to human nature. The need to support the police is temporarily undermined by their use, or the threat of their use, as strikebreakers. No one recognizes the precariousness of imposed needs better than those who job it is to keep them in existence. The reason they are precarious is that they are tools used against the people with them. So long as people have not ceased to struggle, they will not incorporate these tools into what they are. The death of struggle against domination in advanced industrial countries was announced in the 1950s and 1960s.[5] The announcement was not heeded; strikes and popular resistance continued and then in the late 1960s intensified.

Even racism, which appears to have a settled rather than a precarious existence, is not entirely an exception. Consider for the moment only those forms of racism that are related to jobs. So long as whites are led to fear they will lose their jobs to blacks, there is the basis for white supported job discrimination that splits black and white workers and is harmful to both. The fear is not without foundation.[6] The famous 1919 steel strike in the US was broken by the owners sending blacks across the picket lines. In 1940 Henry Ford used a black goon squad to attack white auto workers in an attempt to keep the union out of Ford Motor Company. The 1968 Ocean Hill-Brownsville strike of the New York City teachers union was used by the union leadership to intensify the fears of white teachers about their jobs in communities that were predominantly black or latin. But if the owners and the union leaders were to desist from efforts to split workers along racial lines, the racial antagonisms stemming from job discrimination would be difficult to sustain. Moral pleas will certainly not be sufficient to get them to desist. The imposed need for job discrimination rules out a unity between black and white that would be a threat to the continued domination of ownership over labour.

Can we erect precariousness into the sole criterion for distinguishing imposed from internal needs? There are imposed needs for which this criterion is unsuccessful. In these cases, the imposed needs do belong to the nature of the social person. These imposed needs no longer require the constant external efforts of an alien group to keep them in existence. Yet in the end, if the society does change in a way dictated by the internal needs, these imposed needs which had become a part of human nature will cease to exist. It is true that the origin of such non-precarious imposed needs is in an alien group. But that does not make them accidental to the persons with them. The social theory of the person emphasizes the extent to which persons are formed by their groups. It is possible, though, that persons are social also by being partly formed by groups to which they do not belong. Only by allowing that some imposed needs are part of the core person can efforts at social control be fully justified for a dominant group. Those efforts aim at changing our very nature. The surest control is not a penal system but humans who by nature behave in the interests of those who dominate them.

Consider, for example, racism of another sort, this time a non-economic racism. The white compensates for the alienation from his or her internal historical needs by behaviour expressive of white supremacy. The need to do this has become so deep that it can no longer be called precarious. That it will disappear in a new social order is in no way to deny that it is now part of the nature of some white workers. Analogously, the general strike in 1974 conducted by the Ulster Workers' Council in Northern Ireland was, in part, an expression of the imposed feeling of Protestant supremacy and not an expression of the workers' internal class needs. Those who pushed them into the strike appealed to that imposed feeling. Yet their bigotry, imposed during centuries of effort by British owners to avoid a united Irish movement of lower class Protestants and Catholics, has for long had a life of its own, and can no longer be called precarious.   Does ethical naturalism require that one try to realize 'natural' imposed needs? If morality really has a basis in one's group, one should not try to realize imposed needs. They are imposed to aid an alien group. Ethical naturalism, though, seems to point in another direction. It tells us that human nature is the basis of ethical validity. But some imposed needs form the core person. Is there a way out? The postulates of ethical naturalism were formulated in Chapter II before any inkling was given of the importance of conflict. Yet conflict is the hallmark of the materialist interpretation of history. The idea of a person who, by nature, is the seat of conflicting socially based drives had not been considered.

When there is a conflict of needs within a person, the question to be asked is which needs can be eliminated. And the answer in this case is that only the imposed needs can be eliminated. The answer is arrived at as follows. On the one hand, something must give when there is a conflict of needs. Otherwise people would nullify their efforts to realize certain of their needs by the efforts they would have to engage in to realize needs conflicting with these. On the other hand, it is clear that if one set of needs *cannot* be eliminated then keeping a conflicting set intact will mean restricting the realization of the first set. The internal historical needs cannot, in general, be eliminated. If there were easy mobility in and out of groups, one set of internal historical needs could be replaced by another. But mobility is very limited. The reasons for this are obvious for race and sex. Mobility between classes is restricted in a capitalist society; most people have to be workers if there are to be enough profits for growth, and so only a small fraction of the 60–70 per cent of the population who are workers can cease to be so in a limited period of time. Statistically speaking, then, internal historical needs are irremovable. So the pursuit of imposed needs will inevitably restrict the realization of these internal historical needs, with which they will conflict.

Either one eliminates the needs that come from outside. Then the internal needs can have all efforts devoted to their realization. Or one keeps the needs that come from the outside. Then, though one is unable to do away with the internal needs, one must severely restrict their realization. Everything favours choosing the first alternative. The second alternative implies the sort of nullification of conflicting efforts that incapacitates one for overcoming alienation.

Ethical naturalism needs to be restricted to coherent human natures. Coherent human natures are the basis for ethical validity. In case imposed and internal needs are both part of what a person is, the basis for ethical validity must be restricted to that part of the person which cannot be eliminated. So ethical naturalism applies only to what the person would be upon becoming coherent. This requirement extends the coherence postulate of Chapter III, Section 3, which excluded from ethical life persons whose internal needs conflict because of independent membership in conflicting groups. Since internal needs are not eliminable as imposed needs are, the person with conflicting internal needs cannot become coherent and thus there is no way consistent with naturalism of determining what that person should do.

3 Struggle as a methodology How does one tell what needs are internal in respect to one's group and what needs are imposed in order to perpetuate a system of domination? The method proposed here is that of struggle, rather than of intellectual reflection. Struggle against domination undermines certain needs—the imposed needs—and brings others to awareness—the internal needs. The dominant trend in the history of ethical writing is to propose a method of intellectual reflection for determining the factors most important in judging the validity of ethical principles. This method can succeed only when it employs a fully critical technique. This is necessary since the intellectual level is subject to the worst distortions of imposed creeds and values. The only motive for being fully critical will, though, be that of overcoming domination. And this motive atrophies without struggle. Thus the method of intellectual reflection can succeed in distinguishing internal from imposed needs only when allied with the method of struggle.

Since they have not allied themselves with the struggle against domination, most ethical writers have accepted uncritically the intellectual assumptions of their period. These assumptions have always been a reflection of the need of the dominant class to maintain its position. Thus, for example, modern, western ethical writers take it for granted that there is some obligation to support the nation-state to which one belongs.[7] Of course, if it is an open tyranny, they admit there is no such obligation. But so long as there is political representation and a juridical system that maintains a semblance of fairness, such an obligation exists. It exists, these writers would maintain, despite class divisions within the nation-state. There is not the slightest hint that it may be impossible for the institutions of the nation-state to function except insofar as their prime goal is to perpetuate relations of domination. It is only through struggle that lower groups break through the resulting imposed consciousness about the obligation to support their nation-state.

The struggle of blacks in Detroit and other urban areas in the US in 1967 was a turning point as regards the patriotism of black soldiers in Vietnam. Why should they be fighting overseas in an army that was part of the military-political-economic apparatus that confined them in the ghettos at home? There was no obligation to take up arms for such a nation-state. Blacks set up separate compounds from which white officers were excluded; they vented their frustrations on whites placed in the brig with them; if and when militant black units could be got to go on patrol, their white officers sometimes did not return with them. The struggle of their brothers and sisters in the cities was a big factor in convincing them that their enemy did not inhabit Vietnam.[8]

In a study published in September 1966, a British sociologist concluded from a questionnaire study of workers in a car plant that the workers were disposed to define their relation with management more as one of 'reciprocity and interdependence than, say, one of coercion and exploitation'.[9] Three-quarters of the workers had a cooperative view of management and they did not see that conditions in the plant were likely 'to give rise to discontent and resentment of a generalized kind'. But in October of the same year, 2,000 workers tried to storm the offices of the plant, 'singing the Red Flag and calling "string him up" whenever a director's name was mentioned'.[10] When events did finally spark a struggle, the workers became aware that management was coercive and exploitative. Yet earlier the workers were guided, at the verbal level at which they responded to the questionnaire, by an imposed mentality of cooperation with management.

On the one hand, the existence of struggle situations shows that there has *not* been, as Marcuse had claimed there was, an 'effective suffocation of those needs which demand liberation'. Those needs are the driving force behind the unending, though variably intense, struggle of lower classes and groups. On the other hand, there is no guarantee that these struggles will go very far in peeling away imposed beliefs and needs. According as the struggle is more protracted and widespread, the layers of imposed consciousness and needs are peeled away until there is less and less that conflicts with internal historical needs. But there are tremendous forces lined up against letting struggles go so far. Union officials and liberal politicians are quick to come out against 'excesses' in mass struggles. And the military might of the state is ready to stop struggles forcibly.

In addition to these external forces, imposed consciousness itself restricts the intensity of struggles. The myth of the common good of society is most effective in restricting struggles. It blinds workers to the fact that the effectiveness of the institutions they have set up for economic security is very limited so long as the society as a whole remains capitalist. For the myth of the common good portrays what preserves capitalist domination as the common good. Imposed consciousness thus often prevents economic struggles from developing into political ones, that is, struggles against the state and other institutions of the sum group. 'The working class spontaneously gravitates towards socialism; nevertheless, most widespread (and continuously and diversely revived) bourgeois ideology spontaneously imposes itself upon the working class to a still greater degree.'[11]

To counteract all these forces, there is a need for those persons in the struggle whose consciousness is most advanced to mobilize themselves in an organized way. They will have advanced farthest in peeling away imposed consciousness and in seeing the necessity for giving a political thrust to the struggle. To combat the power of the state and other institutions of the sum group, they must function together as a revolutionary party. It is only because people are uneven in consciousness, due to various causes, that a revolutionary party is needed. The experience and consciousness of the party's members will enable it to propose to others involved in mass struggle a direction for the struggle to take that if followed would be likely to erode the imposed consciousness of successive layers of persons who by their circumstances were less advanced. The struggle method of overcoming imposed consciousness in capitalist society is incomplete without requiring the formation of a revolutionary party to provide leadership in struggle.

An important qualification in our methodology for distinguishing imposed from internal needs has to be emphasized. Not any struggles, but only those against domination help distinguish these needs. The New York teachers' strike of 1968, the Teamsters' raid on the United Farm Workers in 1973, and the Protestant workers' strike in Belfast in 1974 are all examples of reactionary workers' struggles. They all glorified the imposed consciousness of the workers engaged in struggle. In these cases it seemed that it was the internal historical needs, rather than the imposed needs, that were being peeled away. It would be surprising, though, if such things did not happen. One of the aims of creating imposed consciousness is to make them possible, thereby splitting the lower classes in their opposition to domination. How then can struggle be a methodology for separating out imposed from internal needs?

The problem in the three cases mentioned is that one group of workers is pitted primarily against another group of workers. They are pitted against one another by agents who put the interests of workers after their own. Of course, in any conflict workers are pitted against one another; scabs and policemen are, after all, workers. Still, a conflict initiated by strikers against scabs is primarily directed at the owners. Only the owners, not the scabs, can grant the terms the strikers want. It is clear that in situations in which the conflict is primarily between groups of workers the immediate direction of the group that takes the initiative is not the direction of working people generally. It is not a struggle against domination. This is clear since the agents who get them to take the initiative do not put the interests of workers first. Thus the officials of the New York teachers' union had little real concern for blacks in the community; the Teamster officials were indifferent to the interests of the chicanos in the UFW; and the hired thugs who drove the Protestant workers off their jobs and into the general strike were able to ignore the interests of the Catholic workers.

The struggle methodology is then limited to struggles against domination. When the struggle is primarily one that pits members of the working class against one another, the needs it expresses are not necessarily the internal as opposed to the imposed needs of the working class. A similar qualification applies to any lower group in regard to its internal needs.

4 Intellectuals of the ruling class Some members of the unproductive working class have as their profession the development and communication of ideas that become part of imposed consciousness. Because of their profession, it is difficult for them to accept the historical materialist view of these ideas. They must flatter themselves by holding that they teach ideas that have been fashioned in a social vacuum—in the pure medium of 'objectivity'. Part of their own imposed consciousness is to think of themselves as detached intellectuals, not as agents in the process by which the ruling class perpetuates its rule.[12] If they overcame this false view of themselves they would be less useful in this process, for part of their effectiveness derives from their communicating their own conviction about the ideas they have. Their job is to convince people that the good of the society stands above 'petty class squabbles'; that there is no alternative to the system of domination by a ruling class; that people are not to be trusted with the industrial and political control of their lives; that the 'responsibility' of a great world power allows no retreat from the policy of imperialism.

In other words, institutions of higher education, public relations offices, the bar, and the media include many people whose profession is to give the society an ideology. These ideologists stand outside the struggle that might overcome their false view of the purity of their own ideas. As a group, they are incapable of conducting a criticism of the morality of the times. As Nietzsche, who was a devastating critic of accepted morality, would have said, these intellectuals are incapable of raising the question of 'the value of these values' of their own time.[13]

If their job is to spread false consciousness, do these intellectual workers have an obligation to overcome their own false consciousness? There is a certain polarity built into their situation. Because of this polarity, it may be impossible to formulate a consistent ethics for them and hence impossible to say whether they have an obligation to undo their own false consciousness. This limitation will not appeal to those whose profession is to spread so-called universal values, but it is a limitation that is inherent in the role that they play. The polarity is this. On the one hand, because of the work they do, they need to be removed from circumstances that would reveal the structure of domination. They thus enjoy a position—high salaries at the top and generally good working conditions—for which they are in important ways dependent on the ruling class. They can then expect little direct support from the lower classes. On the other hand, these intellectuals are not free but, like other unproductive workers, hired. As a group, their freedom to pursue intellectual research is limited by the goal of thwarting tendencies of the lower classes to challenge domination. Whether aware of them or not, these facts are the source of latent needs that place these intellectuals in opposition to the ruling class.

Putting both sides of this polarity together gives a picture of the intellectual of the ruling class as the locus of a conflict of internal needs. An ethics based on the nature of such an intellectual would command *both* an alliance with the ruling class *and* an alliance with the productive working class. Following such an ethics would lead to abandonment by both of these major classes. Yet people whose position does not allow them to have a valid and a consistent ethics will devise a false ethics that is consistent.

Notes

1   'Empirical observation must in each separate instance bring out empirically, and without any mystification and speculation, the connection of the social and political structure with production' (Marx and Engels, *The German Ideology*, p. 46).

2   Leon Trotsky, *The History of the Russian Revolution* (1932–33), trans. M. Eastman, Sphere Books, London, 1967, Vol. I, p. 15.

3   Milton Fisk, 'Dialectic and ontology', in *Issues In Marxist Philosophy*, Vol. I, eds. J. Mepham and D. -H. Ruben, Harvester, Sec. X, 1979.

4   For a general critique of simplistic resolutions of conflicts, see Karl Marx, *The Poverty of Philosophy* (1848), International Publishers, New York, 1963, pp. 111–12.

5   Herbert Marcuse, *One-Dimensional Man*, Sphere, London, 1968, Chs. I–II.

6   Philip S. Foner, *Organized Labor and the Black Worker, 1619–1973*, International Publishers, New York, 1974.

7   For example, David Hume, *An Enquiry Concerning the Principles of Morals*, Sec. V, Part II, p. 225, footnote.

8   See the general discussion of dissent in the US army in Vietnam by Matthew Rinaldi, 'Olive-drab rebels', *Radical America*, Vol. VIII, Sec. 3, May–June 1974, pp. 17–52.

9   John H. Goldthorpe, 'Attitudes and behaviour of car assembly workers', *British Journal of Sociology*, Vol. XVII, Sept. 1966.

10 *The Times* of London, 19 October 1966. (The quotations in this paragraph were found in Robin Blackburn, 'A brief guide to bourgeois ideology', in *Student Power*, p. 200.)

11 V. I. Lenin, *What Is to be Done?* (1902), *V. I. Lenin: Collected Works*, Vol. V, 1961, p. 386, footnote.

12   Milton Fisk, 'Academic freedom in class society', in *The Concept of Academic Freedom*, ed. Edmund L. Pincoffs, University of Texas Press, Austin, 1975, pp. 5–26.
13   Friedrich Nietzsche, *On the Geneology of Morals* (1887), trans. W. Kaufmann and R. J. Hollingdale, Vintage, New York, 1969, Preface, Sec. 6.

PART FOUR

An Account of the Conditions of Human Action

XII
Virtue and the Good

OUR focus has been on the way the human person is moulded by groups. Group relativist ethics has been worked out within this focus. It is important, though, that another aspect of ethical life not be neglected. The theory of the social person, just laid out in Part Three, provides a framework within which to consider human action. Yet little has been said about human action itself. It is as though we had laid out the boundaries for the field of human action without describing the field. We know that whatever humans do will be done by agents who have been shaped by groups. But we have not yet asked what the doing itself is like.

Ethics cannot neglect an analysis of action since it is, after all, a study of human action, even if only from the perspective of the resolution of conflicts between action benefitting the group and action benefitting the person. In analyzing action, we run into questions about moral character, motivation, voluntariness, and responsibility. The theory of the social person will remain relevant, since the actions of a social person and not of an atomic person are in question.

The present chapter provides a bridge from society to action through virtue. Virtues are bases for actions that are good. Asking how virtues function as bases of action will lead to other questions about the structure of action, which will be explored in this part of the book. The social criteria for virtue and hence for goodness will be the main subject of the present chapter.

1 **Virtue and role** The ancient Greek philosophers explained virtue in terms of function. Humans have a function or role that other entities do not have. This is to engage in rational action, that is to exercise their capacities in conformity with a 'rational principle'.[1] If someone has the capacity to make speeches, then that capacity is not to be used to act the clown or to bore people to tears. Otherwise, it is not being used in order to realize one's human function. To function as a human, one must use this capacity to make speeches reasonably. If one has the capacity to perform feats of strength, then one is not to use it to harm people or property needlessly. Otherwise, one is not functioning as a human

when performing feats of strength. Humans function as humans when they limit the use of their abilities by reason.

Where then does virtue come in? A virtuous person is a person who consistently functions as a human. That which makes a person virtuous is a capacity to limit the exercise of other capacities so that their exercise conforms with a rational principle. Virtue is then a capacity to limit the exercise of other capacities so that one functions as a human. The rational principle behind such a limiting capacity is not to be looked for outside the practical activity of humans. It is not, at least on the Aristotelian theory of virtue, an extra-physical ideal. What then is it?

The individual crafts are characterized by special ways of using our general capacities. These special ways are called skills. The woodcarver's skill is the control of the general ability to move the hands by the aim of making decorative designs in wood. This aim provides the rational principle appropriate to the woodcarver. The skill is then a capacity that limits the exercise of the hands by a rational principle.

This tells us about the function of craftspeople but not about the function of humans as such. In thinking about the function of humans as such, the ancient Greeks left the crafts behind and considered the role of the citizen. To function as a human is to play the role of the citizen. The rational principle by which the virtuous limit their action is then determined by what is rational for the citizen. The analogue of this subordination of the crafts to citizenship is today the subordination of special occupations to the overall social structure. The way the occupations relate to one another and the actual division of occupations itself is dependent on the overall social structure. Many occupational divisions are designed to fragment the working class and thus strengthen capitalism. There is no definition of the occupations independent of the overall class structure. For that reason many of the needs often found in the various occupations must be considered as imposed rather than internal needs. The struggle for industrial rather than craft unionism was a struggle to overcome the imposed needs found in the crafts that led to strife within the working class. Nonetheless, following the Greek analogy, we would have to say that to function as human in the West today is to play the role of a member of capitalist society. The rational principle by which the virtuous limit their action is then determined by what is rational for the member of capitalist society. The aim of perpetuating the profit system becomes the touchstone for rationality and hence virtue.

The aim of the sum group to perpetuate the existing system of domination becomes on this account the touchstone for rationality and hence virtue. Aristotle felt that those who could most easily learn to be rational in this sense would be members of the ruling class themselves. And it was for them that he wrote his ethics. The virtues were then the capacities the ruling class of the city-state could afford to acquire that would enable them to retain their domination. Since to function as human was to be virtuous, true humanity was a real possibility only for the ruling class.

We need not accept the interpretations of virtue in terms of the sum group and its aim and of the ruling class and its aim as the only ones. Aristotle's general theory of virtue, outlined above, allows other interpretations. It admits of interpretation in a fully relativist fashion. Humans as humans would then have no one function, but as many functions as there are classes and other groups to which people can independently belong. Each function has its own rational principle, namely the principle that capacities are to be exercised so as to advance the tendencies characteristic of the group corresponding to that function. Aristotle went so far in applying his general theory as to think that the low born, the ugly, the dispossessed, and those without influential friends were incapable of virtuous actions. The virtuous was then the noble. Rather than argue for an absolute opposed to Aristotle's aristo-cratic absolute, it is best to reinterpret his view of virtue relativistically—as one that is valid only for the ruling class of a city-state.

Another way putting this is to say that a virtue is a capacity needed to adjust the person to the group. Virtue channels other capacities in directions that fit with a social purpose. If I am virtuous, the actions I perform and the emotions I express are performed or expressed 'at the right time, on the right occasion, towards the right people, for the right purpose, and in the right manner.'[2] But, of course, what is right and fitting in all these ways for a member of one group may not be so for a member of another group.

2   The social content of the good   The notion of obligation was discussed in Chapter X, Section 3, but as yet nothing in detail has been said about goodness. As we saw, an act is obligatory for a person relative to one of that person's groups if its not being done would be likely to make it more difficult than it already was to realize the internal historical needs of members of the group in question. The key idea is indispensability. By contrast, goods are optional. Not creating them puts no obstacle in the way of the group. This is far from saying that anything one is interested in is a

good. Only those things that advance the realization of the needs characteristic of a group are goods in the moral sense. Of course, there are personal goods that are not moral goods, or that are even morally bad things to pursue. A personal good is something that advances one's own needs, whether those needs are compatible with the needs of a group or not.

Since the needs characteristic of a group are internal historical needs brought about by group membership, the moral sense of goodness can be spelled out as follows:

An action is a good one to do relative to a given group provided it helps advance the realization of some of the internal historical needs persons in such a group have.

Several comments on this will be helpful before going on to the relation of goodness to virtue: First, a good action may be good for some group other than the agent's. In this respect goodness differs from obligation.

Second, a good action relative to a non-class oppressed group will be good relative to some lower class overlapping that group. Thus what is good to an oppressed race, most of whose members are workers, will also be good relative to the working class. For the advancement of the working class will be furthered at the same time steps are taken to overcome that racial oppression. Conversely, actions that are good relative to a lower class are good relative to oppressed groups whose overarching goals can be realized only by joining with that class. This does not mean that all morality simply reduces to class morality. Many acts that are good relative to a class are so not just because of the goals of the class but also because of the goals of a non-class group. The active support of many of the members of this non-class group would advance that class toward its goals.

Third, a good action is optional in that without it the group struggle need not be set back. Without it no obstacle that was not already there would have to have been created. Of course, without either it or some other good act in its place the struggle will have been made more difficult than it already was. For inaction within a group weakens it in relation to an alien group. This is the basis for the general maxim that people are obliged to do something good relative to their group when the opportunity arises.

Exploring the connection of goodness with virtue illuminates the connection of the group to the person. The virtuous person is in tune with the tendencies characteristic of his or her group. Since classes are the most important groups as far as domination is concerned, the virtuous person is, in the final analysis, one who is in tune with class tendencies. This is because virtue requires a disposition that points actions and emotions in the direction of class goals. The virtuous have then internalized their groups. Their conformity to their groups is a result of the inner force of their own dispositions and not of the external force of an alien institution.[3]

Those who have an inner source of behaviour consistently in tune with the tendencies characteristic of their groups are called 'good people'. The good person is not just a person who is sincere, who acts out of a sense of duty, or who has a heart of gold. The genuinely good person—the morally worthy character—must succeed on the side of performance as well. The good person has the dispositions for guiding action into channels that advance the realization of internal historical needs.

Undeniably, then, the actions of virtuous people tend to be good. For their virtues enable them to do what in their class amounts to an advancement of social purpose. Is not this merely a deductive consequence of the definition of virtue? It is indeed, but it is important to see that more is involved. For if it is merely an exercise in logical thinking to say that the virtuous do good, then it could be concluded that there is no need for virtuous people in a world in which there is good action. People might just do good by chance. This is, though, an impossibility. The definition of good action or emotion, which seems formally correct, turns out to have no application without the existence of virtuous people. Virtue is not just a sufficient logical condition for good action. It is also a necessary ontological condition for good action.

The definition of goodness makes reference to a social entity, the group, whose purpose is advanced by doing good. Social entities do not exist without, in the first place, people and, in the second place, tendencies people have that are the reflections of groups in these people. If there were people but they had no tendencies that made them behave in the manner of members of groups, then there would simply be no social groups. You can guess now where this leads.

Virtues are among the tendencies needed for groups. Virtues are behind the systematic and continuous efforts to advance group interests without which a group could not persist. And so if social entities do not exist without virtues and if good actions advance the purposes of social entities, then good actions do not exist without virtues. The mere tautology that the actions and emotions of virtuous people are good hides behind it an important philosophical truth, one that it does credit even to the great profundity of Aristotle to have seen. The hidden truth is that, since social entities are not alien to people but exist only if people have virtues, virtues are a real basis for the existence of good actions. This is because virtues, as tendencies in people, are a real basis for the existence of groups, in relation to whose purposes actions and emotions are good or bad.

3   The primacy of feeling Beyond the dispositions of humans there is no otherworldly standard of goodness or abstract principle of rightness in terms of which dispositions are judged good or bad.[4] The standard of goodness is not isolated from human dispositions, since it is ultimately the purpose of a class, which depends on human dispositions. To say that one disposition is a virtue and another a vice is to evaluate them relative to the class they perpetuate or undermine.

This might seem to imply that there is no ideal, that the present is perfect, and that virtues are inherently conservative factors. To the contrary, the goals of a lower class represent thwarted internal possibilities. It is these thwarted possibilities that are the 'ideals' in terms of which some dispositions within the lower classes are labelled virtues. Virtue itself is neither conservative nor revolutionary. The virtues of a dominant class are conservative in that their effect is to preserve the relations of domination. The virtues of a lower class include revolutionary virtues whose effect would be to break the relations of domination.

Aside from looking for an otherworldly ideal of goodness, there is another direction in which one might turn away from society. One might turn to personal feelings in order to obtain a standard of goodness. This tendency dominates modern ethics and is paralleled by an inward turn in the areas of metaphysics and theory of knowledge.

Just as Hume drew all questions in the theory of knowledge and metaphysics back to sensous impressions, so too he tried to draw all questions in moral philosophy back to sentiment or feeling. For him a virtue is a state of people that gives others 'the pleasing sentiment of approbation'.[5] What a stark contrast with Aristotle's social conception of virtue! Instead of advancing a social purpose, virtue, in the eighteenth century, creates a pleasing sentiment in spectators. It does this either because it is productive of 'agreeable' acts such as acts of wit, gallantry, and 'ingenious knowledge genteelly delivered' or because it is productive of 'useful' acts such as acts of fairness, kindness, and diligence.[6]

Under the heading of useful acts will be ones that do in fact advance social purpose, but acts are not virtuous for Hume simply because they advance social purpose. They are virtuous if they proceed from a state that causes the feeling of approval in someone.

We begin to see what is wrong here when we recognize that, through imposed consciousness, a vast change could be made in what we actually feel approval for. Hume thinks the approval of socially useful acts is an inherent tendency of humans. There is, though, no reason why the range of what gets approved cannot be greatly varied by social forces acting on consciousness. In short, by being put on an inward basis, virtue ceases to have a constant significance, even in the same social group.

A defender of Hume will say that Hume was talking about a *disinterested* spectator. Yet the above objection rests on the possibility of subjecting the spectator to social biases. The appeal to a disinterested spectator confronts one with the myth of a human nature common throughout the kind, which was criticized in Chapter VIII. If indeed persons are social and society is conflictive, spectators are never immune to changes in consciousness that would vary the range of what gets approved.

The consequences of this subjectivizing of virtue are best understood in terms of the social conditions responsible for it. The effects of the development of a capitalist economy on the realm of thought were, like that development itself, revolutionary. The relatively settled social hierarchy of the middle ages was crumbling in face of the widening of the market and the growth of enterprise outside the restrictions of the guilds. In that older social hierarchy, relations between lord and serf and between guild master and journeyman were ones that involved a personal dependence. Added to this was the fact there was a widely accepted theological rationalization of the social hierarchy. One's place was not only one that set one into personal relation with members of other classes but also one that was natural within the order of creation.

The new economic order shattered all of this security. It broke down the personal relations and made the theological rationalization irrelevant. It left a vacuum, though, that if unfilled would lead to widespread despondency, doubt, and insecurity. The social relations of the competitive market in goods and labour replaced the fixed social universe of feudal times. There was then a great need for some source of satisfaction that would compensate for the loss of the satisfactions inherent in the earlier system. The dispossessed wage labourer of the capitalist epoch suffered the uncertainties of the labour market without compensating personal ties to the potential boss. Even the employer needed something to give enterprise a fixity and certainty that everyday dealings between independent producers lacked. What would fill the gap? Externally there was only insecurity; so a retreat to the security of inner feelings was not surprising.

The retreat to feeling showed itself in different ways. In religion it showed itself in the search for an inner certainty of being saved. Practising the capitalist virtues of frugality, honesty, and hard work was considered as, at best, a way to overcome doubts about being saved.[7] In philosophy it showed itself in the search for an inner certainty of truth. The economy was no longer based on feudal restrictions and privileges but on a rationality in production and exchange that gave priority to mathematical accounting. Descartes generalized this by making the clarity and distinctness characteristic of mathematics the test for true ideas.[8] Hume is part of this tradition since for him insecurity in the moral arena is overcome by the inner certainty of feeling. There is no mistaking one's own approval or preference, and these sentiments are the basis for valuing things. The spectator who judges behaviour as virtuous or vicious is as certain in these judgments as he or she is about the feeling of approval or disapproval. The insecurity of the market is compensated for by an inner certainty on moral matters.

What was the consequence of the primacy given to feeling in morality? If feelings determine what is good and virtuous, then values should be eliminated from social science. The truly 'scientific' spirit does not rely on feelings. Value-freeness in social science easily becomes a convenient political weapon. The claim that values are determined by feelings and not by a scientific method can be used to perpetuate relations of domination. The inner certainty of feeling is ruled irrelevant when the time comes to propose social schemes from a purely 'scientific' viewpoint. It is expertise not feeling that is relevant to successful social schemes. The experts, though, generally do little more than find the means for realizing the ends of the ruling class. So the mantle of science cloaks the interests of the ruling class after the appeal to science has ruled out the value judgements of the lower classes.

Thus, one influential proponent of value-free social science, the economist Samuelson, 'proves' that rent for land is necessary if there is to be efficient production. Those who claim that there is no right to rent for land are, says Samuelson, expressing a value judgment that may reflect the interests of tenants, but economics is unconcerned with such an 'ethical nicety'.[9] Having put down the ethics of free land as unscientific, the road is open for Samuelson to use his 'scientific' economics for the purpose it is intended to serve, to maintain the relations of domination in capitalist society.

Samuelson's 'scientific' argument is based on the notion of efficiency. If the efficient use of land means that millions of the poor are sleeping in doorways and in the parks, then at least rents are avoiding 'inefficient overcrowding' on more desirable land. So 'charging a rent for God-given land is necessary if such scarce land is to be rightly allocated'. The notion of rightly allocating useful resources means there is no other way of using them that would avoid making someone worse off. Some could be made better off by using them another way only by hurting others. To allocate more land to the poor, when it has already been 'rightly' allocated by rents, would deprive the rich.

This optimal allocation of resources will clearly be different for different income distributions. For, with greater equality in income, the lower classes will be able to command the use of a greater proportion of available land. The 'scientific' argument above must then assume uncritically that the economic system, which supports the existing unequal income distribution, is the right system. If it were not, then an optimal allocation relative to the existing unequal income distribution would have no claim at all to being right. After using the slogan of value-freeness to rule out the advocates of rent-free land, Samuelson puts forward his programme of efficiency which makes sense only on the ethical assumption that the economic system giving rise to the existing unequal distribution is the right one. This is a double standard with a political vengeance. For it gives supporters of the ruling class, like Samuelson, a moral basis for being morally unconcerned with the oppression and misery perpetuated by the economic doctrines they espouse. Insisting on the primacy of the social in ethical matters is a way of combatting and exposing this consequence of the ethics of feeling.

4 Universal virtues   Some virtues are obviously bound to a particular group at a particular time. In Aristotle's list of virtues we find courage and 'greatness of soul'. The courageous person fearlessly confronts a noble death, that is, a death in battle; one has greatness of soul if one claims, and is worthy of, the greatest things, including honours. Glorifying such dispositions brings on patronizing smiles today. Fearlessness is now associated with the foolhardy person or with the excessively ambitious person whose desire for the rewards of heroism eliminates fear. The great-souled person would now generally be taken as part of the problem rather than as the epitome of virtue.

Other virtues are not so obviously bound to a particular group at a particular time. Fairness, temperance, and practical wisdom would seem to be virtues in all circumstances. It should not be concluded from this that these dispositions are virtues because of factors transcending social and historical differences. It is one thing for a virtue to be a virtue in every context; it is quite another for there to be one factor common to all contexts that is the basis for its being a virtue. It may be a virtue in all these contexts because it advances quite different social purposes in each of them. The same distinction applies to the consideration of the good. There are some things that are goods in every context. But from this it does not in any way follow that being good is an absolute matter.

Conversely, one must be on one's guard not to accept as universally good actions and emotions that in fact function to advance social purpose only in a limited number of contexts. It would be a mistake to list, say, authority, income, wealth, and self-respect as goods in all contexts.[10] Think of the contexts in which these things are not goods. There is the anarchist possibility of a non-authoritarian society. There is the socialist possibility of a society in which goods are distributed according to need rather than income and in which there is no productive private wealth. There is the communitarian possibility—allegedly realized in some primitive societies—of an integration of the individual into group efforts that eliminates an orientation to personal goals, which is necessary for self-respect. All of these must be ruled out as historical possibilities before the proposed list of goods can be pronounced universal.

How could one tell what virtues and goods are genuinely universal? The method for showing their universality proceeds piecemeal from group to group. The reason that fairness is a virtue within the class of modern productive workers is that this disposition regulates interaction within this class in a way that promotes the realization of the needs that are characteristic of people in this class, in other words, promotes the social purpose of the class. For any other class, fairness must be looked at in light of the distinctive needs of that class. That it will advance those needs cannot be determined without seeing what those needs are. There is little basis for saying that from the general idea of social purpose it can be deduced that certain dispositions will be universal virtues. A piecemeal, as opposed to a general study, seems the only way to find universal goods and virtues.

Notes

1   Aristotle, *Nicomachean Ethics* 1098a7–10.
2   Aristotle, *Nicomachean Ethics* 1106b21–24.
3   See John Dewey's use of this idea, as the depression was beginning, in calling for a transformation of US society from one in which socialization leads to mechanical uniformity to one in which association is internalized, in *Individualism Old and New* (1930), Capricorn, New York, 1962, p. 49.

4 John Rawls attempts to find such an ideal in order to define virtue in *A Theory of Justice*, p. 192.

5 Hume, *An Enquiry Concerning the Principles or Morals*, App. I, p. 289.

6 Hume, *An Enquiry Concerning the Principles of Morals*, p. 269.

7 Max Weber, *The Protestant Ethic and the Spirit of Capitalism* (1904–05), trans. T. Parsons, Scribner, New York, 1958, Ch. IV.

8 René Descartes, *Meditations* (1641), trans. L. J. LaFleur, Bobbs-Merrill, Indianapolis, 1951, Meditation IV.

9 Paul A. Samuelson, *Economics: An Introductory Analysis*, 5th ed., McGraw-Hill, New York, 1961, Ch. XXVII.

10 This mistake is to be found at the very foundation of Rawls' absolutist conception of a fair distribution of goods (John Rawls, *A Theory of Justice*, pp. 93, 440).

XIII

Causes, Ends and Motives

ARE the actions of persons no more than automatic responses to the surrounding society? If persons are important only as outlets for social forces then these forces act as fate. This chapter counters the attempt to deduce fatalism of this social sort from the social view of the person. This form of fatalism denies that factors internal to deliberative processes are relevant to bringing about actions and hence to changing the world. It will not mean, though, that human actions are predictable from external, social circumstances, but only that the operative factors in bringing about an action will be external, social circumstances.

Human actions have a complicated structure. They cannot be interpreted as results of the social situation in the way the motion of one billiard ball is the result of an impact with another. Social forces are indeed reflected in the person. But the way they are reflected in the person and ultimately show up in action is a product of the person. This chapter describes three conditioning factors of action—causes, ends, and motives. Needs are behind each of these factors. It is because needs play this basic role in energizing agents that human actions are not automatic responses to social forces. Our case against fatalism rests on needs.

1 **Causes of human action** Compare the following situations. First, a ball hits a window pane and the window pane cracks. The ball, or the event of its hitting the pane, is the cause of the cracking. Second, as I walk out of the house, I espy a threatening black cloud coming over from the west. I do an about face with the intention of getting an umbrella. The cloud, or my becoming aware of the cloud, caused me to go back inside. Despite the fact that there are causes in both cases, there is a difference between the two cases. The window pane could not have decided to remain whole in face of this attack upon it by the ball. But I could have decided to chance getting to work before the angry cloud burst. Human actions seem, then, to be different from natural events. Whatever it is that causes my action, in the full sense of a human action, did so through my dispensation. I let it

become a cause of what I did. In itself the cause lacked sufficient power to bring about my action.

Do not be in hurry to press the difference too far. If I had not been ill-disposed to getting wet, I would not have gone back in to fetch an umbrella. It is this disposition that plays the major role in my reacting to the cloud. My going back in was not the result of just a whim. Similarly, it was because the glass was not reinforced with a plastic sheet in its middle that it cracked. Suppose the situation had been different in that I liked being rained on and the pane was reinforced. Is there that much difference between qualifying myself with a favourable disposition towards getting wet and qualifying the pane with an inner reinforcement? The favourable disposition toward getting wet would have kept the cloud from turning me around and the reinforcement in the pane would have kept it from breaking. The difference noted above between human actions and physical events seems to have evaporated.

Should we then say that the pane 'let' the ball cause it to break because it lacked the dispositions a reinforced pane would have had? After all, I let a cloud turn me around since I lacked a favourable disposition to getting wet. We should not say this and the reason is as follows. Staying dry when I am dressed is an *end* I pursue whenever there is a good chance of precipitation. One is to interpret my letting the cloud, or my awareness of it, force me inside to get an umbrella in terms of this end in view. Given my aim of staying dry, realizing it when there was a threatening sky seemed to require that I go inside and get the umbrella. Circumstances can become causes of human actions only in their relation to human purposes. There is, though, nothing goal-directed, or teleological, about the doings of the window pane. It has no needs and hence no ends. Consequently, its breaking is not for it a means that in the circumstances is required to realize some end. It does not 'let' the ball or its being hit by the ball break it. For it does not aim at keeping the pressure on its surface from building up beyond a certain point. Thus it does not let the ball crack it in order to realize this or any other aim.

The best way to describe the difference between human actions and physical events is to describe human actions as means to ends. Consequently, whatever it is that causes a human action does so only if that action becomes a reasonable means to an end of the person in the context provided by whatever is the cause. The cause of a physical event need not satisfy this teleological condition. Causes of human action are then circumstances in which it becomes appropriate, and even sometimes necessary, to take action if a certain end is to be realized. Animal action is also teleological. Thus causes of animal actions are likewise not just external circumstances but circumstances with a special relation to ends.

This view of the relation of human action to its causes[1] is totally opposed to the view of the social determinist. Here social determinism is just another expression for fatalism of the kind described above. The social determinist sees external social circumstances—including events and social structures—as the direct sources of human action. The internal factor of purpose is not needed for social structures and social events to bring about human action. This view makes human action a response to its causes in exactly the same way that physical events are a response to their causes. But in actuality poverty does not cause discontent in the way that rain makes crops grow. If the poor are not engaged in the pursuit of ends that their poverty stands in the way of, then their poverty will not bring them to collective action against the system that makes poverty inevitable. With an appropriate set of ends, though, poverty will be the cause of actions that are then means for realizing these ends. This is not to say that lack of ends in view is the only factor preventing poverty from being a cause of action. There might be cynicism about the possibility of moving toward the ends in view. There would then be a general lack of motivation and the external circumstances of poverty would not be an effective spur to action.

As against the social determinist view, the teleological view of human action allows us to say that people make their own history. This is true in the sense that it is the human selection of ends that allows external circumstances to become causally relevant to human action. In the absence of ends in view no external circumstances cause human actions. Nonetheless, the selection of ends is not arbitrary, and the range of actions useful in reaching these ends is limited by the circumstances. 'Men make their own history, but they do not make it just as they please; they do not make it under circumstances chosen by themselves, but under circumstances directly encountered, given, and transmitted from the past.'[2]

2   The beginning of ends   If ends are not arbitrary, how do they come into view? In the last section we were watching out for the pitfalls of social determinism. In this section we must be on our guard against the pitfalls of an idealist view of teleology. If I think of my coming to have an end in view as turning my eyes around from the mire of the actual situation until they are gazing at values in a supra-physical heaven, then my approach to ends is indeed an idealist one. The naturalistic approach rules out this way of thinking. Coming to have an end in view can be no more mysterious than anything else that happens in a way that depends on changes of a spatial or temporal sort. The basic difficulty with abandoning the naturalist approach here is that we would then need to split a person into two parts, one for dealing with existing circumstances and one for envisioning goals. But there is only one person that acts; once the person is split, this condition of unity can no longer be satisfied.

The theory of human nature developed in Part Three is useful here. There are tendencies of various sorts at the root of the system of ends that any human has in view. (1) There are the survival needs for food, sex, the occasion to deliberate, and human support. (2) There are the needs that emerge from these through social patterning. In this category there will be both internal historical needs and imposed needs. (3) There will also be needs that reflect the distinctive nature of each individual. Needs of this third kind may arise from the peculiarities of an individual's genetic make-up, or from the unique way the individual reflects social forces—that is, from the unique set of angles, as it were, at which the various social forces impinge on the individual. This constellation of needs of the three types tends to give rise to human purposes precisely when some of these needs are not satisfied. And here we have an answer to the idealist view of teleology. The goals of our purposes are not actual situations in the present. They are ideals in the sense that they are future satisfactions of unsatisfied needs. But our apprehending these goals or holding them in view is in the present and is fully accounted for by a structure of needs. This structure is itself brought about in material and social conditions of the past and present. No idealist account of ideals is needed.

There is an apparent threat of circularity in our account of needs. Needs that emerge from social patterning are dependent on groups. Yet the groups they depend on do not exist ready-made apart from these needs. This would be an insurmountable problem if the account of needs was simply that social entities cause needs. The historical materialist procedure gives an alternative to such an account: the group is not itself the cause of needs but its emergence is at least part of a system underlying the causal process of the coming into being of these needs. This means that these derived needs come to be in appropriate causal circumstances from the basic ones only in the context of the emergence of a new group characterized by these needs. The system that supports the causal relation will include previous groups and the process of the emergence of the new group. This process takes place among and in conflict with the previous groups. The new group does not then have to antedate the needs it depends on.

The needs of the three types mentioned are enduring needs. People aim at many ends that are based on less enduring needs. Writing this book is an end I have had in view for only a fraction of my life. It will soon be realized, and I will no longer have a need to write this particular book. Still all such temporary projects are means to realizing the enduring needs. The enduring needs stand behind what we think of as our fundamental ends. These fundamental ends arising out of the enduring needs are part of the 'character' of a person. Motives, as will appear in Section 3, are the other part of character.

A good person was defined, in Chapter XII, Section 2, as one whose dispositions lead to actions that advance needs characteristic of that person's groups. (Because of the primacy of class, we can speak merely of the needs characteristic of that person's class.) The ends such a person keeps in view will not then correspond to all of the needs such a person might have. Needs are not automatically reflected in purposes but only tend to be. Character as a system of purposes represents a selection from needs. A person's character is good only if that person keeps in view ends that are characteristic of his or her class to the exclusion of ends inconsistent with those of this class. Objective conditions will then cause the good person to take actions that are in the interests of the class. Those objective conditions in isolation from the ends the good person holds in view are incapable of being the source of such actions. Either the objective conditions would evoke no human response, since no ends are envisioned that could be realized by actions feasible in those conditions, or the objective conditions evoke a response based on ends that come into view because of imposed needs, and hence a response that will more than likely conflict with the interests of the class. The good person, in this class relative sense, is precisely one who is able either to eliminate or to reject the needs imposed from an alien group. Needs are rejected if one does not have as one of one's aims satisfying them. The ability to eliminate or reject imposed needs is the ability to build a good character. The person who eliminates or rejects imposed needs does not guide his or her behaviour by ends in view that arise from imposed needs.

If there is no human action without ends in view, how can one require that a person should change character in such a way as to hold different ends in view? This seems to require that one perform an action without an end in view. Before changing character, any end in view will have to be part of one's present character. And one cannot assume that among these ends in view will be the end of changing one's present character. So in general no purposeful behaviour of one's own will be directed to a change of character. A change of character could come only from external coercion.[3] Unless we can resolve this paradox, the appeal made by the advocate of social change to the lower classes to eliminate or reject their imposed needs is vain. It amounts to an appeal to them to perform actions with no ends in view. Any idea of the self-emancipation of the working class would have to be discarded. Those who desire to manipulate social change from above would have the excuse they desired.

The answer to this conundrum is implicit in the treatment given of conflict within persons in Chapter XI, Section 2. A system of needs that contains both internal and imposed needs will be a conflicting set of needs. This is true even if we say that the imposed needs are part of the nature of the persons with them. But conflict is not just a source of change in society, as historical materialism maintains; it is a source of change wherever it is found.[4] In particular, the conflict between imposed and internal needs and between their corresponding ends in view will, in the right circumstances, lead to a change of character. The process involved will not, of course, be confined within individual persons. The conflict within them will trigger changes in them only in the context of external struggles. The methodology of struggle is not only important for distinguishing imposed from internal needs but also for eliminating or rejecting imposed needs. The process triggered by internal conflict will lead either to a human character oriented toward the interests of an alien class or to a human character oriented toward the interests of his or her own class. In the former case, the imposed needs will dominate the internal needs. In the latter case, the internal needs will dominate. But still the question remains as to how these changes can come about through the person's own actions rather than through external compulsion.

The mechanism is as follows. The existence of the conflict within persons need not prevent them from acting. Indeed, action taken for one end in a person's conflicting set of ends may well create circumstances undermining the other ends and thus changing the person's character. For example, because of ends you hold in view on the basis of internal needs, the circumstance of layoffs at your workplace causes you to participate in a strike action. The kinds of needs and feelings to which participating in this action gives rise are such as to reduce significantly the intensity of the imposed need you had to defend cooperation between manage-

ment and your fellow employees. This need had been the
basis for your trying to defend this cooperation. Now, though,
you do not feel the need to defend it. This means a change of
character. The participation in the strike action was behaviour
with an end in view even though it changed your set of ends in
view. The end in view arose from the internal need to avoid the
erosion of job security. Had this internal need not been in conflict
with other needs, it would have been difficult to see how it could
have played a role in changing your character. Yet the strike action
altered the balance between internal and imposed needs in your
character.[5]

3 Virtues as motives One important item has been left out of
the structure of action. That item is motivation. The motive of a
theft was hunger; that of a murder was revenge; that of an insulting
remark was anger; that of going on strike was a sense of injustice
done; that of raising prices was a fear of the stockholders. By
contrast, the end of the theft was to get food; that of the murder
was to be rid of Jones; that of the insult was to put Smith down;
that of the strike was to win jobs back; that of raising the prices was
to increase the rate of profit. The difference is not hard to see. On
the one hand, the *motive* is a tendency for having a special kind of
feeling, one that promotes actions appropriate to a certain end.
Hunger, anger, and fear are tendencies to experience pangs of
hunger, fits of anger, and fright. And these feelings are spurs to
goal-directed behaviour. On the other hand, *having an end in view*
is a tendency that guides action into one channel rather than
another by allowing only certain circumstances to be causal.

The distinction between end in view and motives parallels that
between propaganda and agitation. The propagandist deals with
issues in a way that gives an audience a conviction about the correct
ends. The socialist propagandist will use the issue of unemployment under capitalism to get people to see the need to transform
capitalism into socialism. The agitator tries to rouse discontent
and indignation. This provides the motive for pursuing the end the
propagandist has laid out.[6] Many people do not quarrel with
socialism as an end but they are cynical about the possibility of
developing a mass movement to realize that end. They can be
brought into the effort to build that movement only by strengthening their motivation. The agitator, by motivating people to take
concrete actions, is one instrument for counteracting this cynicism. And the basic class struggle is another since it constantly
generates outrage and fury at arbitrariness and greed as well as a
feeling of solidarity and dignity in the fight to overcome them.

But having noted the difference between ends and motives, it must also be noted that motives and ends have a common root. My motives indicate to me what my needs are. My hunger indicates that I have a need for food and more than likely have food as an end in view. So a system of needs lies behind both the system of ends and the motives that push me in the direction of those ends.

This is not to say that the motives just are the needs, any more than it is to say that the ends in view just are the needs. A plant's need for water is, as far as we know, never translated into either the motive of thirst or the awareness of watery stuff as an end to be pursued. In the case of humans, though, needs have as their natural development, on the one hand, dispositions for feelings that are a spur to actions implementing the realization of these needs and, on the other hand, a disposition to direct deliberation toward the satisfaction of these needs. These are natural developments of needs since it is in the human organism's groping efforts to realize these needs that motives and ends in view make their appearance as helpful instruments. They are not added on from a supra-physical level. The elimination or rejection of imposed needs in the course of social struggle qualifies this natural development.

From our characterization of virtues, we can readily infer that virtues are a type of motive. A virtue is a capacity for limiting the exercise of other capacities of a person so that he or she acts in accord with the tendencies characteristic of his or her group. How do virtues act as limits? They do so by being capacities for certain emotions, feelings, sentiments that promote actions of one sort rather than another. If you have the virtue of class loyalty, then you will feel loyal to your brothers and sisters when they go out on strike over layoffs. This feeling will promote your participation in the strike.

Their connection with virtues provides a basis for saying when motives are good. A virtuous person is a person with certain good motives, and these good motives are just the virtues of that person. As Bentham noted, there is 'no such thing as any sort of motive which is a bad one in itself; nor, consequently, any such thing as a sort of motive which in itself is exclusively a good one'.[7] Motives are judged in terms of their consequences. Does class loyalty lead to actions that promote the realization of the tendencies characteristic of my class or not? If so, it is a good motive; if not, it is indifferent or a bad motive. This of course was not Bentham's test, since as a utilitarian he would have been concerned with whether class loyalty led to actions generating a universally greater balance of pleasure over pain.

The introduction of motives also supplies the missing element in character. Human character is not just a system of ends in view. It also consists of a system of motives. This is understandable since ends in view by themselves would not lead to action. A person's character includes tendencies for the feelings that are a spur to action. Both sides of character are then based on needs. One can, though, form one's character so that one's ends and motives do not reflect certain of one's needs. Good character eliminates or rejects imposed needs. The motives of the person of good character are, then, tendencies for feelings that do not promote actions opposed to the goals characteristic of his or her group. Among these tendencies must be some for feelings that do in fact promote the group's goals.

4 Fatalism   Ever since the advent of Newtonian mechanics in the late seventeenth century, the bogey of fatalism has in some form plagued moralists. Their worry has been that humans might be determined in regard to what they do in precisely the way material particles are determined in their motions. This worry should have little to do with whether human actions are predictable in detail. On the one hand, we want a modicum of predictability in our associates, who we do not think are any the less human for being moderately predictable. On the other hand, predictability in detail is not even a necessary feature of deterministic science.[8] What then really worried the moralists? It should not be—though it sometimes was—that once all the internal conditions of action are fixed then, in the context of the external conditions, a certain action is determined. For who can object to humans determining their own actions? That is precisely what we want moral agents to do.

The worry at bottom was that, if the analogy of Newtonian material particles is applied to persons, persons would be treated as inert, for material particles change solely on the initiative of the forces acting on them from without. The bogey of fatalism for the moralist lies, then, in the prospect that humans would not initiate changes in their behaviour. Dispelling the bogey of fatalism amounts to showing that the similarity between a human being and a material particle is far less important than the difference.

If we look for the counterpart of a need within a Newtonian material particle we would find that indeed it has one tendency which, with some sympathetic stretching of the imagination, can be called a need. This tendency goes under the label of 'inertia'. A material particle has a tendency to remain at rest or in uniform motion unless acted upon by an outside force. Humans, however, are not inert; they tend to strive for food, for participation in deliberation, and for support from others. These human needs, to consider only the basic ones, mediate outside influences on humans. In the case of the material particle, it is only its inertia that mediates the effect that forces have on it. When you pull on a stone to move it, your efforts are mediated by its inertia; when you try to get a child away from a candy counter, your efforts are mediated not just by physical inertia but also by the need the child has to satisfy a craving for sweets. The human agent—and of course animals generally—have the character of their actions fixed not just by the interaction of their physical inertia with outside influences, but by the interaction of numerous needs with outside influences. Moreover, whereas inertia is a resistance to change, the structure of needs is a positive potential for change.

It would be sheer obtuseness to continue to wonder whether human action, like the motion of a Newtonian material particle, belongs to the realm of external determinism. If it did it would result from external initiating factors mediated only by a resistance to change on the part of the human agent. Many human needs are, of course, the result of the patterning of survival needs by social forces. So such historical needs might be cast in the role of 'external' influences themselves. This would, however, be to confuse the origin of these needs with the actual role they play, as internal determinants, in generating actions. Even so if we ignore historical needs and consider only basic needs, it is inappropriate to talk about human action as merely externally determined, for the basic needs, unlike inertia, actually initiate change.

Hobbes, who understood physical inertia, distinguished humans from material particles very clearly when he said that there are 'small beginnings of motion within the body of man'.[9] These he called 'endeavour'. These beginnings of motion, which provide the inner dynamic of humans, modify all external forces. This human endeavour, arising out of needs, makes it useless to think of human action in fatalistic terms.

Having said that human action is not determined externally, is it settled that human action is 'free'? Certainly not. What we have said so far shows merely that human action is always characterized by endeavour. However strong the force of social circumstances at a given time, it determines action only in conjunction with an inner endeavour. There is, though, a stage at which the influence of social circumstances is of such a nature that humans subjected to it are no longer acting freely, if indeed they are acting at all rather than merely being moved about. We need then to ask, in Chapters XV and XVI, at what stage this happens.

Notes

1　A somewhat similar view was elaborated by Jean-Paul Sartre, *Being and Nothingness* (1941), trans. H. Barnes, Philosophical Library, New York, 1956, pp. 445–51.
2　Karl Marx, *The Eighteenth Brumaire of Louis Bonaparte* (1852), International Publishers, New York, 1963, p. 15.
3　On this paradox, see Aristotle, *Nicomachean Ethics* 1114b12–25.
4　For a general account of the 'dialectics' of change, see Mao Tse-Tsung, 'On contradiction' (1937), in his *Four Essays on Philosophy*, Foreign Language Press, Peking, 1968, pp. 30–5.
5　The price of ignoring conflict between classes and, internally, between needs has been a retreat to idealism in order to account for changes in social structure and, internally, changes in character. Jürgen Habermas pays this price when he appeals to an awareness of ends that develops by its 'own dynamics' in 'Towards a reconstruction of historical materialism', *Theory and Society*, Vol. II, 1975, pp. 287–300.
6　V. I. Lenin, *What Is To Be Done?* (1902), in *V. I. Lenin: Collected Works*, Vol. v, 1961, P. III, Sect. B, pp. 409–10.
7　Jeremy Bentham, *Principles of Morals and Legislation*, Ch. X ('Of motives'), Sec. 3, Para. 29.
8　Richard N. Boyd, 'Determinism, laws, and predictability in principle', *Philosophy of Science*, vol. XXXIX, 1972, pp. 431–50.
9　Thomas Hobbes, *Leviathan*, P. I, Ch. VI.

XIV

Choice and Deliberation

SOME human actions involve more than the three factors, cause, motive, and end. They involve the additional factor, deliberation. When I pour a glass of water from a pitcher after I have been looking for water and while I am thirsty, I do not deliberate, unless there is some special reason for caution. The motive—thirst—, the end in view—water—, and the cause—the observed presence of the pitcher—give rise of themselves to the action of pouring the water from the pitcher. In what sort of case, then, does deliberation become an important factor? A familiar sort of case arises when the cause in conjunction with the end leaves open which from among various alternatives will be the action actually taken. A choice needs to be made from among various alternatives. If the choice is not made just on a hunch or a prejudice, it is reached after deliberation. Are there any strategies for choice based on deliberation that might provide a standard for 'rational' choice? If there are, it will be of interest to ask whether this standard is absolute or not.

1   Means and ends   Deliberation is often said to concern itself with means rather than ends. It will be useful to point out just how this is true and just how it is false. It is true in that there must be an end in view for any process of deliberation to be carried through to its conclusion. It is false in that it is always possible for one to deliberate about a part of one's system of ends in the light of the rest of that system.

The truth behind the claim is, then, that in deliberation one cannot get totally outside the system of one's ends in order to ask what one's overall system of ends should be. Deliberation takes place within the framework of some ends in view. Since ends in view arise on the basis of needs, this will also mean that in deliberation one cannot get totally outside the system of one's needs in order to ask what one's overall system of needs should be. Deliberation over whether to be guided by imposed needs will take place in the context of other needs, the internal historical needs.[1]

When one deliberates about whether one should hold a certain end in view, one is in effect asking whether doing so would be a means to realizing all the better certain other ends one has in view. Even in this case, deliberating about whether to pursue an end involves treating this pursuit as a means to assumed ends. Deliberation about ends does not then emerge out of the blue. I do not, for example, question whether I should change my character unless the course of events makes me aware of its conflictive nature.[2]

There can thus be a change of character that is not an automatic response to a change of environment. It can be the result of deliberate effort. In fact, any part of human character can be called into question by deliberation, though not all of it can be called into question at once. There are then no 'ends in themselves' from the point of view of deliberation. An end in itself would be something that of itself directs toward it the actions of those humans who become aware of it. To deliberate about an end in itself would be absurd, once there has been full congnizance of it. Since one can in fact deliberate about holding any particular end in view, nothing is an end in itself. The doctrine that some things are ends in themselves is an attempt to insure that there is always a background of ends for deliberation.[3] But the doctrine is too strong for what is actually needed. All that is required is that at any given time there be *some* ends in view that give meaning to our deliberations. It is not required that on all occasions some of the ends in view be the *same*.

2 **Principles of choice**   We have said something about the scope of deliberation—it extends to ends as well as to means. We turn now to consider whether there are any formal principles of choices of the kind based on deliberation that are necessary for the rationality of these choices. Such principles govern the relation of deliberating to choosing by telling us which alternative to choose on the basis of features of the various alternatives revealed by deliberation. They are, then, not the same as specific ethical claims as to what is right or just. For these principles do not say in particular what is right or just, but say how in general to determine in a rational fashion which among the various alternatives is the right or just one to choose.

In the atomistic philosophical tradition, where form is independent of content, these formal principles of choice are quite independent of the contentual ends that are held in view during deliberation. In this tradition, the theory of choice is value free, in the sense of Chapter XII, Section 3. A value-free theory of choice makes rationality a function of form and hence independent of the specific ends guiding deliberation. Ethics, as a normative discipline, would be concerned with these ends in view. Thus Arrow presupposes just such an independence when he begins his influential work on the theory of choice. For him 'it is formally possible to construct a procedure for passing from a set of known individual tastes to a pattern of social decision-making, the procedure in question being required to satisfy certain natural conditions'.[4]

In this section, three formal principles of choice are introduced. They are far from being the only such principles. In the next section, their alleged neutrality, as regards commitments to ends, is discussed. The criticisms, though, will extend beyond these three principles to the independence of any such formal principles. There is a dialectic between form and content that rules out a value-free theory of rational choice.

First, we shall consider *the principle of maximum expectation*. It calls for choosing the action from which the most is to be expected. The members of a union local are meeting to take a strike vote. Each member is deliberating over whether to vote for or against going on strike. The central issue is the right of management to require involuntary overtime. There are, let us suppose, two possible outcomes of choosing *to go on strike* (S). First, the strike might be *won* (W). In that case, involuntary overtime will be abolished. Second, the strike might be *lost* (L). In that case, the union will come out in a weakened position in relation to management, though with a small concession on the overtime issue. There are also two possible outcomes of choosing *not to go on strike* (not S). First, management might resume *negotiations* (N). A compromise will then be reached on involuntary overtime which puts an upper limit on it of five hours per week. Second, if further negotiations are not agreed to, the option of *arbitration* (A) of the dispute will be used. Management's position of unlimited involuntary overtime will then stand.

Now to each of these outcomes we assign several magnitudes. We consider, first, how likely it is that any of these things will happen given that the indicated choice is made. Is it, for example, more likely that the strike will be won than lost, given that the union chooses to go on strike? (Here we let $p(W/S)$ stand for *the probability of winning given that the union chooses to go on strike*.) We consider, second, what value individual union members would assign to each of the four outcomes on the basis of the indicated effects they will have on the union. (Value here is merely a preference ranking and should not be confused with moral goodness.) Is it better to emerge with the union in a weakened position as an effect of losing the strike or for unlimited overtime to

Table 1

Alternative actions	Possible outcomes	Probabilities	Values
Strike (S)	Win (W)	$p(W/S) = 0.1$	$v(W) = 100$
	Lose (L)	$p(L/S) = 0.9$	$v(L) = -50$
Not strike (not S)	Negotiate (N)	$p(N/\text{not } S) = 0.6$	$v(N) = 30$
	Arbitrate (A)	$p(A/\text{not } S) = 0.4$	$v(A) = -10$

stand as an effect of arbitration? (Here we let $v(L)$ stand for *the value of losing the strike*.)

Let these magnitudes be as in Table I. In deliberation, one considers not just the values of the outcomes, but as well the probabilities of those outcomes. One does not, then, vote to strike simply because the highest value is associated with winning the strike. One must also consider the chances of winning it if the union chooses to go on strike. To take into account both probability and value, one simply adds together the products of the probability and the value of each of the possible outcomes of any one of the actions. This sum is the 'expected' value of that action. So each action has an expected value equal to the sum of the products of the probability and the value of each of the possible outcomes of that action. The expected values for the two actions—$e(S)$ and $e(\text{not } S)$—are calculated in Table 2. Thus the expected value of the strike action is considerably lower than that of taking the consequences of not striking. The reason for this is, in part, that the chances of success for the strike are very low.

The principle of maximum expectation tells us that, if in the process of deliberation one finds that one course of action among

Table 2

Alternative actions	Possible outcomes	$p \times v$
Strike (S)	Win (W)	$0.1 \times 100 = 10$
	Lose (L)	$0.9 \times -50 = -45$
		$e(S) = -35$
Not strike (not S)	Negotiate (N)	$0.6 \times 30 = 18$
	Arbitrate (A)	$0.4 \times -10 = -4$
		$e(\text{not } S) = 14$

all the alternatives has the highest expected value, then that action should be chosen. This principle calls for a vote against the strike. The principle is applicable only when calculating expectations is a part of deliberation. Such deliberation will by no means be easy since it requires getting magnitudes for a host of probabilities and for a host of values. The principle applies when there is a reliable way of getting these.

A major problem will be the comparability of values, which came up in Chapter V. Suppose I am told that, if I throw any of the sides *one* through to *five* of a die, I will win a million dollars; whereas if I throw side *six* I will lose all my possessions and my job. I dread changing the basic circumstances of my life, and thus refuse the wager. Did I act irrationally? One cannot say until the value I place on the dollar can be compared with the value I place on stability. This means translating a sense of stability into dollar terms. There is no reason to suppose a justifiable procedure exists that makes this possible.

Second, *the principle of maximizing the minimum* gives rather different outcomes than the principle of maximum expectation.[5] Maximizing the minimum tells us to pick the alternative whose worst possible outcome is better than the worst possible outcome of any other alternative. In our strike example, the worst possible outcome of striking—losing—was represented by a value of -50; whereas the worst possible outcome of not striking—arbitration—was represented by a value of -10. Clearly then the principle of maximizing the minimum would direct voting not to strike, since -10 is the best of the worst outcomes.

In that particular example, both principles direct voting no-strike. Suppose, though, the probabilities and values were as in Table 3. The maximum expectation—equal to 14—is still that from not striking, whereas now the best of the worst consequences

Table 3

Alternative actions	Possible outcomes	Probabilities	Values	$p \times v$
Strike (S)	Win (W)	$p(W/S) = 0.1$	$v(W) = 100$	10
	Lose (L)	$p(L/S) = 0.9$	$v(L) = -5$	-4.5
				$e(S) = 5.5$
Not strike (not S)	Negotiate (N)	$p(N/\text{not } S) = 0.6$	$v(N) = 30$	18
	Arbitrate (A)	$p(A/\text{not } S) = 0.4$	$v(A) = -10$	-4
				$e(\text{not } S) = 14$

is losing the strike rather than going to arbitration—being − 5 as against − 10. Thus the principle of maximizing the minimum directs one to vote for a strike, on the grounds that, even if one loses, what happens will not be as bad as what could happen if one does not go on strike at all.

The principle of maximizing the minimum is preferred in cases where no reliable calculations of probabilities can be made. It in no way involves probabilities. Yet if one knew that there was a nine out of ten chance of losing the strike, the fact that none of the possible consequences of going on strike are as bad as the worst possible consequence of not striking at all seems to have less importance. It is perhaps better, then, to view the two principles as applying under differing circumstances rather than as competitors. The principle of maximizing the minimum also has troubles as regards the comparability of values.

Third, and last, we shall consider *the principle of the highest indifference curve*. It plays an important role in consumer economics.[6] So far no consideration has been given to the material conditions that make actions possible; only the outcomes of actions have been appealed to in order to determine which action should be chosen. Now we introduce the requirement that a person can do only what is within his or her means, where means are identified with income.

For purposes of illustration, we limit deliberation to the question of how an income is to be divided between just two consumer goods. Should one use one's income to buy more furniture than food or more food than furniture? There will be several different levels of satisfaction that one can imagine for oneself, independent of whether one's income would allow one to reach the higher levels among them. Each of these levels is called an 'indifference' curve, since all the combinations of furniture and food on any given level provide the same level of satisfaction. Thus the combination of four hams and two chairs might provide the same satisfaction as two hams and four chairs. Both combinations would then be on the same indifference curve. At a higher level, the combination of ten hams and five chairs might provide the same satisfaction as five hams and ten chairs.

The principle of the highest indifference curve tells one to use one's disposable income to buy that mixture of goods (a) whose total price is just equal to that income and (b) which alone belongs to the highest indifference curve one can attain with that income. Suppose the price of two chairs is equal to that of three hams. Both the combination of seven chairs and three hams and the combination of three chairs and nine hams will cost the same. (Each combination will cost the same as nine chairs.) If each combination exhausts my disposable income, would it then be rational for me to buy either one? Not necessarily; the principle directs me to reject one of the combinations if it is on a lower satisfaction level. We might guess that seven chairs and three hams would not provide as much satisfaction as three chairs and nine hams. For one wants to be able to feed, for a reasonable period, all the people one can seat. The combination of seven chairs and three hams should then be rejected since it belongs to a lower indifference curve than the curve attained for the same funds with the combination of three chairs and nine hams. Rationality here is a matter of maximizing the satisfaction an individual can derive from available resources.

3 Social nature of rationality It is now time to give a critical look at these three maximum principles. Aristotle placed prudence, or excellence in deliberation, among what he called the 'intellectual', rather than the 'moral', virtues. The moral virtues provide direct motivation for action. The intellectual virtues are in general capacities for attaining truth, and prudence in particular is a capacity for attaining the truth in regard to what will lead us to our ends.[7] Putting this in the context of the principles of choice just listed leads one to say that the virtue of prudence involves a disposition to carry through the calculations required by one or another of the three 'maximum' principles. Of course, there will be other principles that the prudent, or practically rational, person would also tend to follow. In any final list, some modifications even of the three maximum principles might be necessary.

The moral virtues are relative to social purposes. Is the same true of the intellectual virtues? Or are they absolutes to be identified by understanding the nature of the human intellect? If so the earlier general definition of virtue in Chapter XII applies only to the moral virtues. The human person is indeed social, but is there not a part—the intellect—that preserves an identical nature through the social variations in the rest of the person? It would then be possible to determine, once and for all, what true rationality is. Practical rationality or prudence, in particular, would be a virtue with a universal base.

The best way to raise suspicion in regard to the claim that the intellect is a preserve of absolutism is to look at the limitations of the three maximum principles. The principles work reasonably well under the general assumption that deliberating agents have clearly defined sets of values. (The problem of the comparison of values is now being ignored.) There are certain ideal situations for which this assumption seems unquestionably true.

Consider a situation defined abstractly simply as a market economy. That is, the situation is defined by abstracting from everything but the unrestricted exchange of goods. The chief value in the system is the realization of free exchanges between buyers and sellers. Any need that restricts the freedom of these economic agents is excluded. In such an ideal situation we abstract from class conflicts. Also there is no conflict of values within persons, since we abstract from any internal historical needs that might conflict with the primacy of the market.

One of the theoretical niceties about this ideal is that in it there is no blurring of means and ends, such as was discussed in Section 1. Deliberation starts from a given set of ends and in its course these ends are not challenged. No ends, such as those one might have in view because of imposed consciousness, come to be questioned in regard to whether they serve well as means to ends one holds in view because of internal historical needs. For, by abstracting from class conflict, no ends in view can be regarded as imposed.

Another ideal situation that supports a clearly defined set of values has been devised by Habermas.[8] In an ideal speech situation the chief value is the cooperative search for truth. Any need that restricts the freedom of the interlocutors is excluded. Class conflict is abstracted from and thus abstraction is made from any internal historical needs that might conflict with the primacy of unconstrained discourse. There will then be no blurring of means and ends. The rational choice to make will, accordingly, be one that is based on deliberation carried out in dialogue with others in the ideal speech situation.

Such idealizations can be of importance only if it can be shown that they are presupposed by actual practice. Actual economic behaviour is obscured rather than illuminated by examining it in the light of idealized agents defined by a market. The class struggle is the essential framework for the understanding of economic behaviour. Likewise, there is no basis for saying that deliberation through discourse, such as the debate at a meeting called to take a strike vote, contains a standard of truth-seeking that can be fully realized only in an idealized speech situation. There would be such a standard only if it were right to say that ethics is a final arbiter, that the rationality of a debate in a union points beyond a class rationality, and that truth in the realm of value cannot be founded on the social person. The groundlessness of these views has been pointed out, yet they are all assumed when rationality is based on an ideal speech situation.

In actual situations persons cannot have the clear sets of values they have in these idealizations. The conflictive person of actual class society cannot be rational by any standard of rationality that requires clear sets of values. Why not? The conflicting needs in such a person do not have a vector sum that points such a person in an unambiguous direction. Those needs interact in such a way that in estimating the value of a possible outcome of one choice the person lets imposed needs be the guide and in estimating the value of another possible outcome of the same or a different choice the person lets internal historical needs be the guide. What then are the person's values? One cannot get out of the problem by denying the person has any values, for the person very definitely acts like someone guided by values—though different ones on different occasions.

Returning to our first maximum principle, what is the maximum expected value from among the alternative actions? The question cannot be answered unambiguously since one could bring values from either of two conflicting sets of values to any part of the calculation. In making a calculation on a matter like striking one might use imposed values to estimate the value of the arbitrated settlement (that is, $v(A)$ above). After all if a union notable like I. W. Abel of the Steelworkers was against strikes maybe arbitration is not so bad. But one might at the same time use internal values to estimate the value of losing a strike (that is, $v(L)$ above). One might reason that, even if the union loses, the action will have shown the 'sell-outs' in the union leadership that the ranks voted to strike no matter what they told the ranks about management being ready to come up with a sweetener. Such a calculation made with values, from two conflicting sets of values, is clearly worthless. For there is another calculation in which, conversely, $v(A)$ is based on internal and $v(L)$ on imposed needs. And there is no basis for choosing the one calculation rather than the other in deliberation. It is tempting to require that only one coherent set of values be used for a given choice. Yet the calculation arrived at by such a limitation would apply only to a person with a coherent set of values. A person of this kind exists in the idealizations we have rejected but nowhere in actual class society.

Rationality for conflictive persons is not, however, impossible to achieve. But it cannot be premised on the view that ends are given once and for all. The sharp separation of ends from means that every one of the maximum principles presupposes has first got to go. Rational deliberation is simply not a mechanical calculation of maxima on the basis of pre-set values. Yet, for example, in the case of the principle of the highest indifference curve, it is assumed that every combination of commodities has a unique value for the consumer. It has long been recognized that in actuality consumer behaviour is a manifestation of the conflict between internal historical needs and needs substituted for them. It does not result from a single coherent set of values.

What then is rationality? In the process of deliberation, one of the central functions of practical rationality is to sort over, in the context of struggle, the perspectives within which one might take an action in order finally to base one's action solely on internal historical needs. 'Deliberation is rational', says Dewey, 'in the degree in which forethought flexibly remakes old aims and habits . . .'.[9] Rarely if ever am I brought up short and forced to deliberate where there is not at least the trace of the question as to whether my purposes are consistent with other purposes I have. The notion of a value-free science has as a clear corollary a sharp separation of ends and means. This separation implies a value-free consideration of the best means, one independent of deliberation about ends. Without the independence there would be no 'scientific' theory of choice.

Practical rationality is not just the ability to arrive at the correct relation of means to pre-set ends. It also involves the ability to restructure one's system of ends. It thus includes the ability to make correct value judgments. Rational choice is not, however, the outcome of an arbitrary reshuffling of ends, for it depends upon a process of deliberation in which ends that conflict with ends based on internal historical needs are dropped. Practical rationality is the ability to pick ends conforming ultimately to the goals of a class. Form and content here are not independent, since the rational form found in choice is dependent on a content of ends limited by internal historical needs. Practical rationality is clearly relative to groups. No theory of rational choice can, then, be value free. The theory must begin by recognizing that the only rational choices are those advancing internal historical needs.

Having said all this, one still has to admit that the maximum principles do describe what it is to be rational strictly within the confines of certain occupations in contemporary society. For within those occupations the conflictive nature of the person is kept latent, and the goal of strengthening the capitalist order acts as though it were an eternal imperative. By abstracting from everything but those occupations, imposed consciousness is not recognized as such. There is, then, a clear set of values on the basis of which the maximum principles can be used to define the person of practical rationality, or prudence.

Outside such occupations deliberation has the task of peeling away layer after layer of imposed consciousness. The maximum principles are then no longer the standard of practical rationality.

Where deliberation has this task, a clear set of values is in the making but is not yet realized. William Hinton remarked, in connection with the change of consciousness during the late stages of the Chinese revolution, that consciousness cannot be refocused in a single night. At first, change in consciousness spreads from one part of the personality to others until the whole self is involved in an explicit conflict between the old and the new. It is only in a social struggle that this explicitly recognized conflict can be resolved.[10] Thus the process of deliberation is not independent of social interaction. One does not 'remake old aims' in one's head. Rather deliberation blends into the practical struggle it is an instrument for. It advances the remaking of old aims already initiated in that struggle. It is only if one denies the interaction of deliberation with practice that one will think of deliberation in mechanical terms as the fitting of means to pre-set ends.

4   Choice as endeavour   It remains to carry deliberation through to choice. When there is a break in the course of activity that has been set in progress by causal circumstances, ends, and motives, deliberation assumes the task of putting things back on their course. One considers, in a process involving an interaction of thought and practice, the several alternatives that the causal circumstances allow; one considers one's purposes against the background of other, perhaps more far-reaching, purposes; and finally the deliberative interlude is ended and one is acting again.

There is a mistake that has to be avoided. Intellectual analysis backed up by struggle does indeed come to the rescue of a certain general course of action when obstacles to it occur. These obstacles take the form either of conflicting motivation, of indeterminacy of causation, or of causal circumstances that physically thwart the desired action. Yet even though intellectual analysis sharpened by struggle comes in at such a point, one must not make the mistake of thinking that it is capable, of itself, of regenerating action along the given general course. This would be the mistake of thinking that from judgments one obtains overt action. Against this mistake it has been common to say that judging must be supplemented with willing. But willing is only a name for the problem, not its solution.

Deliberation makes one aware of alternatives and their important aspects. Action is regenerated only in conjunction with the *feelings* aroused by this awareness of the alternatives. These feelings are based on needs, and they act as motives for what the agent will do. (These feelings are not the same things as the valuations spoken of in connection with the maximum principles.

The valuations are only *estimates* of the intensity of one's feelings. They are estimates made on the basis of things one normally aims at and thus usually has positive feelings for.) Deliberation can at best lead to the judgement that one of the alternatives it has brought to awareness has a feature another does not have. The feature may be the conformity to group purpose of one of the alternatives. But feeling may not be mobilized behind this alternative however rational the deliberation. How can there be a coincidence of the course recommended by rational deliberation with positive motivation for taking that course?

What is missing for such a coincidence is good character. A good character enables rational deliberation to be effective. The feelings that get one back on the track of action are ones that come from needs that have been selected in a certain stage in the process of character building. Suppose that stage is not very advanced. The needs whose realization would advance social purpose might still be either blocked or rejected. The most sensitive deliberation imaginable—one that criticizes ends incompatible with this social purpose and ranks means in respect to it—might be of no avail. Why not? The feelings required to implement the results of this deliberation are simply absent. Without the feelings arising from internal historical needs, deliberation that comes up with the means for realizing those needs will be useless. Of course, if deliberation does contribute to such a purpose, the reason will be that character building has advanced beyond the elementary stage, releasing feelings based on internal historical needs. Rational deliberation must meet with good character to insure a rational choice.

A choice is made when deliberation brings to awareness features of a course of action that engage intense positive feeling. The choice itself is not the action chosen, but it is the endeavour or the beginning of the endeavour to perform that action. This endeavour is the result of the deliberation only insofar as the deliberation gave rise to a desire to perform the action. The choice is not just the mental recognition that I want to do something. Such a recognition does not commit me to do anything. Rather the choice must be marked by some beginning toward the action, such as writing a note for myself to get paint on my way home after becoming persuaded by deliberation that if I do not start painting the house now it will not get done for another year. Writing that note is the beginning of the endeavour to paint the house. Writing it is choosing to paint the house soon. Deliberation engaged feeling with the writing of that note.

Notes

1   Thus in Rawls' view of deliberation, the choice of our character involves an acceptance of some of our desires as 'fundamental' and a criticism of others after consideration of the conditions under which they arose (*A Theory of Justice*, Sec. 64).

2   John Dewey, *Human Nature and Conduct*, p. 190.

3   Aristotle, *Nicomachean Ethics* 1094a19–30.

4   Kenneth J. Arrow, *Social Choice and Individual Values*, 2nd ed., Yale University Press, New Haven, 1963, p. 2.

5   For details, see R. D. Luce and H. Raiffa, *Games and Decisions*, Wiley, New York, 1957, Ch. XIII.

6   Samuelson, *Economics*, Ch. XXI, Appendix.

7   Aristotle, *Nicomachean Ethics* 1139a21–31.

8   Jürgen Habermas, *Legitimation Crisis*, trans. T. McCarthy, Beacon Press, Boston, 1973, p. 108.

9   John Dewey, *Human Nature and Conduct*, p. 198.

10 William Hinton, *Fanshen*, Vintage, New York, 1968, p. 609.

XV
Philosophical Freedom

Is not all this talk about virtue, motives, and choice peripheral? Surely the nub of the matter is freedom. For ethics, all that is really important about human action is that it be free. Only if action is free can the agent be morally worthy or reprehensible. Is it not strange to wait till the end of the discussion of human action to tack on the most important feature of it?

The only excuse is that freedom has already been discussed, without actually calling it such. In fact, put down what has already been said about human action in this part of the book and you have an account of the elements of freedom. To make clear we have all the elements, they need to be synthesized with the problem of freedom directly before our eyes. This will be done here after first criticizing a conception of freedom that requires more than has already been introduced. Freedom will be a mere capacity. This capacity is called 'philosophical' freedom. It is only a precondition of ethical life. It differs from 'social' freedom, which is the topic of the next chapter. Social freedom exists where people have won the struggle to have certain rights recognized.

1 Is choice uncaused? When actions were characterized as morally good or bad, nothing was said about how they came into being. Their goodness or badness was said to be a function of how they fit with a social pattern. It was not claimed that good actions must be the ends in view of agents. One can do a good thing without intending to do it. Where then does the question of freedom come in at all? It comes in with obligation: to be obliged to do something, one must be free to do it. This freedom implies an ability to act otherwise. If one fails to do what is obligatory, then at least one could have done otherwise than what one has done. In particular one could have done precisely what was obligatory.

Let us follow up on the idea of being able to do otherwise. There are several components here. First, there is the component of causal insufficiency. The causal circumstances in isolation would not have brought me to do what I did do. Second, there is the component of compatibility. The causal circumstances were compatible with different motives, deliberation, and ends, and the agent has the needed abilities to perform an alternative action on the basis of these different internal factors. Third, there is the component of adequacy. Given the presence of the bodily and mental abilities to perform the action, the causal circumstances, the motives, the deliberation, and the ends together brought me to do what I did. Merely because I saw water, did not bring me to drink it. I had to be motivated by thirst or in some other way. But having seen the water, I might have had a motive that led me not to drink. When all three components—insufficiency, compatibility, and adequacy—are satisfied in the above way, we shall speak of being able to do otherwise in the *weak* sense.

It might be objected that some stronger sense is needed. The objection is to the compatibility and the adequacy components, and not to the component of causal insufficiency. The compatibility component should, the objection runs, be strengthened. Not only are different internal factors—motives, deliberation, and ends—compatible with the causal circumstances, but also a different action is compatible with the causal circumstances together with the internal factors. It follows from this that the component of adequacy must be revised. For the causal circumstances together with the three internal factors, in the presence of the needed bodily and mental abilities, did not, in isolation from some other factor, bring me to do what I did do. We shall show how accepting this *strong* sense of being able to do otherwise leads to a rejection of naturalism. In Section 2 a conception of freedom that requires being able to do otherwise only in the weak sense is defended.

Suppose freedom implies ability to do otherwise in this strong sense. Freedom of this kind we can call 'strong' freedom. The causal circumstances, the motive, the end in view, and the process of deliberation will, then, leave the choice of an action open if it is to be free. An important factor needed in bringing about choice is still missing. Suppose, however, freedom implies ability to do otherwise only in the weak sense. This kind of freedom we call 'weak'. In this case one's act can be free even when the four factors in the list are the only ones needed in bringing the act about. (This, of course, does not mean the action is predictable in terms of these four factors.)

According to the conception of choice in Chapter XIV, Section 4, when deliberation presents an alternative in such a light that one is motivated to endeavour to realize that alternative, deliberation at that point is terminated by choice. Strong freedom implies that such an endeavour to action is *not* brought about solely through the presence of the collection of the four above

factors—deliberation, motive, end, and cause. In short, the
engaging of the motive, which is the beginning of the endeavour to
realize the action, is either a chance event or an event that has a fifth
factor contributing to its occurrence.

Which alternative will engage the backing of which motive is,
without such a fifth factor, as much a matter of chance as the time
of fission of a radioactive atom. An appeal to chance is not, though,
available to advocates of strong freedom. If my choice were a
chance event, how could I be obliged to make the choice I do?
Being told that I have an obligation to participate in a strike would,
if choosing were a chance event, be like being told that I have an
obligation to throw a six when I throw a die.

What then is the fifth factor for advocates of strong freedom?
For them choice is open from the point of view of the causal
circumstances and of both the motives and the ends based on our
needs. The fifth factor is a supra-natural one. Thus strong freedom
has two sides: the insufficiency of natural factors and the necessity
of a supra-natural one for bringing about choice.

Kant stated a position like this when he defined freedom as 'the
property which the will has of being a law to itself'.[1] Thus when I
act freely, and not from 'alien' forces, I am determined to act by a
law or moral principle that comes from my 'pure' practical reason.
Such a law is the supra-natural fifth factor. How does the mere
presence of a law in reason determine action? It was, after all,
shown in Chapter XIV that deliberation without feeling would
never give rise to action? In this case, Kant sees the law as
generating its own 'motive', which is the motive of 'reverence' for
the law.[2] This motive is not then derived from a natural need. So
when I freely choose to participate in the strike, I am brought to do
so by a law that pure practical reason proposes and that generates
its own motive for obeying it. I do my duty for duty's sake and for
no other motive.

To justify this kind of strong freedom, one must justify laws of
pure practical reason. There is no basis for supposing for a minute
that there are what Kant calls laws of pure practical reason. Such
laws would both be learned and have validity independently of 'the
influence of alien causes'. Since the social-physical world is alien to
pure practical reason, this view conflicts with a naturalist account
of knowledge. Even if there were such laws, why on earth should
we be motivated to make our choices conform to them? Kant was
led to posit a reverence for pure law not based in needs out of
desperation.

Moral principles are, in fact, formulated precisely because of the
conflicts and uncertainties in the social circumstances where our

actions take place. They are—like descriptive thoughts about the world—partially a result of our interaction with the world. Once formulated, they serve a role as instruments in the struggles we are engaged in. There is no basis then, for setting moral laws above our needs. They are not derived from a supra-natural region such as pure practical reason. Like needs themselves they come from our physical and social nature.

One can account for the motive of 'duty for its own sake' easily enough without abandoning the level of naturalistic thought. When it is hard to give reasons everyone can agree to, people are simply told to do things because it is their duty. They then accept duties either on the assumption that the reasons can be supplied or because of the authority of those who promulagate duties. Gradually, though, these duties come to be detached, simply by being obeyed, both from the presumption of reasons and from the backing of moral authorities. At this point, people are motivated by an impulse to do whatever is widely accepted as a duty. This motive is not then generated by a pure practical law.

2 Freedom as a capacity for action There is, then, good reason to abandon the view that freedom requires, in addition to the four natural factors of action, a fifth supra-natural condition. The four factors are natural since they are changed by social or physical influences. We shall now attempt to describe human freedom, as a precondition of obligation, within the framework of the four natural factors. The freedom so described will imply the ability-to-do-otherwise only in the weak sense.

The exercise of freedom is best viewed as a special way of having an effect in the world. Everything in the great chain of beings changes the world in its own special way. Stones create a gravitational pull on other bodies. Trees hold the earth and provide umbrage. Humans affect the world in a still different way. Stones and trees do not have ends in view and they do not deliberate. Dogs and apes might have ends in view and do things for motives, but they do not ponder alternatives—as far as we know—in a process of deliberation. They are creatures of performance, not of deliberation. The exercise of freedom[3] means realizing a capacity to have an effect in the world or to refrain from having that effect through an interaction of end in view, motive, causal circumstances, and deliberation in the light of the available facts. It is assumed that both having this effect and refraining from it are things that are possible within the range of one's strength, endurance, intelligence, and skill. If one exercises freedom in not writing an angry letter, it must be within the range of one's ability to write it; if one exercises freedom in breaking a cup, it must be within the range of one's ability to handle it carefully.

This description of freedom needs qualification. The whole structure of cause-motive-end is grounded in needs. It is needs that come to awareness as ends in view. It is ends in view that make it possible for certain circumstances to be causes of action. And finally it is needs that take the form of capacities for feelings, which capacities, when appropriate ends are in view, function as motives. Suppose one's needs are, though, in some way 'alien'. The message *Drink beer!* is flashed on the TV screen at a level below conscious awareness. This produces a strong desire for beer. At half-hour intervals one leaves the screen to open another beer can. Even deliberation is involved, since one has to decide when one will miss out least in getting the next beer from the refrigerator. We would not have freedom, if all, or most, of our behaviour were, like this, an outcome of artifical needs. A completely manipulated civilization is not free. The qualification required is that in being free one must have a capacity for bringing about an effect in the world by ends and motives that come from needs that are *one's own*.[4] Problems about what counts as one's own will be taken up in Section 3.

Now an explanation. Why was deliberation in the light of the available facts included in our original description of freedom? Not all human action is deliberative; sometimes the cause-motive-end structure is all that is involved. But with only this structure required, it is possible for a compulsive action to be an exercise of freedom. Compulsive action can be intentional in that associated with it is an end in view, but it cannot be deliberative. The compulsive person cannot stop and view the alternatives.

Saying that a person has freedom is not the same as saying that the person's actions are all free. You have freedom when you have the capacity to bring about changes by the four factors. It is assumed these four factors satisfy the qualification that the needs behind motives and ends are one's own and that deliberation takes place in the light of available information that is not part of imposed consciousness. Clearly an exercise of freedom will be a free action. A complication arises, though, if we try to insist that the converse is also true. Not every free action is an exercise of freedom since there are free actions for which the motives and ends are based on needs that are not one's own or for which deliberation sets out from imposed consciousness.

A racist act deriving from alien needs or imposed beliefs or both is not an exercise of freedom. It does not come from what the racist is as a result of the groups to which he or she belongs. To say, though, that the racist act is not free because of this is to imply that racists are never responsible for their acts of racism. Surely racists are to be held responsible for at least some of their racist acts. It is no easy matter to say which.

A beginning can be made by noting that when one acts freely one at least *could* exercise freedom. The racist does not exercise freedom when acting from alien needs or imposed beliefs, but he or she could, in the circumstances, exercise freedom by choosing on the basis of non-alien needs and non-imposed beliefs. If an alternative set of needs and beliefs of this kind does not exist, then the act is not free. It is not necessary to inquire why, in the first place, the alternative set is not operative in bringing about a choice. It may be that the opportunity has not arisen through struggle to weaken the set of alien needs and imposed beliefs. In this case the racist cannot be blamed for the failure to undertake the obligation to overcome imposed needs and consciousness. Nonetheless, the racist is acting freely and has responsibility for his or her racist act.

In sum, freedom the capacity can be given the following formulation:

I   One has 'freedom' when one has a capacity to bring about or to refrain from bringing about an effect in the world, where both bringing it about and refraining from doing so are within one's range of abilities, by having an end of one's own in view, by experiencing a motive of one's own in the context of causal material-social circumstances, and by deliberating in the light of available information that is not part of imposed consciousness.

A separate formulation is needed for free action, since some free actions are not exercises of freedom in the sense of I:

II An action is 'free' when (a) it is brought about by a motive, an end, a cause, and deliberation, and (b) the agent has a set of needs and beliefs on the basis of which, in the causal material-social circumstances, the agent could exercise freedom in bringing about or refraining from bringing about the action.

If the motive and end referred to in II (a) are based on an alien need or the deliberation is based on imposed consciousness, then the action cannot be free unless there is in the agent some set of non-alien needs and non-imposed beliefs that are the basis for the possible exercise of freedom referred to in II(b).

How are freedom and free action related to the ability to do otherwise? In the weak sense of Section 1, to be able to do otherwise is not to be restricted by the causal circumstances to what one actually did. The causal circumstances—including not just external factors but also the agent's own abilities—do not, then, in isolation bring about what one does. One's range of activity is narrowed down to what one actually did by adding to the causal circumstances the motive, the end, and deliberation. This leads to the following:

III An agent 'could do otherwise' when (a) there is an alternative action that, in the circumstances, would be within the agent's range of abilities to perform and (b) those circumstances would be compatible with the different motives, ends, and deliberations that would bring about the alternative action.[5]

The notion of bringing-something-about used in I–III is left unexplained. It is appropriately explained in a theory of causation. In theories of causation that interpret it differently, I–III will have different meanings.[6] By saying, as in I, that there is a capacity to bring something about in the causal circumstances by the various internal factors one implies that those circumstances are not themselves causally sufficient.

The needs and beliefs involved in an exercise of freedom are not the only ones compatible with the immediate circumstances. The immediate circumstances are capable of sustaining non-alien and alien needs, non-imposed and imposed beliefs. This is because the immediate circumstances include influences both from one's own groups and from alien groups. Thus one's own needs and non-imposed beliefs, which are operative in the exercise of freedom, are supported at best by only one side of the immediate circumstances. The circumstances are always rich enough in conflict to be compatible with alien needs and imposed beliefs, which could then be the basis for acting otherwise. Moreover, the abilities needed to act otherwise are guaranteed since an exercise of freedom involves the abilities needed both to perform and to refrain from an act. When one exercises freedom one could do otherwise. The compatibility of an alternative structure of motive, end, and deliberation with the immediate circumstances is needed to make obligation intelligible. Without such an alternative one would inevitably act as one does and thus could not be obliged to act. It is still possible that where the immediate circumstances do not contain conflicting influences, alternative sets of the internal factors are compatible with those circumstances. All that we have been interested in showing here is that in a society with conflict freedom involves the ability to do otherwise. (It is fairly obvious from II, moreover, that an agent who performs a free action could have done otherwise. Either the free action is an exercise of freedom or the agent could replace it with an exercise of freedom.)

The notion of exercising freedom provided by I captures the valid core of the notion of 'rational self-determination' that Kant felt was so important to the idea of freedom. To examine one set of ends in the light of another set or to examine a set of alternative means in the light of given ends is certainly to make a contribution from the side of practical reason to bringing about one's behaviour. This contribution, when it is not based on imposed consciousness, comes from the person and thus amounts to self-determination. It is not, though, the only contribution since there are also needs and causal circumstances. Thus rational self-determination is not, as Kant thought, the only aspect of exercising freedom, but it is nonetheless an essential one.

Hegel repeated Kant's mistake in order to set the state above conflicting groups. So long as society is torn between competing classes, there is, Hegel thought, no freedom. Each class is limited by and hence constrained by its particular interests. There is no genuine universal principle governing this society. Compromise can blend these particular interests together into formally universal procedures that apply across class lines.[7] But people are constrained to accept these universal procedures on the basis of their particular interests. The universality of the procedures does not derive from anything universal but from limited interests. To reach freedom one must get beyond the limitations and compromises created by class interests. Only human nature itself as the basis for organizing a state that is above classes can be the source of freedom. For human nature is not limited in the way class interests are. By definition, the human as such is not constrained by any limited interests. To be free is to be self-determined by the principles that express human nature, which is a truly universal basis for these principles. Since these principles are developed in the state, the state is where people are free.[8]

This involves two mistakes we are already prepared to pick out. First, rational self-determination by the idea of human nature is abstracted by Hegel from motives and ends that develop in group existence. Such an abstraction is needed for freedom in the sense of determination of choice by the purely universal. But there is no choice apart from the motives and ends that develop in group existence. Second, the state is abstracted from the particular aims of classes and given a universal aim. This is necessary if the state is to be where people are free in Hegel's abstract sense. But as a sum group the state will serve to perpetuate the domination of one of the sub-groups and it will not then pursue a universal principle.

3   Voluntary action and alien needs   A free action is not the only kind that one does without being overwhelmed by the causal circumstances. For deliberation is not essential if internal factors are to play a role in bringing an action about. Free actions, in the

sense of II, involve deliberation in the light of available information. But motives and ends are involved in generating actions
that though not deliberated over are voluntary. Actions that either
are free or could be if deliberation were present are 'voluntary'
actions. Of course, when it does not involve deliberation, a
voluntary action must nonetheless be one done with at least an
awareness of the available circumstances. Otherwise it might be
something that one would not have willingly done had one been
aware of the circumstances. Like free actions, voluntary ones are
actions performed in circumstances in which one could have done
otherwise. So a non-free voluntary action is not an action brought
about by the causal circumstances in isolation, but rather one that
does not involve deliberation. As mentioned above, when one acts
compulsively—that is, acts from an intense motive that precludes
deliberating—one is not acting freely, even though what one does
may well be voluntary.

A voluntary action, like a free one, may be brought about by a
motive or end that is not the agent's own. Since, though, the action
must satisfy II(b) in our formulation for free action, the agent who
performs a voluntary action could act from a motive or end that is
his or her own. A voluntary action must satisfy II(b) since it is
either itself free or misses being free just by the element of
deliberation. The agent who performs the voluntary action like the
one who acts freely could exercise freedom in bringing about or
preventing the action.

What motives and ends are the agent's own? We have assumed
that whatever is the agent's own is not alien, in the sense of coming
from a group to which the agent does not belong or does not
independently belong. Thus motives and ends that are the agent's
own are not imposed and do not derive from imposed needs.
Where imposed needs have become part of the agent's nature, we
nonetheless say here that these are not the agent's own on the
assumption that they would be eliminated in developing a coherent
self.

Considerable falsification is involved in some groups' attempts
to say what motives and ends are an agent's own. Those committed
to perpetuating domination will praise the patriotic worker. But
behaviour that is not an exercise of freedom cannot be used as a
model. So the worker's motive of patriotism must be regarded as
the worker's own. If it were imposed from some other group, then
the patriotic worker is a dupe and not a model for behaviour.
However, since war sets members of the working class of different
nation-states to killing one another, there is good reason to say that
patriotism is not a motive of the worker's own. To overthrow

domination workers need to unite across national boundaries against the international ruling class. The worker's enlisting is not, then, an expression of freedom since the motive for it is not the worker's own.

Against this it might be argued that freedom and hence alien needs are, like goodness, relative to groups. From a ruling-class or a sum-group perspective, the worker exercises freedom by enlisting and the motive of patriotism is the worker's own. From a working-class perspective, the worker does not exercise freedom by this act and the motive is not his or her own. The connection between needs and obligations might seem to support such a relativistic freedom. The institutions of the sum group teach obligations that serve the end of continued domination. To motivate people to obey the institutions of the sum group, needs must be created that are in accord with perpetuating domination. Suppose, though, these very needs were to be judged alien to the people who have them. The actions based on these needs would not, then, be exercises of freedom. Because freedom is required for obligation, no one could be obliged to follow those teachings regarding obligation.

Plainly the ideological tail is now wagging the scientific dog. The obligations the sum group promulgates are given legitimacy by calling the needs that get people to obey them internal rather than alien needs. But to determine scientifically whether or not such needs are alien, the observer must be prepared to ignore these assumed obligations. Just because the schools, the politicians, and most of the churches teach that military service is an obligation, it in no way follows that the need to perform patriotic acts is an internal historical need of the worker. All that follows is that such a need must be the worker's own *if* such an obligation is to be valid. The method of struggle is required here to decide whether patriotism is based on an alien need. This method will show that patriotism is based on an alien need of the worker under capitalism and that the claim of institutions of the sum group that patriotism is based on a need that is the worker's own is sheer ideology.

Alien needs depend on who one is rather than on the group perspective from which one is viewed. Freedom is not, then, group relative in the way goodness is. However, there is an important way in which freedom is relative. This is the way in which obligation, as distinct from goodness, is relative. Since an obligation is for a given person in a fixed set of groups, an obligation is relative only in the sense that it might not be the same if that person were to belong to other groups. The same is true of freedom: one who does not, as a worker, exercise freedom by enlisting may do so as a member of an upper class. The list of alien needs has changed. What is being denied is an absolute freedom based on a universal set of needs that are each person's own. Since freedom is a precondition of obligation, it is not surprising that freedom is relative in precisely the way obligation was seen to be relative in Chapter X, Section 3.

4 Responsibility and morality People are regarded as responsible for what they do voluntarily and *a fortiori* for what they do freely. Moreover, they are regarded as responsible for some of the consequences of what they do voluntarily or freely. Responsibility is important since ethical life involves sanctions designed to prevent the breaking of norms. Nonconformists are fined, scorned, fired, imprisoned, blacklisted, and tortured. These sanctions are appropriate only where agents are responsible for their acts and the consequences of their acts.

How, though, are criteria for responsibility established? Are they established from a perspective that does not reflect a group purpose? One of the factors in establishing such criteria is surely this: a group will develop a practice of sanctioning people who freely or voluntarily act in a way that blocks the tendencies of the group. The act that blocks the group tendencies need not itself be the event for which the person is sanctioned. But once the person is sanctioned by members of a group for any event, the event is treated as one for which the person is responsible and hence as an event that is either a voluntary action that blocks the group's tendencies or a consequence of such an action. One becomes responsible for what one is fined, jailed, or beaten for. The cart of punishment goes before what is usually taken to be the horse of responsibility.[9] Where responsibility is settled in this way, it is group relative. (Responsibility also emerges from praising and rewarding, but we limit ourselves to the negative cases.)

Consider the case of responsibility for violence. The owners allege that the picketers were responsible for the violence that erupted as people tried to cross the picket line and exercise their 'inalienable right to work'. The striking workers allege that they were merely 'protecting their workplace from interlopers' during a period when they temporarily vacated it to insist upon fair conditions of employment. If the owners do not try to impose sanctions for violence on the picketers, then they would be letting the strikers know that they could keep scabs out of their place of work with impunity. Yet the use of scabs is one of the most powerful tools by which owners break strikes and thereby avoid having to meet the demands of workers. Thus the tendencies of the owning class would suffer a setback were it not insisted that sanctions be imposed on the strikers for any violence that erupted. If the strikers do not try to make the owners pay in some way for the violence, then they would be letting the owners know that they could get away with any tactics needed to get scabs into the workplace. Yet it is necessary to exclude scabs if there is to be a good chance of a successful strike. Thus the tendencies of the working class would suffer a setback were it not insisted that the owners be made to suffer for any violence that erupted because of their effort to bring scabs across the line.

How is this to be analyzed? The strikers acted voluntarily to protect their place of work from interlopers. This was the act that was against the interests of the owners. What the strikers are held responsible for is, though, the violence. The violence becomes, thereby, a consequence of the strikers' behaviour from the perspective of the owners. Conversely, the act of employing scabs was, from the strikers' perspective, the one that led to violence.

The relativity of responsibility here corresponds to the relativity of rights. From the perspective of the owners, the strikers have no right to protect their place of work from outsiders and have responsibility for the violence that erupts in violating this right. From the perspective of the strikers, the owners have no right to send outsiders to work and have responsibility for the violence that erupts in violating this restriction. Since rights and good acts are relative to any groups, including ones to which the person who has the rights or who does the good acts does *not* belong, responsibility is relative in the same way. This is not the way obligation is relative, since it is relative only to those groups to which the person with the obligation could belong.

It is class tendencies that determine whether the strikers or the owners will be responsible for any possible violence. A fact-finding mission can illuminate misconceptions each side might have about what actually transpires when violence breaks out. But so-called hard facts alone will not amount to an ascription of responsibility.[10] A fact-finding mission can ascribe responsibility only by taking sides with one of the classes.

Responsibility is also relative where the focus is more on the action itself than its supposed consequences. In 1970 James Johnson, an autoworker in Detroit, brought an M-1 carbine into his plant in his overalls and killed two foremen and a job setter. There was no question that his shots had done the killing. Conditions in the plant were abominable. Johnson's defence lawyer, Kenneth Cockrel, took the jury into the plant to judge conditions themselves. Ten of the twelve jurors had worked in Detroit. The jury found Johnson 'not responsible for his acts'. The irate Judge Colombo recommended to hospital officials that Johnson be kept in custody the rest of his life.[11]

The question is not whether the deaths were consequences of Johnson's acts but whether the causal material-social circumstances—plant noise, oil slicks, defective machinery, dismissal by a foreman, Mississippi boyhood, cousin lynched—were compatible with other motives, deliberations, and ends than Johnson acted from. The jury said, no; the judge said, yes. Psychological study could not be expected to yield a neutral answer. The point is that the working-class jury did not want to describe Johnson's acts in a way that, when followed up with sanctions, might help Chrysler maintain discipline under abominable conditions.

Since Johnson was not responsible, he did not act freely or voluntarily. And thus we find a point at which relativity affects free action and voluntariness. The compatibility of causal circumstances with alternative inner factors is not so much a fact of the world as a construction to fit social purpose. In the case of needs, the method of struggle could be used to distinguish alien needs from others. But without an empirical methodology for the case of compatibility with causal circumstances, relativity must be admitted for free action.

In sum, relativity affects free action, the exercises of freedom, voluntariness, and responsibility. This is understandable since they belong to the normative views of things groups develop in order to advance their interests. To allow that they were insulated from these group-relative normative views and based on an assumed universal human nature would lead to absurdity. For obligations valid for a group might be ones that this group is not free, in the absolute sense, to obey. The assumed universal human nature might not include the motives needed to get people to obey these obligations. Or, people might not be held responsible, in the absolute sense, for doing things that they have no right, relative to the group, to do. The attempt to make people believe that free action, the exercise of freedom, voluntariness, and responsibility are absolute in nature is, then, all one with the attempt to get them to believe that ethical claims themselves are absolute.

Notes

1 Kant, *Groundwork of the Metaphysic of Morals*, trans. H. J. Paton, p. 114.
2 Kant, *Groundwork of the Metaphysic of Morals*, p. 69, n. 2.
3 Aristotle called the exercise of this capacity *praxis* to distinguish it from other

things within the more general category of the exercise of capacities—*energia* (*Nicomachean Ethics* 1139a20–21).

4 For this qualification, I am indebted to Nancy Holmstron's, 'Free will and a Marxist concept of natural wants', delivered to the Radical Caucus, American Philosophical Association, St Louis, April 1974, and printed in *Philosophical Forum*, Vol. VI, Sec. 4, 1976.

5 This follows the suggestions of J. L. Austin in 'Ifs and cans', in his *Philosophical Papers*, Clarendon Press, Oxford, 1961, p. 173.

6 An appropriate sense of bringing-about can be found in Milton Fisk's 'A defence of the principle of event causality', *British Journal for Philosophy of Science*, Vol. XVIII, 1967, pp. 89–108.

7 Hegel, *Philosophy of Right*, Sec. 186.

8 Hegel, *Philosophy of Right*, Secs. 260–70.

9 For more on this, see Oliver Wendell Holmes, Jr., *The Common Law*, Little, Brown and Co., Boston, 1923, Lecture II.

10 For a technical treatment, see H. L. A. Hart and A. M. Honoré, *Causation in the law*, Clarendon Press, Oxford, 1959, pp. 58–64.

11 Dan Georgakas and Marvin Surkin, *Detroit : I Do Mind Dying*, St Martin's Press, New York, 1975, pp. 8–11.

PART FIVE

A Prospectus for a Theory of Rights

XVI
Social Freedom

THE transition from philosophical freedom to social freedom is one from a *capacity* humans have to perform actions in a certain way to the *rights* humans have to exercise that capacity. Under the heading of social freedom fall such rights as the right to free speech and the right of nations to determine themselves. Rights are very obviously social since having them puts certain restrictions on other people. So here, in this last part of the book, we are not just talking about the way the social formation of a person is relevant to the moral principles valid for that person. We are also talking about the way the needs of a person are the basis for moral restrictions on other persons. This particular type of moral relationship—which constitutes the rights a person has—adds something new to what was uncovered in the earlier discussion of goods and obligations.

1 **Individualist freedom** The classical liberal conception of social freedom was tied up with the atomic view of the person. The person was viewed as a centre of action functioning in a distinctive way in a variety of social settings. Thus each person is capable of a special spontaneity, which is not only desirable but always possible where society does not grind individuals to indistinguishable grains of sand. The person has an inner nature, and the important thing for the classical liberal is that this nature be developed to the full, which is impossible where the person is overwhelmed by forces of social conformity. The fully developed person is, in this view, a person with a distinctive individuality. Individuality is the prime virtue for the classical liberal; one acquires individuality while struggling against conformity. The cultivation of individuality gives happiness to those who cultivate it and satisfaction to others, since 'all wise and noble things' emanate from individuality and not from collectivity.[1]

A 'right to non-interference' was based on this conception of human nature. The atomic person is best fulfilled when left alone by society. So the individual has a right against society, a right not to be interfered with. There is one qualification: if the individual is doing things harmful to others, they, for self-protection, have a right to interfere with the individual.[2] The claim that all persons have this qualified right to non-interference from the group will be called the *liberal principle of non-interference*. This principle sounds so elementary. We drank it in from our earliest childhood as part of the morality taught within liberal democracies. Yet this conception of social freedom is so fundamentally wrong that it is not a dependable guide.

In the *first* place, one cannot begin to have an understanding of human behaviour without granting at the outset that humans are social in nature. The right to non-interference can, though, be derived only from a non-social view of human nature. This is plain once we recognize how a case of perfectly legitimate interference can be defended. Persons would be at odds with themselves did they not allow some of their wants to be curbed through pressures from the group. One does not need to raise the spectre of totalitarianism in order to think of examples. In family activity, a certain effort to be cooperative can be expected on the part of the members even when doing so causes inconveniences. Here the group 'interferes' with the recalcitrant member without the excuse that this is 'self-protection' from harmful acts. The claim that humans have a right to non-interference, except in cases of self-protection by others, is clearly too strong.

Only on the aspect theory of the person is all interference allowable. As indicated in Chapter I, Section 3, if persons are only aspects of a social entity they have no rights against it. By contrast, the social theory of the person, which is a middle ground, gives no comfort either to totalitarianism or even to the sort of domination that liberal democracies tolerate. For on the social theory of the person, the internal historical needs of the person form the basis for a struggle of the person against the kind of social interference that results in needs being imposed on the person.

In the *second* place, one cannot begin to have an understanding of human behaviour by thinking that the dichotomy between individual and society is exhaustive. One needs at least the trichotomy individual-group-sum group. What bearing does this have on the liberal principle of non-interference? It shows that the principle is as well too weak, since interference for self-protection is sometimes not justified. Suppose the individual is a member of a lower group and the sum group performs its usual function of continuing the domination of a dominant group. That individual has the right *not* to be interfered with by the sum group, even when he or she is attempting to eliminate the system of domination and in doing so harms the sum group. To say the individual has this right is of course to say something that is true only relative to the lower group. But there is no such right at all if the individual-society dichotomy is taken as exhaustive. For then the society as a whole is the only group to be considered. The effect of not viewing the situation in terms of a social system perpetuating domination over lower groups was to allow liberal theorists to propose rights that were apparently absolute. Those rights had no basis in the realities of some of the individuals to whom they applied, since those individuals were formed by lower groups.

The liberal principle of non-interference is not a dependable guide since it is both too strong, by being based on the atomic view of the person, and too weak, by being based on the individual-society dichotomy.

2 Freedom and social change These two criticisms suggest an alternative to the liberal principle of non-interference. The alternative cannot, in view of the first criticism, neglect the social character of the self, and it cannot, in view of the second criticism, ignore the relativity of morals in a society involving classes. This alternative to the liberal principle of non-interference lays down the conditions under which a person has a right to exercise freedom as a capacity.

Sometimes we are not happy about the things people do when they exercise their rights. Otherwise, we would have no need to accord them rights. They have rights precisely because people who are not pleased with what they do might interfere with them. A right is a bulwark against such interference. A right is an effective bulwark if it is more than a permission. Permitting people to do something means desisting from interposing obstacles. Whereas, when people have the right to do something, they have a call upon one to keep others from interfering with their attempt to do it.

These remarks, together with the two criticisms, suggest the *relativist principle of non-interference*, which is as follows:

A person has a 'right' relative to a given group to exercise freedom by an action of a certain kind when it is likely that it would be incompatible with advancing the interests characteristic of that group *either* for its members to place obstacles in the way of that person's exercising freedom by an action of this kind *or* even for its members to allow others to place obstacles in the way if members of the group are in a position to block these obstacles without a greater setback to their group than would result from allowing them.

First, some brief observations on this lengthy principle. This principle is equally a statement of what a right is. The person who has a right to an exercise of freedom, relative to a group, need not be a member of this group. When members of a group defend someone's rights, they go beyond what they are obliged to do if their defence can be successful only by making a greater sacrifice in relation to group interest than would be made by allowing those rights to go undefended. At least for lower classes, rights relative to a class and rights relative to lower groups imply one another.

Now, some detailed comments. Recall, first, that freedom is a capacity to act from motives and ends based on *needs of one's own*. One does not have a right to freedom in the sense of having a right to perform any free act. For one can act freely even when the motives or ends are not one's own. The principle of non-interference says only that one has the right to certain exercises of freedom—certain acts done from one's own motives and ends. Imposing needs on people tends to push their own needs into the background. This creates an obstacle in the way of their exercising freedom. For a group to allow itself to have needs imposed on it when it is in a position to initiate a successful attempt to avoid this is for it to ignore its members' right to exercise freedom. This right requires an attempt to prevent the imposition of needs and to eliminate them once they have been imposed. Defending rights is a matter of shielding not just from physical force but also from psychological force.

The right to exercise freedom by an action of a certain kind thus implies a corresponding obligation to eliminate already created imposed needs and to avoid the creation of new ones. There will be an obligation to combat racism within the working class, since the need to be racist is one imposed for the sake of splitting the different racial groups in the working class, thereby weakening the tendency of the working class to act on the basis of its internal historical needs. Racism substitutes for the exercise of freedom action that is based on alien needs. Promoting racism interferes with the right of the working class to exercise freedom.

Recall, second, that freedom is a capacity to take actions that are backed by *deliberation* in the light of the available information that is not part of imposed consciousness. To act without seeking out available information is to act out of ignorance and hence is not to exercise freedom. Moreover, withholding available information relevant to a rightful exercise of freedom is restricting the liberty guaranteed by the non-interference principle. Secrecy on the part of one segment of a group in the process of making plans that will affect the entire group will inevitably be a restriction on the rights of other segments of the group. This is why elitist leadership within a group violates the liberties of members of the group outside the elite.

Because of class-relativity, there is no unrestricted right to be allowed the information needed for deliberation. Why, for example, should I make information about the Symbionese Liberation Army available to the FBI? That information might enable the FBI to exercise its freedom. But whose interests would be served by this? The FBI is an institution that perpetuates the domination of the ruling class. If people cooperate with the FBI, they strengthen its ability to suppress all groups opposed to that domination, and not just groups like the SLA whose tactics were objectionably elitist. Interfering with the FBI's attempt to get available information does not violate any right it has relative to the lower classes.

The third comment links *alienation* and freedom. A group must overcome alienation to exercise the right to freedom. Where there is alienation there are obstacles that a given form of society has put in the way of the internal historical needs of a group. So there are obstacles to the actions needed to advance the interests of that group. One clearly has a right to exercise freedom in advancing the interests of one's group. And hence one is obliged to do what one can to attempt to overcome these obstacles and thereby to overcome alienation.

Here is where the importance of freedom to social change emerges. Dealienation can be effected only by a change of social forms. Hence, the right to exercise freedom by actions in the group's interest implies an obligation to dealienation which in turn implies an obligation to push for the realization of internal historical needs by changing the form of society that is blocking their realization. This obligation to change society implies a right to change it. (For, in general, if obstacles to a certain act could be allowed to stand then the failure to perform that act would not set the class tendencies back, and hence would not be obligatory.)

Since a society based on a relation of domination will contain alienation, the right to exercise freedom within the lower classes of such a society implies a right to revolution. For revolution means a change from one form of society to another and, hence, a change of the class structure of the original society. In the context of contemporary capitalist society, the right to revolution is a right to a socialist revolution. Thomas Jefferson noted in *The Declaration of Independence* that, when a form of government no longer secures the right to liberty, 'it is the right of the people to alter or abolish it'. Likewise, when a form of society no longer secures the right to liberty it is the right of the people to alter or abolish it.

3 Free speech and the class struggle The principle of non-interference does not say that there is a right to exercise freedom by doing any action. The action must be congruent with group purpose. We now turn to ask if free speech is a right under this principle. If there is such a right, does it extend to people outside the group relative to whose interests it is valid?

Since rights relate one person to others, a phenomenon appears with them that did not appear with obligations. If A has an obligation to do X, then the validity of the obligation rests on how doing X affects the interests of a group to which A belongs. But if B must respect A's right to do X then the validity of the right rests both on how B's insuring A the opportunity to do X and on how A's doing X will affect the interests of, not A's group, but B's. The reason for this is that if, instead, A's right were valid relative to A's group and B happened to be a member of an antagonistic group, then, because of the relativity to A's group, B's obligation toward A, which derives from A's right, would be based on A's, not B's, group. But this plainly contradicts our account of obligation according to which it rests on the interests of the group of the person who has it. So the special thing about rights as distinct from duties is that a person in a group antagonistic to yours may have a right that exists because of the positive effect it has on your group. Before discussing, in the next section, how this rather abstruse point has a bearing on free speech, let us consider the effects of a denial of free speech.

Who benefits when free speech—the exercise of freedom by speaking or writing—is denied? The Smith Act of 1940 and the McCarran Act of 1950 laid the basis in the US for a broad attack on free speech. Both acts were in explicit violation of the First Amendment to the US Constitution which forbade Congress to make any law 'abridging the freedom of speech'. The Smith Act was first used in the Minneapolis Labour Trial of 1941 in which leaders of General Drivers Local 544 (CIO) and national leaders of the Trotskyist Socialist Workers Party (SWP) stood trial.[3] Eighteen of the defendants were convicted under the Smith Act for publication and circulation of literature and the establishment of an organization and membership therein whose purpose was 'to teach, advocate and encourage' the 'overthrow of the government by force and violence'.

Neither the defendants, nor indeed any true Marxists, advocated then either the immediate overthrow of the US government or the future violent overthrow of the US government. They advocated an overthrow of the capitalist government when a new form of government would be a genuine expression of the lower classes. They did not advocate that this future overthrow be violent. They did, though, claim the right to use violence in the future overthrow when it would become necessary in response to the violence used by the ruling class to prevent the lower classes from establishing state power. Such distinctions were lost on those prosecuting revolutionary socialists under the Smith Act.

The indictments had been engineered by Dan Tobin, President of the Teamsters (AFL). Roosevelt was indebted to Tobin, the chairman of the Democratic Party's National Labour Committee. The Minneapolis truckers had originally belonged to the Teamsters but, when they voted to leave and go into the militant CIO, Tobin fingered them to FDR as subversives. FDR then sent in marshals and FBI agents to raid the Minneapolis and St Paul SWP headquarters. Tobin had been chagrined that, through the earlier organizing efforts of the Minneapolis truckers, the Northwest Council of the Teamsters had grown strong and had become a threat to his conservative power. FDR, for his part, did not want the anti-war stance of the Trotskyists of Local 544 to spread and pose a threat to realizing the imperialist aims of the coming war. The defendants had wide support among civil libertarians, inside and outside labour, yet once they were convicted the Roosevelt Supreme Court refused three times even to review the case. Not until 1958, did a US Court of Appeals hold that mere teaching or advocacy of overthrow of the government, forcible or otherwise, is not a call to action and is not felonious.[4]

Who benefited? Immediately, Tobin and the trucking firms, both of whom were opposed to strikes and militant union organizing. Consequently, the immediate losers were the truck drivers themselves. Ultimately, by quelling sentiment against the war within labour's ranks at the very start, the way was prepared for organized labour's no-strike pledge during World War II that was to mean low wages despite higher prices.

This is not an exceptional case; the denial of free speech generally has serious repercussions for the lower classes. The exercise of free speech has been vital for the development of militancy among workers, women, and minorities in advanced industrial countries. The efforts of the US government to prevent dissident groups from continuing to speak for change did not start with the killing of Black Panther Fred Hampton in Chicago in 1969, or with the Minneapolis Labour Trial in 1941, or even with the Palmer-Hoover Raids on communists in 1919. The capitalist state has been perpetually vigilant. In a context in which there is no huge movement to act on the message but in which the important thing is to spread the message to be acted on, the right to free speech is worth considerable effort to defend.

4 The relevance of time to the denial of free speech Let us turn our perspective through 180 degrees. As we just saw, members of lower classes need to have the right to free speech. But should members of lower classes accord to spokespersons of the ruling class the right to free speech? The question here is not whether the right is absolute. The question is only whether, in general, it is in the interests of the lower classes to allow free expression to members of other classes.

It is important to be clear about the context.[5] The present context in the US is one in which, because of the absence of a mass opposition movement, reprisals for the militancy of dissidents can be so fast and thorough as not to disturb the social equilibrium. It would be ludicrous to propose the systematic denial of free expression to spokespersons of the ruling class in the newspapers, in the classroom, and on TV. Those who attack these forums must reckon themselves strong enough to take on the state, whose power is internally uncontested. In this context there can be no systematic attempt to deny spokespersons of the ruling class the right to free speech without the loss by the left itself of the important tool of free advocacy for its own position.

This conclusion is not based on the old ground that everyone should have the right to free speech since only through an exchange of ideas can the truth emerge quickly.[6] We should have no illusions about what the ruling class does with the right to free speech. It is not used to allow for philosophical debate of the widest possible alternatives. Rather it is used by the ruling class, through its spokespersons, to disseminate values designed to thwart militancy and to put safe limits on debate. Why should one grant a right that will be used against one? It is better to grant the right than to have the ruling class retaliate when one is defenceless.

But there is another context. There is a context in which a huge opposition movement poses a serious challenge to state power by the lower classes. The militant movement has laid down the gauntlet in the contest for state power. The factors in the debate over free speech have different weights now. Greater weight goes to the fact that it is not in the interest of the lower classes to be subjected to the imposed consciousness that results when freedom of the press is accorded to representatives of the dominant class. The elimination of this source of imposed consciousness becomes more important than retaliation for restricting freedom of the press. In fact, once this movement of the lower classes is in a position to make a bid for state power, it has a right to wrench the media from those who have the potential for subverting this movement.

On 17 November 1917, the Bolsheviks, without unanimity, proposed to the other socialist parties that the capitalist press in Russia be closed. State power had, only a few weeks earlier, been taken by the Congress of Soviets, but it was still contested. Some members of the Congress objected to the suppression on the ground that earlier the Bolsheviks had defended the free press against the Czarist censors. Was not this a simple inconsistency? Trotsky replied in support of the resolution for suppressing the capitalist press by noting that now there was a contest for state power; 'The victory over our adversaries is not yet achieved, and the newspapers are arms in their hands.' Lenin followed:

If the first revolution [that of February 1917, that overthrew the Czar] had the right to suppress the monarchist papers, then we have the right to suppress the bourgeois press. It is impossible to separate the question of the freedom of the press from the other questions of the class struggle . . . . Now that the insurrection is over, we have absolutely no desire to suppress the papers of the other socialist parties, except inasmuch as they appeal to armed insurrection, or to disobedience to the Soviet Government.[7]

Double standard! Certainly, but *two* periods and only *one* basis of validity! The single basis for validity is the interest of the lower classes. The first period was one in which the Czar suppressed the advocacy of change and in which the liberals and socialists did not have the power to contest the control of the state. Then the opposition press had a right to be free. The second was a period in which the peasants and workers were contesting control of the state with the owning class. The power of the capitalist press was obviously a factor in this contest. Now the capitalist press did not have a right to freedom. In each period the operative consideration in determining the right to a free press was the same: was the freedom of the press something with long-term harmful or helpful implications for the advancement of the interests of the peasants and workers?

None of this implies that, if the capitalist counter-revolution were weak, the Bolsheviks would have had a right to close the capitalist press. The counter-revolution was, however, strong enough to provoke a civil war that, when it ended in 1921, left Russia devastated.

The question is most decidedly not: did not this suppression of the bourgeois press give rise to a penchant for suppressing freedoms which became the motivation for Stalin's brutal purges? This question turns freedom of speech into a fetish by making it an absolute, and it fails thereby to dig behind freedom of speech in order to determine whether in distinct periods the conditions for its justification, relative to the same class, are equally present. Suppression of freedoms does indeed provide a link between the suppression of the capitalist press in 1917 and the purges of Stalin. But behind this there is an important dissimilarity. In the former case—that of November 1917—the suppression of the press was a measure taken to protect the interests of an alliance of workers and peasants. In the latter case—that of Stalin's purges—the denial of freedoms was a measure to protect the interests of a new ruling class—a bureaucracy that still rules the USSR—at the expense of those lower classes. Here we have two periods and not one but two standards of validity.[8]

In a harmonistic society conditions would not justify a removal of a right to free speech once the right had been justified under earlier conditions. For the claim that there was no longer such a right would be correctly regarded as merely a selfish break with cooperative endeavour. Here we have not been talking about ideal harmonistic societies but about actual antagonistic ones. And for such societies free speech needs to be viewed differently in different periods. In periods in which the dominant class is unchallenged, there is in general a right, relative to the lower classes, to free speech for spokespersons of the dominant class. But when the lower classes themselves are able to constitute an effective challenge to the dominant class, the right, relative to the lower classes, of free speech for spokespersons of the dominant class no longer exists, for such a right would then conflict with the internal historical need of the lower classes to throw off domination.

Notes

1   This, in brief, is the view of John Stuart Mill, *On Liberty* (1859), in *The English Philosophers from Bacon to Mill*, ed. E. A. Burtt, Modern Library, New York, 1939, Ch. III.
2   John Stuart Mill, *On Liberty*, Ch. I.
3   For a dramatic personal account of the Smith Act arrests and trials of West Coast members of the US Communist Party in 1951–52, during the McCarthy era, see Al Richmond, *A Long View From the Left*, Delta, New York, 1972. Ch. X–XI.
4   A detailed account of the trial is given by one of the socialist truckers, Farrell Dobbs, in his *Teamster Bureaucracy*, Monad Press, New York, 1977; see also Ralph C. James and Estelle James, 'The purge of the Trotskyites from the Teamsters', *Western Political Quarterly*, Vol. XIX, March 1966, pp. 5–15.
5   Hal Draper, 'Free speech and political struggle', *Independent Socialist*, Vol. IV, 1968, pp. 12–16.

6   'But the peculiar evil of silencing the expression of an opinion is, that it is robbing the human race . . . . If the opinion is right, they are deprived of the opportunity of exchanging error for truth; if wrong, they lose, what is almost as great a benefit, the clearer perception and livelier impression of truth, produced by its collision with error' (John Stuart Mill, *On Liberty*, Ch. II).

7   Quotes from John Reed's notes on the meeting in his *Ten Days That Shook the World* (1919), Mentor, New York, 1967, Ch. XI.

8   Such distinctions are ignored by Alexander I. Solzhenitsyn in *The Gulag Archipelago: 1918–1956*, trans. T. P. Whitney, Harper & Row, New York, 1973, Ch. VIII–X.

XVII

Equal Rights

THE question here is no longer what rights to free action people actually have but whether people have such rights equally. Does everyone have the same rights, and if not under what conditions must certain rights be granted to everyone? 'Equality!' is a rallying cry for reform, rebellion, and revolution. Is it possible to have an objective basis for saying that people have been wronged when a right has been denied them while granted to others?

The denial of a genuine equal right is said to be an injustice, so the terrain here is that of the theory of justice. Of course, since denying any genuine right—equal or not—is a matter of injustice, Part Five in its entirety deals in one way or another with fairness or justice.

1 **Equality in historical perspective** The notion of a right underwent its full development in the modern period after originating in Roman law. The notions of good and virtue, however, underwent their development in ancient Greek moral thought, which they dominated. The development of the notion of a right reflected the basic social changes that led to the modern period of western history. It was not, then, a simple matter of moral blindness that rights were not a part of the moral terrain covered in such classics as Plato's *Republic* and Aristotle's *Nicomachean Ethics*. Our third moral notion, the notion of obligation, comes into modern western thought from the moral tradition of the decalogue—from the Judeo-Christian tradition in which the role of divine commands is central. In modern ethical life the notion of right did not, of course, replace the notions of obligation and good. All three are operative for us still, making it important to get some grip on the changes that have brought them to us.

These changes in moral conceptions will be seen to support the theory of historical materialism. They were generated by the class struggle as it existed at different times. Only if morality is relative to historical factors, such as the class struggle, is the history of morals relevant to morality itself. History is irrelevant to absolute morality; it is not a tale of the emergence of such a morality—since absolute morality is fixed—but a tale of human misperceptions of it. In fact, there is nothing to morality but the history of its role in advancing various interests; so morality provides a striking confirmation of historical materialism.

Emphasis on the good and virtue is appropriate for members of a dominant group who are confident they can absorb any challenge to the structure of the society in which they live. Virtue is important for such a people because it guarantees consistency in doing what is fitting within the framework of the existing society. And the good is simply that which insures a better existence for those in such a society. Even Plato, who did advance a conception of a society with an intellectual ruling class to replace the commercial society of Athens, was more concerned with outlining the virtues that would stabilize such a new society than with issuing directives for a movement to overthrow the old society.

With the downfall of the Greek city-state, this perspective did not change, since the new task of stabilizing a Hellenistic kingdom or a Mediterranean Roman empire was equally a task to be carried on primarily through the predictable behaviour of virtuous people in the dominant classes. Virtue was, then, no longer what was fitting in the city-state, the *polis*, but what was fitting in the imperial world, the *cosmos*.[1] It is significant that the ancient slave societies of Greece and Rome did not disintegrate through aggressive bids of slaves to supplant the ruling classes. Rather, the mode of production based on slavery became unable to generate sufficient wealth to prevent the impoverishment of the masses of free people. The majority of the free people were the losers as land, industry, and commerce became concentrated in the hands of a few. This prepared the society not for internal revolution but for the change to feudalism that resulted from the conquest from outside by the Germans and Arabs. While the slave mode of production kept the society alive, wide penetration of the society by the thought of a new social order was thwarted by the suppression of the Spartacus slave revolt, the Quamran commune, the Zealots, and so on. Without wide penetration of a mission for internal social change, a sense of obligation did not become a major theme within the dominant strata of society.

Obligation was, however, a reality for the Hebrews and the Christians. They had a deep sense of mission, originating in the need to overthrow national oppression and evolving into a desire for an unearthly kingdom. Moses led his people away from the exploitation of the workshops and fields of Egypt before giving them the ten commandments. Some of the early Christians distinguished themselves from the militarist nationalists, who were for the forcible overthrow of Roman colonialism, by binding themselves to a law of love that would prepare people for the coming of the Kingdom of God. The emphasis in either case is on change rather than stability for oppressed people: what is required is not the stability of character that enables the dominant group to do what is fitting in the given order, but the dedication to divine command that enables an oppressed people to make witnesses of themselves in face of the established order. We noted earlier that obligation, as opposed to goodness, is associated with urgency. This urgency is the spirit of a people whose mission is to overcome oppression. It was first characteristic of the revolt from below, or of what Nietzsche called the 'slave' revolt.[2] But when oppressed nations and their lower classes challenge the established order seriously enough to shake the confidence of the ruling classes, a sense of urgency to defend the system of domination makes obligation a reality for the ruling classes too. Aristocratic virtue and noble coolness give way to the urgency of command in wars against national and class liberation. Obligation replaces virtue and goodness as the major theme within society's dominant strata.

In the idea of virtue there is the embryo of the idea of a right. For in doing what is beneficial to the community, one must behave in certain ways in regard to others. One must give them enough room to perform the functions they have in the community. Thus when the principles of virtue come to be codified as laws, the functions people perform in the community are given legal support. This is done by formulating the laws in terms of the rights of people in the various social categories, which were defined by the social functions. This development did not, though, change fundamentally the outlook of the ancient Greeks. Even for the Greeks social purpose, operating through the patterns of virtuous behaviour, left enough room for various people to do their jobs. Roman law simply articulated how much room there was for people in the various categories.

However, it is only in the modern period that rights, as we think of them, come into their own. That room we allow to people to do their thing in is, in the modern period, not there just because of some community or of some cosmic plan. It is there because of 'the importance of the individual', whatever his or her role. Rights are then no longer derived from virtue, and hence from social structure, but from the individual.[3]

In the sixteenth and seventeenth centuries, the capitalist form of society was emerging victorious over the feudal order. This meant that the agent's room for action was no longer to be defined by the old social order. On behalf of the new social order, no new structure of privilege and status was proclaimed; instead, the laws of production and exchange were proclaimed the new order. The agent was not restricted by privileges but only by the market. The individual could, then, be thought of as an autonomous centre from which rights emanate as far as the individual could defend them.

Of course, the social difference was not as dramatic as the ideologues of the new conception of rights—such as Hobbes and Locke—made it out to be. The laws of production and exchange implied their own structure of privilege and status since they implied economic inequality. The individual was subject to this structure and was thus not fully autonomous. In short, the new concept of rights that differed so dramatically from the socially based concept of rights in Roman law, represented the individualist ideology about the new capitalist order more than the reality of that order. But that ideology had great appeal and it served well as a verbal justification of the new order.[4]

The modern conception of rights arose in social conditions that made plausible the view that the individual has a nature that does not change with changes in social structure. Because of this, the modern conception of rights became associated with the conception of universal equal rights. How did this come about? No social position distinguishes the nature of one such individual from that of another. The individual is then atomic. So whatever rights one individual has, every individual has.

By contrast, for Aristotle, giving an individual his or her due involved a consideration of the station of the individual; in different societies the stations would be different, but there would always be the station to consider.[5] There was for him no universal equality. But the bourgeois revolution tore down the idea of social stations, leaving individuals free to participate in commerce on an equal basis. The labourer who sells labour power to a manufacturer does this, not as a requirement of birth or because of allegiance to a lord, but supposedly as an equal in a contract.[6] Such social changes were the conditions that gave great appeal to the modern idea of rights, which was associated with the idea of universal equality. But the theoretical notion of the atomic individual on which both the idea of rights and that of equal rights came to be based was part of the individualist ideology needed both to convince people that the new order would not reproduce old privileges and to legitimate the market and hence the inequality in wealth based on it.

Once cut loose from the ideology of the atomic individual, the ideas of rights and equal rights can be given a solid enough base in

the social view of the person. On this new basis, these ideas will not
be the same as they were for Hobbes and Locke. The social person
is capable of freedom and, in virtue of this and class interest, has
rights and indeed equal rights.

2 The extent of equality Citizens are supposed to have equal
rights as regards voting for elected officials. But a member of the
Board of Directors of General Motors has a right to vote on
corporation policy that is denied to a worker on the assembly line at
a GM plant in Detroit. So in the one case rights are equal and in the
other they are not. What is it that makes for the difference between
rights that are equal and those that are not?

One answer might be that it is the laws of a society which define
the limits of equality. If laws are genuinely universal, then all
people are equally subject to them. Along with this *formal* legal
equality there are *substantial* legal restrictions on equality. For the
laws themselves not only specify certain rights that are common,
but also limit the rights of people in certain categories. The
member of the Board of Directors who owns considerable stock
and the assembly-line worker have equal rights to license the
automobiles they buy. Despite a number of such equal rights,
though, workers in the US have a limited legal right to strike, in
view of the power of the courts to enjoin them to return to work and
of laws denying some workers the right to strike at all. Yet owners
can 'strike' by withholding capital from certain enterprises in
order to force prices up, change government policy, or invest
where it is more profitable. In the legal view, the limits of a
person's equality with others are, then, defined by two things.
First, formally everyone is equally subject to the laws. Second,
there are some substantive rights granted by law to everyone.
These rights are for the most part the so-called civil rights: the
right to vote, to have complaints heard in court, to criticize
authorities, to have access to equal public education, to trial by
peers, and so on.

This is a very superficial view of equality, one that cannot serve
the explanatory role we are after. In the first place, laws are often
constructed to give legitimacy and force to preexisting views of
equality, views which historical materialism tells us arise from the
mode of production in the society. Laws may win acceptance for
the view that the right to withhold what one contributes to
production—labour power or capital—is not an equal right. It is
not, though, because there are these laws that the right the owner
has is not shared by workers. The source of substantive equalities

and inequalities lies deeper in the way production is organized in the society.

In the second place, beyond the civil rights, the equality guaranteed by a rule of laws will be dominantly formal in nature, making it of little consequence to those who suffer substantive inequality. The law says that no one is to sleep under the bridges of Paris. The weight of the law falls fully on the lumpenproletariat, while the well-dressed bourgeois manages to find better shelter even after an evening of debauching. Nonetheless, if a bourgeois did try to sleep under one of the bridges of Paris, justice would, in theory, be done without regard to class. Also, if the worker who drives cars off the assembly line to the shipping dock were to drive a car into the streets and sell it in order to split the proceeds with all the workers on the line, then management would have that worker arrested for theft. True, the workers made the car, but the property laws in a capitalist society are such that it is not workers but owners of means of production who also own the products of labour. Nevertheless, there is still formal equality: if Henry Ford III were to drive a car off a General Motors line in order to add a touch of variety to his fleet of personal vehicles, he would, in theory, be subject to justice without regard to class. In short, in class society a rule of law of itself will not guarantee significant substantive equality of rights.

A second approach to the limits of equality starts with the atomic view of persons. In themselves, these persons are unrestricted since of themselves they are not integrated into a social structure. In themselves, their rights are then unlimited. However, those who accept this view also recognize that persons are in fact in interaction and that unless persons agree to limit their rights their chances of survival are limited. This gives a basis for deciding on the limits of equality for atomic persons: each person has an equal right to as many sorts of free action as are compatible with others engaging in similar actions.[7] The idea, then, is very simply to define the limits on equality by building up the biggest set of rights for oneself compatible with others exercising similar rights. Rights outside such a set need not be shared equally.

The difficulty here is that the approach starts with useless abstractions. One does not discover one's rights, and *a fortiori* one's equal rights, in a vacuum. Yet this is what one would be doing if one treated the problem as the logical one of building the largest consistent set of claims as to what people have a right to do. For example, suppose one starts building a set of equal rights by putting the right to have access to equal public education in the set. People can exercise this right in such a way that they do not interfere with others exercising it. But there have been plenty of societies in which public education is not a possibility since in those societies the material conditions for educational institutions do not exist. This, of course, will not prevent one from putting this right in the set. The set will then contain rights that, relative to the society as a whole, do not exist and hence are not equal. Or, again, one starts by putting in the set the right to an income equal to $16,000 in 1970 dollars. This is a right that, formally speaking, every family in the US could have had in 1970. For every family would have had such an income if total income had been distributed equitably among families. Yet capitalism has a structural need for inequality; divisions within the lower classes, which help keep profits high, are sustained by income differences, and investment by owners in growth would be jeopardized by the cutback in income from ownership that equality would require. An equal right, relative to capitalist society, to $16,000 in 1970 did not exist. Starting from the atomic person means ignoring the fact that it is a social structure that gives content to rights.

3   The class basis for equality   It is now time to look at the question of equal rights from the point of view of the social theory of persons. It is hard to turn our heads around from the tradition of equality based on a universal human nature toward the theory of equality based on group perspective. The former position is not necessarily associated with conservatism. Just as often, radicals look for justification in a universal human nature.

William Hinton points out that, in the revolution in the countryside in China, there were two views of the basis for changing consciousness. The one was a form of 'idealism, a demand for abstract justice in an unchanging world'. The other was a form of 'historical materialism, a demand for justice based on the concrete conditions of human life, a justice which changed as conditions changed'. Hinton says, 'The first considered the demand for equality to be right in itself; the second considered that demand to be right in one context, wrong and harmful in another.'[8] Whether members of a class are to be equal to members of other classes, in respect to a certain right, is not a matter to be decided idealistically, that is by reflection on the nature of the right in question, or on some universal conception of human nature. Rather it is a matter to be decided in terms of what will advance the interests of members of the class. The attitude of the moral idealist—whether a radical or a conservative—is to insist, prior to all consideration of empirical class relations, that people have certain rights equally.

If reformers struggle simply for equality as such, then their task is even larger than they themselves conceive of it. For such a struggle commits them to getting recognition of the fact that whatever right anyone has everyone else has it too. To cut the task down to something that sounds more realistic, equality if often limited to that set of rights—called civil rights—thought to be characteristic of liberal democracy—the right to organize a faction, to express one's thoughts, to due process in handling grievances, to compete in a free market, to representation in governance. Why have liberals chosen to struggle for equality in these rather than other regards? The historical answer is that at first the struggle for equality in these regards was associated with the emergence of a ruling class that would be able to establish itself all the better against feudal restrictions with widespread recognition of the equality of these rights. And this historical answer is part of the justification for taking these rights to be equal. They are equal rights since defending their exercise without regard to persons was in the interest of the development and consolidation of the power of the new owning class. Later, the lower classes needed them.

The criterion for equality can be put as follows:

Relative to a given group, a right to exercise freedom by an action of a certain kind is 'equal' when everyone has the right, relative to that group, to exercise freedom by an action of that kind.

This formulation describes equal rights on the basis of the group relative notion of rights developed in the last chapter. A common popular justification of the equality of a right is that if we were to deny the right to others they might turn around and deny it to us. But their denying it to us is an objectionable state of affairs only if it is, in the first place, our right. And how is this established? Our group relative interpretation of equal rights provides the answer while remaining within the spirit of this popular justification of equality.

From the perspective of a lower class, or any dominated group, the struggle for equality has two distinguishable parts. (Here equality means the recognition of equal rights.) First, there is the struggle for equality *within* the class and, second, there is the struggle for equality *between* this class and the dominant class. In both cases the notion of struggle comes in quite naturally. People struggle together to overcome inequality and, indeed, are often obliged to. For, as members of the same class, they have an obligation to attempt to remove obstacles in the way of exercising rights that exist relative to this class. Then solidarity is more than a feeling; it is an obligation. This solidarity may be for the purpose of realizing either equality within a class or equality between a lower class and a dominant class.

Consider the first front, the struggle for equality within a class. The struggle for equal rights for women—not just in the economic but in all areas—as carried on within the working class is a struggle to overcome those differences within this class that are detrimental to women. As already explained, these differences will also be detrimental to the working class as a whole. This does not mean that the demands of women for equality must first arise as demands that come from sexually mixed organizations of the working class. The initiative for calling attention to unmet needs, to special forms of oppression, and to appropriate remedies will come from women themselves. They are the ones who suffer directly from inequality. They are in the best position to check their demands to determine whether they represent internal historical needs of the group of women. If they do represent the true needs of women, they will not run counter to the internal historical needs of the working class and pursuing them will not weaken the ability of the working class to overcome the domination of the ruling class. Since in a class society, class domination is the reason for the being of other forms of domination, the legitimate demands of women for equality will never be in more than apparent conflict with the interests of the working class. The struggle of women for equality will in fact advance the interests of the working class by leading to a unification of the struggle against the ruling class. The struggle of working women for equal rights thus requires behind it the solidarity of the entire working class.

Consider now the second front, the struggle of lower classes for equality with the dominant class. This front cannot advance far without challenging the basic structure of the society. Its completion is inconceivable without revolution, an end to domination by the existing ruling class. Nonetheless, demands for equality in respects that would imply a loss of control by the present owning class need to be voiced at every opportunity to give direction to a struggle that may be a long one. It is thus essential to raise demands, in appropriate contexts, for free necessities, for workers' control of corporation policy, and for an end to the state which functions for the owning class. To be effective the struggle for these demands will require solidarity between all lower classes.

4 Equal national rights Do nations have equal rights? In particular, does a nation have the right to control itself through setting up a state? No rigid definition can tell us what a people or a nation is. A group might demonstrate that it is a nation merely by engaging in a struggle to be treated as a nation. Being a majority group in a fixed location is not a necessary condition for being a nation since there have been wandering nations and dispersed nations. Moreover, nationhood does not seem to require a complete cultural continuity, for a people can have their cultural heritage virtually blotted out as a result of national oppression, leaving merely a common heritage of being specially oppressed. Still, a common origin and a common heritage, that may well not stretch back to the point of origin, are often important in constituting a nation. They have helped constitute the blacks in the US as a nation.

In the 1950s and 1960s there was an upsurge of national liberation struggles in various parts of the world. These struggles involved the effort by nations under the domination of other nations to achieve equality in political respects in order thereby to go on to achieve equality in other respects as well. This was true of the Vietnamese in their struggle against the US, the Algerians against the French, and of certain black organizations in the US against the oppressing white nation and the state set up by that white nation. It is, of course, one thing to demand rights as citizens—civil rights—within an existing nation-state, but quite another to demand the recognition of national rights, among which is the right of a nation to determine its own affairs by setting up its own state. In the course of the 1960s the struggle of blacks in the US for civil rights was transformed into a struggle with a strongly nationalist character. Certain black nationalist organizations even projected the idea of a black nation-state. Have blacks in fact the right to form a nation-state within the territory of the US?[9] If not, what is the ground of their inequality in respect to the oppressing white nation, for which the nation-state in the US is geared to function?

Here a distinction is relevant that was drawn in Chapter XVI. The distinction is that between one's having the right to do something and its being good to do it. When a nation has the right to political self-determination, not allowing it to struggle for self-determination would produce harmful consequences in respect to some social purpose. Nonetheless, political self-determination, if achieved, may generate harmful consequences in respect to the same social purpose.

We saw in the case of free speech that allowing the right of free speech to spokespersons of the ruling class had, by itself, the harmful effect of deepening the feeling of support for the sum group. However, this effect must be considered along with other effects of granting the right of free speech. One of these other effects is that with free speech respected it becomes more difficult for the ruling class to attack the democratic rights of opponents of domination. These opponents can then publicly criticize the arguments of spokespersons of the ruling class that generate support for the sum group.

In like manner, national self-determination inevitably involves drawbacks that make it in some cases a mistake. These drawbacks can be traced to the fact that a nation is not uniform as regards class. A ruling class emerges in a new nation-state often leaving the original lower classes almost as powerless as before.[10] If, for example, the blacks in the US were to form a nation-state, a group would emerge from the more privileged among the blacks who, either for themselves or for the alien whites, would control the new state at the expense of the black lower classes. This prospect must be weighed against the advantages and disadvantages of a quite different course of action: a struggle for racial equality in which independent black groups play a vital role that prepares the way for a united struggle by the lower classes for the elimination of the domination by the owning class. In the US this second approach—the struggle for a united struggle—has many strong reason in its favour. Even so, the question of the right to political self-determination for blacks in the US is not necessarily to be answered in the negative.

The reason is the same as in the case of free speech. If the lower classes of an oppressing nation do not support the right of an oppressed people to secede, the split between the lower classes of that people and the lower classes of the oppressing nation will be widened. This is because agitation for secession represents for the oppressed people their rebellion against oppression by another nation. Not to support their right to secesseion is then to remain indifferent to their oppression. Nonetheless, while respecting their right to national self-determination, it is obligatory to point out that, should the drive for self-determination succeed, the domi-nation of an indigenous ruling class will be a new factor in postponing the date of unity among lower classes of the oppressed and oppressing nations. But supporting the right to secede may itself avoid secession and its drawbacks. The very success of the struggle to win the right to secede reduces the felt need to secede. For winning this struggle for this right will imply winning a generally greater degree of equality for the members of the oppressed nation.[11]

So the equal right of nations to form independent states is not a matter to be decided just on the basis of the fact that forming such a state might set back the unified struggle of the lower classes. Equal consideration must be given to the fact that denying an oppressed nation the right to self-determination will widen the split between the lower classes of the oppressed and oppressing nations even further. Likewise, one cannot neglect the fact that supporting the right to self-determination will itself reduce oppression thereby diminishing the cause that made self-determination seem a necessity in the first place. Only in the light of all three of these considerations is it possible to gain the right to say that, relative to the interests of the lower classes, an oppressed nation, such as the blacks in the US, have, in relation to the whites, an equal right to form a politically autonomous state. Still, having the right to form a state does not mean forming it is a good thing to do.

Notes

1   For details and needed qualifications, see Alasdair MacIntyre, *A Short History of Ethics*, Macmillan, New York, 1968, Ch. VIII.
2   Friedrich Nietzsche, *On the Genealogy of Morals*, First Essay, Secs. 7–10.
3   This change has been described by Leo Strauss, *The Political Philosophy of Hobbes* (1936), University of Chicago Press, Chicago, 1963, Preface and Ch. VIII.
4   See the penetrating social critique of the new theory of rights by C. B. Macpherson, *The Political Theory of Possessive Individualism*, pp. 78–87.
5   Aristotle, *Nicomachean Ethics* 1131a25–30.
6   See Frederick Engels' historical materialist account of the origin of the idea of moral equality in *Anti-Dühring* (1885), trans. E Burns, ed. C. P. Dutt, International Publishers, New York, 1939, Ch. X.
7   This is based on Locke's idea of limiting unrestricted natural liberty to a set of liberties that discourages incursions (*Second Treatise of Government*, Sec. 129). By contrast, Rawls assumes a definite list of liberties to be "basic" and then requires that there be an equal right to exercise the basic liberties as fully as is compatible with everyone exercising them to the same degree (*A Theory of Justice*, p. 60).
8   William Hinton, *Fanshen*, p. 606. In agreeing that the idealist view of equality is wrong, it is not necessary to agree with Hinton that from the perspective of the lower classes the Chinese Communist Party correctly applied the historical materialist view of equality.
9   On the history of black nationalism, see Robert L. Allen, *Black Awakening in Capitalist America*, Ch. III; for a critique of integration and a defense of a separate black nation-state, see *The Autobiography of Malcolm X*, Chs. XIV–XV, XIX.
10   The drawbacks are discussed by Franz Fanon, *The Wretched of the Earth*, pp. 148–205. They are demonstrated in practice in Malawi, Zaire, Zambia, etc., where the process set in motion by national liberation was killed before reaching class liberation. The result is that even national liberation has at best been partial.
11   On this problem the considerations adduced by Lenin are still of fundamental importance ('Theses on the national question' (1913), *V. I. Lenin: Collected Works*, Vol. XIX, 1963, pp. 243–251; 'Critical remarks on the national question' (1913), *ibid.*, Vol. XX, 1963, pp. 19–51).

XVIII

Economic Justice

DEFENDERS of the capitalist form of society do not defend a right to economic equality. Economic inequality is, they argue, to everyone's advantage. Yet some of these defenders of capitalism are also supporters of liberal democracy. They must then recognize limits to economic inequality beyond which even capitalism should not go. Vast concentrations of economic wealth are sources of political power that strangle the basic liberties of a democratic society. But many defenders of capitalist society maintain that in the US at least these limits to economic inequality have not been reached.

The purpose of this chapter is to show that the arguments justifying the existing high degree of economic inequality fall apart. To show this it will not be necessary to defend, or to reject, the right to complete economic equality. Nonetheless, this chapter points in an egalitarian direction. For it shows also that the degree of economic inequality inevitable within even a reformed capitalist society cannot be justified from the perspective of working-class morality.

1 Economic inequality According to many writers on US society, the stage of widespread affluence has been reached within the US. There is, on the one hand, a reduced level of economic inequality, and there is, on the other hand, an elimination of the lower classes as a majority in favour of a large and prosperous middle class. The misery and inequality that characterized nineteenth and early twentieth-century capitalism have been redeemed with the arrival of the 'affluent society'. This picture, however, conceals the urgent problem of economic inequality within the US. As Gabriel Kolko notes in his pathbreaking dissenting work on income distribution, 'The predominantly middle-class society is only an image in the minds of isolated academicians.'[1]

First let us look at the distribution of before-tax personal, as opposed to corporate, income during the period 1910–70 to get some idea as to whether there has been a significant trend toward equality. To do this we can consider families as broken up into five groups of equal size, ranging from those with the highest to those with the lowest income. (People living in families make up roughly 90 per cent of the US population.) *In the sixty-year period considered, families in the highest fifth received between 40 and 45 per cent of all family income.* That is, they received at least two times more than they would have if every family received the same income. Despite variations from year to year, there is no overall trend in this period toward a significantly smaller share of the national income for the richest fifth. The middle fifth has received between 15 and 18 per cent of all family income. This means that it received over the entire sixty-year period less than it would have if income were egalitarian. For this group the trend, within these narrow limits, has been for a slight rise in its share of income, but after World War II that rise stopped completely. Finally, what about the families in the poorest quintile? That group has received between 4 and 6 per cent of the national personal income, which runs up to five times less than it would receive under equality. The overall trend has been for families in this bottom group to get proportionately the same during the sixty-year period. As regards income in the US, then, there is significant and continuing inequality.[2] The top fifth as a whole takes six to ten times more of the national family income than does the bottom fifth. (Data for non-family persons shows even greater inequality.)

Our data has so far been taken on before-tax income. Will not taxation make the picture one of greater equality? It does change the picture as regards equality but only in an insignificant way. Many taxes are regressive: they are a larger fraction of lower than of higher incomes. Social security taxes, property taxes, and sales taxes are all regressive. It cannot be expected that these would provide a shift toward equality. But even the federal income tax, which is progressive, has failed to do more than decrease by two per cent the share of national income of the top fifth. The increase in the share of the bottom fifth resulting from federal income taxes has remained a fraction of a per cent. Moreover, the percentage of all taxes coming from the non-owning classes has been rising steadily since World War II. Taxes have, then, failed to equalize income significantly.[3]

We are dealing with a society in which private ownership of the means of production is a fundamental feature. Some personal income comes from ownership, to be sure, but one cannot say exactly how wealth is distributed simply on the basis of knowing how income is distributed. For one thing, a significant but variable share of returns from ownership is invested in new means of production and does not appear as dividend income. Nonetheless, in a capitalist society we can predict that wealth, like income, is unevenly distributed. It is highly concentrated in the hands of a very few owners: they own the plants, the trucks, the warehouses, the mines, the office buildings, the large estates, and the objects of art. The poor are often net holders of 'negative wealth' because of their debts. *Between 1810 and 1969, the concentration of wealth has remained remarkably constant; the top one per cent as regards wealth has held between 20 and 30 per cent of all the wealth in the US.* In 1962 the poorest 20 per cent held less than one-half of one per cent of the nation's wealth.[4]

Nonetheless, some currency has been given to the view that corporate ownership has become widespread and that workers are now significant owners. Stock ownership is, indeed, more widespread, but this has not seriously affected the high degree of concentration of stock ownership in the hands of the wealthiest.

By 1962, the wealthiest one per cent of the population still held 72 per cent of the nation's corporate stock. In that year, the wealthiest one per cent also held 48 per cent of the nation's bonds, 24 per cent of the loans, and 16 per cent of the real estate.[5] Clearly then wealth is even less equitably distributed than income in the US, and the inequality has been one of long duration. Pensions for workers account for nearly ten per cent of corporate stock. This may provide workers with security after retirement, but it does not give them the power of wealth holders. The reason is that they have no control over these pension funds, which merely add power to the financial institutions that manage them.

Is it not possible to have affluence alongside inequality? The thesis that the US has become 'middle class' may still stand if it can be shown that the lower income quintiles are experiencing affluence. Two things are to be noted in this regard. First, the official unemployment rates between World War II and 1975 have averaged 4.8 per cent of the workforce. Many people do not show up in the statistics since they have dropped out of the workforce due to the discouraging job picture. When all hidden sectors of unemployment are taken into account, the actual unemployment figures may have averaged 8 to 10 per cent of the workforce. Unemployment compensation, even for those eligible for it, would not be an adequate means of keeping these workers and their families affluent if they were unemployed for long periods. In 1970, 23 per cent of all factory production workers were unemployed for at least three months. Clearly, then, unemployment alone keeps a sizeable part of the lowest quintile from affluence.

Second, the cost of the means of satisfying survival needs has skyrocketed due to a variety of socio-economic factors. For example, a car is often a necessity for getting to work due to widespread inadequacy of public transportation. A telephone is a necessity when work for those laid off depends on being called-in only a few hours in advance. As a result of these and numerous other changes, the amount of income needed to meet the bare necessities has skyrocketed. The increased purchasing power of workers' incomes does not mean affluence. It signifies the greater difficulty of satisfying survival needs in an advanced capitalist society.

An income that allows a family these more expensive necessities but that provides no savings either for long-term investment or for children's education would be the minimum needed to keep a family beyond the poverty line. The US Bureau of Labor Statistics has defined a 'modest but adequate budget' as one that allows a family to meet the expenses of food, clothing, cheap housing, used car, minimum school outlays, one TV set in ten years, nine movies per year, and no savings. This modest budget lies, then, just above the poverty line. In 1967 an urban family of four could afford this budget with an income of $9,076. Yet 54 per cent of all US families lived on less than this income and thus fell below what is in effect the poverty line. In 1973, $12,626 was needed for this budget, which was $600 more than the median family income. In 1977 the modest-but-adequate line was $17,106, considerably above the median income of $12,436 for families with one wage earner. The supposedly affluent factory worker who is not laid off or put on part-time during the year made, on the average, $8,600 in 1973, which was $4,000 less than the BLS modest budget.[6]

A large prosperous middle class has by no means replaced the struggling lower classes as the majority class. With more than half of the people living below the modest but adequate budget of the BLS, the underbelly of US capitalist society is a deprived majority, just as it was fifty years ago. 'In advanced capitalist societies, the costs of staying out of poverty (i.e. of satisfying invariant subsistence needs) grows as the economy grows. Consequently, there is no long-term tendency in advanced capitalist societies for the incidence of poverty to decrease significantly as the economy grows.'[7] The economic inequality of US society is not just relative inequality, for it is an inequality that means deprivation for a sizeable chunk of the society.

2 Ownership and productivity   There are several strategies used by spokespersons of the ruling class to defend the situation of inequality described above. The first defence rests on the rights of ownership. The second rests on the need for inequality in order to

increase productivity. In the next section, a third strategy will be
discussed: it rests on the notion of a fair wage.

According to the *first defence* of inequality, those who have put
their hard-earned money into a business enterprise have the right
to appropriate the fruits of that enterprise and divide them
according to their own decisions. Thus the product that workers
have made is controlled by owners and not by the workers. Owners
are within their rights to divide the product in such a way that
inequality is great and poverty widespread. An entire web of
ideology has been woven on this basic frame of the rights of
ownership. Part of that web is the system of law, backed by police
force, entitling the owner to the fruits of the worker. From the
perspective of members of the working class, there are several
holes in this defence. These holes show that what is built on the
frame of ownership rights is indeed only ideology.

On the one hand, if ownership rights lead to continued
inequality and poverty, then from a working-class perspective
there simply are no such rights. The attitude that ownership of the
means of production is sacred merely protects the owners at the
expense of those who suffer the resulting inequality. A right is
more than such an attitude; it must be justified and indeed justified
from a class standpoint. Economic inequality can be justified by
ownership rights only if there are such rights. There may well be
such rights from the perspective of the ruling class. Yet the
continued inequality and poverty resulting from ownership are
evidence favouring the view that relative to the working class
owners have no legitimate right to the fruits of enterprise.

On the other hand, the basis given for the justification of the
owner's right to the fruits of enterprise is not adequate. That basis
was the hard work of the investor. Investment, however, is an
on-going process in a viable firm. The initial investment is
followed by many subsequent investments. Let us grant that the
owner has worked hard—whether in the form of the honest toil of
the self-employed person or in the form of the forcible plunder of
the syndicated criminal—to accumulate the initial investment. But
when the plant is rebuilt or expanded, the new investment will be
possible only because of the hard work of the workers. Once new
investment has been made, there is no longer the same basis for
saying that the original owner has the right to control the entire
product of the new investment. The logic of 'hard work' applies
here too. If the owner worked hard to accumulate the initial
investment, it is equally true that the workers worked hard to make
the new investment possible. Thus, in a viable firm, the workers
should, on the logic of hard work, have a right to appropriate an

ever increasing share of the product. The capitalist's own logic backfires!

A modified version of the hard-work defence of inequality has been devised by economists. According to it *both* the contribution of the capitalist *and* that of the worker to the production of a commodity have to be recognized. By measuring what each contributes, one can say what share of the product each should get. The shares will in fact be such that inequality and poverty result. But, according to the modified defence, this arrangement is perfectly just since deserts are strictly according to contributions.

The theory behind this modified defence has recently been shown to be untenable.[8] Very simply, the theory is circular. How does one measure the contribution of the capitalist to determine the capitalist's share of the product? One can do this, according to the theory, by finding out how much added units of capital increase the value of the entire product. But this requires that different kinds of capital goods have a price so that units of capital can be compared. The prices of capital goods do not just drop from the blue. They are determined, it turns out, by the ratio of wages to profits. Here is where the circularity comes in. For wages and profits are precisely the shares going to workers and owners. The defence of unequal shares on the basis of unequal contributions is worthless since it must resort to explaining unequal contributions in terms of unequal shares.

According to the *second defence* of inequality, significant inequality with poverty at the bottom is a necessary condition for making the society as affluent as it is. In a widely published newspaper article entitled 'Morality and the Pursuit of Wealth' appearing in July 1974, the President of the US Chamber of Commerce, Arch Booth, said the realization of equality by the transfer of wealth from the haves to the have-nots would lessen the 'work incentive of the most productive members of society' and endanger 'the ability of the economic system to accumulate capital for new productive facilities'. Booth's solution is to let the rich keep on investing in productive facilities thereby increasing the share the poor get through better wages and higher employment.

There is one glaring fallacy in this argument. It is the logical fallacy of an 'incomplete disjunction'. The disjunction Booth offers us is that *either* we have a forced redistribution of income within capitalism *or* we let the income of the non-owners rise naturally by increasing investment. But the disjunction needs to be expanded to include at least one more alternative: beyond capitalism, it is possible to expand productive facilities through the investment of collective rather than of private capital. In one form of collective ownership, workers would manage the investment of collective capital in order to advance their interests. In this case, the inequality in both wealth and income needed for growth under private capitalism becomes unnecessary. Without significant inequality, private capitalism would lack the centres of economic power needed to put large amounts of labour to work in order to produce a surplus for growth. The model here for a system of collective ownership of the means of production is not that of nationalized industry run by a bunch of officials who are not controlled by workers. This would be the bureaucratic model found in places like the USSR which are no longer private capitalist societies. Rather, the model is that of a workers' democracy in which democracy extends down to the workplace and in which workplaces are coordinated by a council of representatives from each. This socialist alternative is sufficient to make Booth's disjunction incomplete.

But why do we need such a third alternative? The reason is that Booth's two do not solve the problem of poverty. He is demonstrably wrong in holding that continuing to invest will eliminate poverty. As was pointed out in Section 1, growth under capitalism makes staying out of poverty increasingly more difficult. But he is absolutely correct in holding that taking from the rich to equalize economic status will reduce the ability of those still left with wealth to expand productive facilities significantly. Thus sticking with the two alternatives advanced by Booth gives a depressing conclusion: the only way to increase production in order to overcome society-wide scarcity leads to chronic inequality and poverty. This conclusion would be inescapable were it not for a third alternative like the socialist alternative uncovered when asking whether Booth's disjunction was complete.

A workers' democracy can afford greater equality and an elimination of poverty while at the same time increasing productive facilities. It can do this because investments in productive facilities are made from wealth that is not just produced by but also managed by the workers rather than by a ruling minority. If investment is made with private capital, there will be economic stagnation where there is not great inequality. Moreover, where investment is made with private capital and hence for private capital, investment slows down, whatever the human need for it, when profits fall. There is, then, not only chronic inequality and poverty but also a periodic recurrence of shortages of the supply of goods to meet survival needs.

In a workers' democracy all of this is changed. (a) Since capital is collectively controlled by workers, the surplus produced is controlled by those producing it. There is, then, no need for an unequal economic power, as there is when people have to be put to work to produce a surplus they will not control. (b) Eliminating poverty will not result in a setback to constructive growth. In the first place, the vast production of waste items—war materials, luxuries for the rich, advertising—needed to stabilize the system of private profits will be rechannelled into production for the satisfaction of survival needs. This will go a long way toward eliminating poverty. In the second place, poverty is a drain on the productive potential of those caught in it. This potential will be released for producing even more social wealth. (c) The full productive capacity of industry can be employed without the capitalist's fear of driving the rate of profit down. So long as the products of industry provide a basis for making people and plants more productive, there is, in a workers' democracy, no reason to run industry at much less than full capacity. By contrast, capitalist industry slows down when people cannot buy more, not when people do not need more. In short, in a workers' democracy, relative equality, the absence of poverty, and the expansion of means to satisfy needs are compatible goals.

3 **A fair wage**   A *third strategy* for defending the inequality and the poverty that is to be found today in the US introduces the concept of compensation for work. The defence is that labour is sold on the free market and, on the whole, the free market determines a *just* price for things. Thus, since inequality and poverty are, in part, a result of the free market for labour, there is no *right* to economic equality or even to a 'modest budget'. A free market must not involve the use of power by those who exchange their goods and services within it to coerce those with whom they exchange.

This argument seems to leave open the possibility that wages should mount and thus that the worker should come closer to the owner in economic status. But in fact this possibility is not open. As pointed out in Section 1, the range of inequality and the degree of poverty in the US have remained remarkably constant. The majority of the people are at or below the level of existence provided by the modest budget. Because of the greater power and organization of the owning class, the wages and salaries of workers remain at a level that allows them merely to perform their jobs well and to raise a new generation of workers. (Differences between the wages of, say, industrial and clerical workers need to be viewed against the background of a general pull toward this subsistence level.) To perform well and to reproduce themselves they have been forced to purchase the ever more elaborate and hence more expensive means of satisfying survival needs and the needs specific to their jobs. Short-term variations in the supply of and demand for labour are only part of this long-term pattern of compensating workers at a subsistence level. At this level, there is nothing much left over for savings and investments that might narrow the gap between them and the owning class. The BLS's moderate but adequate budget is the changing upper limit of the subsistence wage. So long as the owning class is a ruling class, workers' compensation will be held under this limit.

It is not, then, the free market that determines this long-term level of wages. This level is determined by the power of the owning class. The market only provides variations on it. From the perspective of the owning class, a wage that provides a subsistence appropriate to a worker of a given kind is a fair wage. It is a fair wage precisely because, on the one hand, higher wages would erode profits, and, on the other hand, lower wages would destroy the possibility of having the healthy, well trained, and contented workforce needed for production. The appeal to the free market is only a veil for these interests of the owning class. Ruling-class interest and the power at its disposal, not the free job market, allows the owners to call a wage fair that insures inequality.

What, then, is a fair wage from the perspective of the working class? Suppose we are calves who face the prospect of going to slaughter as one-year olds. The farmers who send us to slaughter find that this is the age at which to realize a maximum profit on us. So one year is the 'fair' time, from the perspective of the farmers, for calves to enjoy themselves before slaughter. An inquisitive calf poses the question, 'What is the true "fair" time for cattle to live before slaughter? Is it two years, or even three?' A selfish calf who has no regard for the farmer and the future of cattle farming generally shouts, 'Stop quibbling; we should demand a moratorium on beef eating. An end to the slaughter of cattle!' Similarly, Marx said that the slogan, 'A fair day's wage for a fair day's work!' should be replaced by the slogan, 'An end to the wage system!'[9] Instead of the wage system, work should be done in such a way that the workers' compensation is not just a function of the greater power of a non-working ruling class.

The wage system is a system that in advanced industrial countries has been central to the domination of lower classes by a ruling class. Through that system people are set to work in order to preserve or increase the control of wealth by and, thus, the power of a minority class. They are thus given from what they produce only what is needed to reproduce their labour. When part of the product of workers is used in this way to perpetuate and strengthen the domination of a non-working class, workers are properly said to be 'exploited'. Acceptance of the wage system and plans to reform it from within do not face up to the key role wages play in domination. When workers themselves decide how they are to be compensated out of what they produce, the wage system has ceased to exist and along with it exploitation.

The struggle of workers for higher income under capitalism is no less important because of all this. But it must be placed in a proper perspective. The struggle is important because without it workers would gain less in prosperity and lose more in recession than would be necessary and the ranks of the unemployed would swell beyond their chronically high bounds. But two things must be remembered. The *first* is that this struggle is not aiming at a wage that is 'fair' in an absolute way. The idea that there is such a thing as an absolute fair wage implies that within the wage system there is some point at which a proper division can be made of the fruits of enterprise between owners and workers. That there is no such point is clear since we are not dealing with classes whose aims can eventually be harmonized but with classes whose inner historical needs are in conflict on the very point of wages themselves.

The *second* thing is that the struggle for higher income begins the organization of people for the collective action that is needed to abolish the wage system itself. This long-term perspective has for some time been forgotten by trade unions everywhere. Their leaders advocate accommodation with the existing system of domination of working people. These leaders talk about a fair wage but they mean only the wages and benefits they think they can wheedle out of the owners. Their conception of fairness and of rights is no longer a class conception. A class conception makes overthrowing the wage system a right of working people.

4 A just distribution   Let us leave defences of present economic inequality and take up a proposal for limiting inequality. If capitalist arguments justifying present inequality fail, then where is the line to be drawn for an acceptable degree of inequality? Our problem is how to distribute a product that has come about through the combined efforts of people in different roles. Since isolated producers are the exception, we cannot start with the assumption that there is a product to which an individual producer is 'entitled' because he or she is 'responsible' for that product.[10] In deciding on a principle of just distribution there are two factors to be considered.

On the one hand, there is the average amount of goods per individual in the population, and, on the other hand, there is the degree of inequality with which goods are actually parcelled out to individuals. Increasing the average amount of goods per individual might increase the inequality of distribution, whereas decreasing the inequality in distribution might decrease the average per individual. In capitalism we saw that inequality of wealth is a condition of economic growth. Also, inequality of income within the working class weakens solidarity, making possible a greater surplus and hence greater growth. If strict equality means poverty all around, we might recoil from strict equality and look for a balance between a large average amount and considerable equality. But so far we have no clue as to where to strike this balance.

John Rawls has recently proposed an interesting way of balancing a high average amount of goods with a low degree of inequality.[11] The idea is that we are to avoid demanding such a low degree of inequality that the worst off are penalized by getting less than they would with a higher degree of inequality. We are to avoid only those high degrees of inequality that are arrived at by preventing the worst off from getting the most they could get.

Rawls formulated this in his Principle of Difference which tells us to 'maximize the expectations of the least favoured position'. If what goes to the most favoured could have gone to the least favoured without reducing the expectations of future goods coming to the least favoured, then it should indeed go to the least favoured. Maximizing the goods that go to the least favoured group has, then, the effect of preventing the kind of drop in the average amount of goods that would cause general deprivation. At the same time, it has the effect of preventing excessive inequality, since distribution to the well off is limited by maximizing the expectations of the least well off. We have the best of both worlds—a higher level of affluence than with excessive egalitarianism and a lower level of inequality than with less benefits for the worst off. A beacon seems to have been lighted for the groping reformers!

Without denying the brilliance of this suggestion, it is well to insert two cautionary remarks concerning any distribution scheme that leads to reform of present inequality. The *first* remark takes us back to historical materialism (Chapter XI, Section 1). It is that Rawls talks about distribution without relating it to production. He assumes wrongly that the validity of his principle is absolute, rather than relative to circumstances within production.

Marx criticized the Social Democracy for its failure to consider that,

The distribution of the means of consumption at any time is only a consequence of the conditions of production themselves . . . . Vulgar socialism (and from it in turn a section of democracy) has taken over from the bourgeois economists the consideration and treatment of distribution as independent of the mode of production and hence the presentation of socialism as turning principally on distribution.[12]

But Rawls has a blueprint for distribution considered in abstraction from any mode of production.

In what kind of organization of human and material potential to overcome scarcity will such a distribution scheme be practical? One thing is certain: in capitalist society there is not the least chance that the Rawlsian scheme could be put into practice. The reason is simply that the organization of production in a capitalist society centres around increasing productive facilities through the making of profits. The class of owners would not advance the interests characteristic of their class by agreeing to maximize the expectations of the least favoured. Given its power, this class would block the realization of the scheme.

Suppose, though, that some mode of production would allow for distribution in accordance with the Principle of Difference. Should not one simply choose to bring about such a mode of production? Certainly—if the Principle of Difference is valid. But its validity is relative to production in the following way. Validity in general is relative to classes, and classes are essential roles in a given mode of production. One should, then, choose to realize the principle only if it is valid relative to one's class. Nonetheless, that class might have to change the existing mode of production in order to realize the new distribution. Even though the capitalist mode of production excludes the application of the Principle of Difference, it may be a valid principle for one of the lower classes within capitalism.

A distributional plan is not just because it is elegant or intuitive but because it answers to needs arising in production. Not only the actual but also the just distribution is dependent on production.

The *second* remark on Rawls' Principle of Difference concerns its relation to the lower classes. Can it function as an ideal for the lower classes? After all, the whole trade-union struggle for higher wages and better working conditions seems to point to the fact that the working class is dedicated to maximizing its expectations, even if this cannot be accomplished within the capitalist system. But there is a fatal difficulty. There is one thing better for the least advantaged than working to maximize the expectations of the group of the least advantaged. That is their working to change the group from being least advantaged. The least advantaged—however this group is delimited—has, as a group, a right to move out of the position of being least advantaged. 'The last shall be first and the first last.'[13]

Moving out of the position of being least advantaged has two possible implications. *Either* some other group is placed in the category of least advantaged. To maintain its advantage the newly advantaged group cannot allow groups under it to maximize their expectations. The situation then reproduces that of the old order. *Or* all groups become equally advantaged relative to their needs, ending the system of differential advantages. The possibility for maximizing the advantages of the least advantaged comes only when there are no longer any advantaged groups to be protected by not maximizing the advantages of the least advantaged.

Thus the Principle of Difference cannot be realized so long as there are differences in advantages and is irrelevant once differences in advantages have been abolished. But it would be utopian to put strict equality on the immediate agenda. The equal satisfaction of needs is an ideal that we can choose to realize only down the road within a fully developed democratic organization of production that has little resemblance either to private capitalist or to bureaucratic organizations of production.

Notes

1   Gabriel Kolko, *Wealth and Power in America*, Praeger, New York, 1962, p. 108.
2   These data are based on tables in Kolko, *Wealth and Power in America*, p. 14, and in Frank Ackerman and Andrew Zimbalist, 'Capitalism and inequality in the United States', in *The Capitalist System*, 2nd ed., p. 298.
3   Kolko, *Wealth and Power in America*, Ch. II, and Ackerman and Zimbalist 'Capitalism and inequality in the United States', in *The Capitalist System*, 2nd ed., p. 303. In Sweden, by contrast, taxes change the ratio of the bottom third to that of the top third from 38 to 48 per cent.
4   Lititia Upton and Nancy Lyons, *Basic Facts: Distribution of Personal Income and Wealth in the United States*, Cambridge Institute, 1878 Massachusetts Ave., Cambridge. Mass., 1972, p. 6, and Ackerman and Zimbalist, 'Capitalism and inequality in the United States', in *The Capitalist System*, 2nd ed., p. 301.
5   Upton and Lyons, *Basic Facts*, p. 31.
6   Arnold Cantor, 'The widening gap of incomes', *The AFL-CIO American Federationist*, March 1975.
7   Bernard Gendron, 'Capitalism and poverty', *Radical Philosophers' Newsjournal*, 4, January 1975, p. 13. This essay appears as Ch. XII of

Gendron's *Technology and the Human Condition*, St Martin's Press, New York, 1977.

8   A major piece in this exciting but technical attack on capitalist economics is P. Garegnani's 'Heterogeneous capital, the production function, and the theory of distribution', in *A Critique of Economic Theory*, eds. E. K. Hunt and G. Schwartz, Penguin, Harmondsworth, 1972, pp. 245–91.

9   Karl Marx, *Wages, Price, and Profit* (1865), Foreign Language Press, Peking, 1970, Ch. XIV.

10   On entitlement, see Robert Nozick, *Anarchy, State, and Utopia*, Basic Books, New York, 1974, Ch. VII.

11   Rawls, *A Theory of Justice*, p. 78–80.

12   Karl Marx, *Critique of the Gotha Programme* (1875), ed. C. P. Dutt, International Publishers, New York, 1970, pp. 10–11.

13   Matthew 20: 16.

XIX

Rights and Social Structure

A theory is an effort to get behind the appearances to something that accounts for them. In this effort there is always a danger: it is easy to take for an account something that only seems to get to a more fundamental level than the appearances themselves. One falls into this trap when one's account is only a formal construction. In a formal construction, notions that supposedly designate explanatory entities are used without the slightest justification that they designate anything at all. They are a mere embellishment on customary thought. The history of science is strewn with formal constructions. There was, for example, the theory of the luminiferous ether, an ether that was to be the medium for electro-magnetic waves. Ethical theories are not immune to these troubles. They often end up containing formal constructions, as when Plato postulated moral ideals outside the space-time universe and when Kant postulated a reverence for duty unaffected by social and physical existence.

In addition to this danger, there is the practical difficulty of gaining acceptance for a theory at a time when there is widespread acceptance of a different theory. The key problem here is gaining acceptance for the theory's central theoretical notions as ones that are determinate enough to be applicable to reality under specifiable circumstances. Without such acceptance, defenders of the established wisdom will say that the theory has fallen prey to the above-mentioned danger: they will object to the new theory as a formal construction.

Gaining acceptance for the applicability of notions is, though, not a matter of pure intellect. It is a matter conditioned in important social ways.[1] Acceptance of new theoretical notions can be upsetting for an established school. Also it can be upsetting for a ruling class, when the implications of those notions undercut the established relations of domination.

The central notion of the ethical theory of this book is that of advancing the interests characteristic of a group. In the past few centuries, considerable effort has been spent in developing the atomic conception of the person and in underplaying the social conception of the person. The effect has been the dogma that if there are interests characteristic of members of a group this is only because members of the group happen to have these interests all on their own. The idea that groups are entities to be reckoned with as part of the furniture of this world was thought to have been discredited. The ethical theory of this book can be accepted only if the bankruptcy of the theories based on the atomic conception of the person is sufficiently unsettling to enough people to make them reflect that another conception—the social conception of the person—might well be intelligible. Granting that it might be intelligible means, though, giving up the carefully elaborated theory of individualism according to which group interests are merely interests a certain number of people happen to have in common.

This chapter focuses on this central notion of advancing group interests. This discussion by itself will not make people shift from the traditional individualist paradigm of persons. But perhaps it will make clear to them one of the reasons they cannot easily shift to the social paradigm of persons. This is that they are integrated into a social system for which the individualist paradigm has been the intellectual coping stone.

1   The interdependence of needs   The good, the obligatory, and human rights have all been interpreted in terms of advancing tendencies characteristic of a group. This is why the central notion in this book is that of advancing a tendency characteristic of a group. That which is *good* advances the realization of the needs characteristic of a group. An act is *obligatory* for a person because, without it, the effort to advance the realization of the needs of that person's group would be likely to suffer a setback. And a person has a *right* to do something when not protecting people from interference by others in performing that kind of action would be likely to conflict with the advancement of the realization of the needs characteristic of a group. The needs characteristic of a group are not just any needs that happen to be common to members of the group; they are, rather, internal historical needs. They are historical in the sense that they arise on the basis of a patterning of survival needs within a given form of society. And they are internal in respect to the group in the sense that they are needs arising from the patterning of survival needs by that group. Thus the needs characteristic of a group do not include any needs imposed on members of the group as a result of their presence in the sum group of which that group is a sub-group.

To understand the notion of advancing group tendencies based on the social theory of the person, it will be helpful to distinguish the above view of morality from the utilitarian one that sees everything in terms of advancing the general welfare. Is the only difference that general welfare has been reduced to group welfare? Not at all, since the point of view of utilitarianism can be adapted to specific groups. Rather than the welfare of human-kind generally, the key notion would be the *aggregate* satisfaction of needs characteristic of a group. To calculate such an aggregate, people in the group are first taken one at a time in order to sum up the satisfactions of each individual's group-related needs. Then, by a further addition, the total satisfaction of group-related needs of all individuals in the group is computed. This provides a way of distinguishing, on a group basis, the better from the good, and ultimately the best from the better. The good will advance group interest, the better will advance it still further by providing a greater aggregate of satisfaction of needs characteristic of the group, and the best, or the right thing to do, will maximally advance group interest.

In group-relative utilitarianism, the problem of distributing satisfactions within a group is that of maximizing the satisfaction of group-related needs. Equality is to be promoted if by it a greater aggregate of satisfaction is realized. With too much inequality a spirit of rebelliousness might develop that would be incompatible with maximum aggregate satisfaction. Is there, then, anything really inadequate about a group-relative utilitarian approach to interpreting the notion of advancing the realization of the needs characteristic of a group?

The full answer to this question has been anticipated in Chapter VII, Section 2, where it was indicated that it is structured and not unstructured aggregates that are important in moral theory. Structure is important because we do not concern ourselves with the sheer quantity of satisfaction resulting from the realization of needs when we speak of advancing the realization of group needs. The reason for this is that group needs are *interdependent* as regards their realization. One does not satisfy them in isolation from one another. And this is also the reason why Marxism cannot be a brand of utilitarianism.

Even the patterning of survival needs by group membership makes the realization of these survival needs interdependent. For example, in view of the fact that eating is typically a social event, the realization of the need for human support becomes in part dependent on the realization of the need for food. Conversely, the realization of the need for deliberation comes to depend on the realization of the need for support, since in the group context decision always has as its backdrop the circle of those from whom one receives support.

More important than the quantity of need satisfaction in this interdependent pattern is the absence of obstacles at key places in the pattern. Because of the interdependence, the pattern itself becomes something to be defended. An obstacle to support from others would block the route to meaningful deliberation. One might compensate by eating more, yet this satisfaction is not enough, just by its quantity, for full compensation. What is wrong is that the system of need satisfaction as a totality has been jarred, not that the quantity of satisfaction has been diminished.

When we consider, not survival needs, but needs characteristic of a class, the phenomenon of interdependence reveals a new aspect. For example, the need for job security is realized in conjunction with the realization of the need for a strong union. The union is a social structure that must be developed in order to realize needs other than needs for any kind of social structure. As before the important thing is not the sheer quantity of satisfaction but the all-round development of this interdependent system of need satisfaction.[2] A threat to job security is indirectly a threat to the union. And conversely, a direct threat to the union is indirectly a threat to job security. In this case there is a novel need. One of the needs—that for a strong union—is a need for a structure which develops means to advance the other needs. It is not, then, just one more need alongside the rest. The car owner needs clean spark plugs, well ground valves, an oil pan that does not leak, and, to be sure, a well-running motor. But this last need is quite different from the first three.

The interconnection of needs should not keep us from recognizing that sometimes needs are realized independently. The characteristic phenomenon, though, is that of getting everything going together before things run well at all. This gives importance to the social structures that develop in and then advance this process. It is also fatal to the interpretation of advancing group tendencies as maximizing the satisfaction of group needs. To make clear the implications of this interdependence of need satisfaction for ethics, something must first be said about the different kinds of needs that are characteristic of being a member of a group.

2 The need for social entities Earlier we distinguished between the patterning of survival needs due to membership in a group and the creation of historical needs as a result of the peculiarities of a given patterning of survival needs. Both factors must be considered in understanding the interdependence of needs. The life of any group integrates the needs for food, sex, support, and deliberation in a distinctive fashion.[3] If a particular individual does not accept the manner of integration resulting from his or her group, then that individual risks losing opportunities to realize the survival needs. Associated with any patterning of survival needs is a distinctive insecurity concerning the realization of these needs. This insecurity often arises out of conflict with other groups and creates the need for strong organizations that will promote security. Before these organizations can be fully effective, a fundamental change of society itself is needed. Thus a need for a new form of society develops. And so a complex web of interdependence is woven, starting with survival needs themselves and including even the need for a new society.

Since they are not themselves historical, survival needs are not characteristic of a group. But the way they are patterned by a group gives rise to historical needs of several kinds. First, there are needs for 'individual' as opposed to 'social' entities. There is the need of the worker for gainful employment by someone else. The worker's gainful employment is the individual entity needed. Second, there are needs for social rather than individual entities, such as the need of workers for strong independent organizations that can protect their interests within the wage system.

Try not to think about this, as the utilitarian would, in terms of the aggregate satisfaction coming from the realization of many needs. At one level there is the realization of each person's need to be gainfully employed. And at another level there is the realization of each person's need for an organization strong enough to protect employment. It would be hard to attribute any practical import to the claim that gainful employment advances the tendencies characteristic of the working class just half, say, as well as gainful employment and strong organization together. When there is high employment the union has a stronger bargaining position. And when the union is stronger it is prepared to fight against layoffs, and it is likely to be successful. Given this interdependence, it is impossible to isolate the satisfactions of these two needs and sum them together. But it would be necessary to make such an isolation of the two satisfactions in order to be able to say that being gainfully employed gives half, or some other fraction, of the satisfaction of being both gainfully employed and having a strong union.[4] In short, there are the two needs, they each receive satisfaction, but the satisfactions cannot be arithmetically summed.[5] This is due to the interdependence of their realizations, and it makes the key notion of utilitarianism—aggregate satisfaction—irrelevant.

The interdependence does not mean that needs for social entities reduce to needs for individual entities. In the first place, needs for social entities may grow out of needs for individual entities, but they rarely remain mere tools for the latter. They always represent something more. In the second place, the social entities for which there are needs are themselves integrated with the needs for individual entities in such a way that there will be a need for some overarching social structure. This overarching social structure, which is itself a social entity, may be unrealizable in the present context. But the advancement of tendencies characteristic of a group depends on whether or not this structure is brought closer to actualization or, if it exists already, is improved.

In the case of the owning class, the existing capitalist society provides this overall structure. From the standpoint of that class, actions that advance a number of tendencies of the class but that endanger this structure do not, in the final analysis, advance the tendencies of the owning class. We judge such actions on the basis of the all-round development they give to the sum group, because the need for this development of the sum group is central to the entire system of needs characteristic of the owning class.

The objection that is sure to come to mind is that the development of an overarching social structure is important only because it is the context for maximizing the aggregate satisfaction of needs. Granted that, because of their interdependence among one another and of their dependence on this ultimate need, lesser needs cannot simply be added together, as regards their satisfaction, in order to determine how much an action advances the tendencies of a class. But, the objection runs, we can use the degree of development of the overarching social structure as an index for judging how much an action advances the tendencies of a class. The greater the development of that structure, the greater the satisfaction coming from realizing the needs of the class.

A response to this objection emerges from the consideration that some needs characteristic of a class may be blocked by the overarching social structure toward which the class tends. As that structure develops, some needs that were characteristic of the class may cease to exist, with the result that the remaining needs are simpler and fewer in number. There is little basis for claiming that realizing these remaining needs affords a greater aggregate of satisfaction by comparision with realizing the needs that existed before the social structure became developed. This undercuts the proposal to use the degree of development of an overarching social structure as an index for greater aggregate satisfaction.

The need for independent workers' organizations leads to a need for workers democracy (Chapter X, Section 1). This need for an overarching social structure will be realized only by organizing the survival needs differently than in a capitalist society. This will be essential if the historical need for gainful employment by someone else is to be transformed within a workers' democracy into the historical need for productive activity directed by and for those who are productively active. A process of advancing the tendencies of the working class that starts out by advancing the need for gainful employment by someone else may end up destroying that need while still advancing other tendencies of the working class. The development of a workers' democracy is not, then, morally obligatory because it realizes a greater quantity of satisfaction in respect to the same needs workers have under capitalism. Some of the class needs will have vanished and will never be realized by the new social order. The new needs may constitute a simpler and less numerous system. There is, then, no reason to claim that realizing these simpler and less numerous needs will afford a greater aggregate of satisfaction than would have resulted without the development of the overarching social structure.

This is not to say that there is something sacred about social entities as distinct from individual entities. The need for a social entity that serves to integrate other needs does not become a 'higher' need than the needs it integrates because, as a Platonist would have it, social entities are otherworldly entities. It is higher only because of the relations of dependence on it that develop in history. These relations make the social entity a key to advancing group tendencies. Reducing unemployment requires collective action that can be all the more determined when it is motivated by a commitment to a workers' democracy. This is the basis for the primacy of social structure over aggregate satisfaction in advancing the tendencies of a group. The need for a social entity is then a higher need not because social entities are otherworldly but because of the key role they play in the group struggle.

3   **Social entities as a basis for rights**   The elaboration of the idea of advancing group tendencies or interests continues here but with a different emphasis. So far the emphasis has been on showing that advancing group tendencies does not amount to maximizing satisfactions of group needs. Here the emphasis will shift to implications for the idea of advancing group tendencies stemming from the fact that there are group tendencies to maintain or create overarching social orders. One cannot judge whether the tendencies of a group are advanced without reference to these special

tendencies. We shall discuss this matter in conjunction with the rights arising from such central tendencies.

Rights are social in two distinct ways. First, they are social in that it is the needs people develop in a social group that justify them. Among these needs is a need for a society of a certain kind. This need is one that, as we just saw, has primacy in respect to the others in group struggle. Consequently, it will have primacy in justifying rights. So, second, rights are social in that among the needs that justify them there is a need, not just for an individual, but also for a social entity. (The same doubly social character belongs to goods and obligations.)

In order to understand the way social entities justify rights, let us begin by recalling the discussion of the history of the idea of rights in Chapter XVII, Section 1. It was pointed out there that the individualist conception of rights that attributed rights to an atomic human nature was correct insofar as it emphasized the growing irrelevance of the feudal hierarchy of ranks as the basis for rights. But it was one-sided insofar as it ignored the fact that the new social order emerging out of changes in the mode of production carried its own hierarchy of groups on which a new set of rights was based. In making an overarching social structure the primary basis for rights, one abandons the individualist's theory of rights based on an atomic human nature. Instead one accepts a theory of rights that was already implicit in the ancient doctrine of virtue. For that doctrine was itself based on the consideration of what was beneficial to the maintenance of the existing social order. Thus the doctrine of virtue gave importance to a social entity.

This doctrine of virtue cannot be developed correctly without a change. It bases rights on the characteristic features of a present or future social order. But rights cannot simply be read off from such features. Great inequality is a characteristic feature of capitalism, but it does not prevent workers from having the right to less inequality now. Equality will be a characteristic feature of a fully developed workers' democracy, but this is no guarantee that workers now have a right to full equality. Instead, rights must be based on the possibilities for change. This change can be of two sorts, either change that reforms an existing social order or change that creates a new social order. The possibilities of reforming and hence strengthening an existing order determine the rights of defenders of that order; the possibilities of creating a new order determine the rights of those opposed to the old. Thus the historical stage of development is crucial to fixing what rights there are. The inadequacy of the old doctrine of virtue stems from its hallowing either rigid custom (Aristotle) or a utopian programme

(Plato). It left no room for a transitional notion—a notion of rights based on possibilities leading beyond mere custom but not on the false assumption that our ultimate ideals have already been realized.

Even the ruling class cannot successfully maintain its position by a conception of rights based simply on the characteristic features of capitalism today. Reforms are needed to channel the force of opposition movements in directions that actually support the existing relations of domination. These reforms challenge customary expectations and, with them, established rights and privileges. People's rights are justified, relative to the ruling class, by whether or not protecting them strengthens the social structure—the sum group—that furthers the realization of the needs of the ruling class. But to strengthen that overarching social structure, it is necessary to protect different liberties at different times.

Similarly, if the need to overcome domination is the basis for a need for an entirely new social order, the protected liberties of that new order do not automatically become the rights of members of a dominated class even before the new order is realized. We noted this already in pointing out that there is no general right to deny free speech to members of the ruling class in an epoch during which civil liberties are important for organizing an opposition to the ruling class. Rights come about not because of what a social structure allows but because of what is needed to maintain it or to bring it into existence. This is the way the present theory of rights differs from that based on the classical doctrine of virtue, even though both give social entities a central place.

4   The rights of working people   There are two conceptions of the social entity on which the rights of working people today in advanced capitalist countries are justified. According to the one, working people's rights are justified within the framework of maintaining the profit system. This is the conception of defenders of the profit system, from all the big owners to most union officials however radical their rhetoric may on occasion sound. This conception is enshrined in the Declaration of Policy of the Taft-Hartley Act of 1947 in the words:

Industrial strife, which interferes with the normal flow of commerce and with the full production of articles and commodities for commerce, can be avoided or substantially minimized if employers, employees, and labour organizations . . . all recognize under law that neither party has any right in its relations with any other to engage in acts or practices which jeopardize the public health, safety, or interest.[6]

Maintaining the profit system is referred to here as upholding the public interest.

According to the other conception, working people's rights are justified within the framework of bringing about a workers' democracy. The need to bring this social entity into existence is one among the needs characteristic of the working class. To show how this need fits with the others, we shall gather together a list of the main categories of needs of working people, including both productive and the majority of unproductive workers.

This list repeats things discussed earlier, but the purpose here is to show that advancing the tendencies of the working class is not a matter of realizing one or more isolated interests of the working class. Classes are not inert but are continually changing the world for the purpose of reforming or creating overarching social structures. An action can be a candidate for advancing the tendencies of a class only when put into relation to this activity regarding social structures. This can be seen as follows.

To begin with, there is the need for a less limited realization of survival needs than is allowed under the profit system. Substitute needs, that can be more easily satisfied, have the effect of diverting attention from the very limited satisfaction of survival needs. Thus, for example, the need to deliberate on important matters is satisfied only in a limited way since it is not satisfied within the workplace. Instead, one is allowed the satisfaction of the substitute need to deliberate over the choice of consumer goods. Moreover, support from those with whom one works is replaced by support within the confines of the family. Finally, the need for basic physical satisfaction is limited through high noise levels, unhealthy air, unwholesome processed foods, and high tension levels. Because of these limited realizations of survival needs, substitute needs are easily developed for being entertained by crime-squad shows, for leadership figures, for repressive social measures, for buying new gimmicks, and for national glory. But there remains the recognition that there is deprivation at a more fundamental level.

In addition, working people are aware that they are the slack in a system that needs continual tightening to be stabilized. Since World War II, as many as one out of five workers experienced unemployment sometime during each year. Inflation freezes their real wages to protect the profits of owners. Military spending puts a floor on demand for basic materials, yet military production is a drag on the more efficient production of enough consumer goods. Unemployment, stagnant real wages, and waste spending are ways the profit system defends itself at the expense of the worker. Workers have, then, a need to be defended against these inroads.

Yet no organizations formed within the present profit system can provide sufficient protection.

What then is needed is a social order that would remove the limitations on survival needs, that would reduce the necessity for substitute needs, and that would eliminate the destabilizing features of the profit system. The need for such a social order has primacy over the other needs since the struggle for their realization is most effectively organized by the struggle to realize that need. To realize the survival needs in a less limited way, deliberation and support must take place within the setting of work itself and not off to its side. The less limited realization of these survival needs requires, then, a workers' democracy, a democracy that is not restricted to electing public officials but extends into the area in which people spend their working lives. Working people will deliberate over their concerns as producers of the scarce goods and services on which the society depends. They will not be limited to receiving support from impersonal bureaucracies while they are working. There will be cooperation and hence mutual support at the workplace, based on the fact that it is run by working people for themselves and other working people.

In addition, the need to be freed from the effects of economic instability can be satisfied only when it is the needs of people and not the profits of owners that regulate production. The need for such an economic system dovetails with the need for a workers' democracy. Once the need for an economy based not on profits but on needs themselves is felt, it will be recognized that democracy cannot be limited to the making of internal decisions within isolated workplaces. Workers will have to make decisions about the distribution of goods and services within the society as a whole.

At the top of the structure of needs there is, then, the need for a workers' democracy within which the profit system and the market have been replaced. This is the need that is central in determining whether the tendencies of the working class are advanced. One cannot determine whether those tendencies are advanced on utilitarian grounds. It is this need for a new social structure that has primacy in determining what are the rights of working people.

Notes

1   Thomas Kuhn, *The Structure of Scientific Revolutions*, 2nd ed., University of Chicago Press, Chicago, 1970, Chs. VIII, XII.
2   For a discussion of the values of wholes in relation to their parts that sheds some light on this point, see G. E. Moore, *Principia Ethica* (1903), Cambridge University Press, Cambridge, England, 1962, Secs. 18–23.

3   See John Dewey's observations on the 'interpenetration' of habits in *Human Nature and Conduct*, Ch. II.

4   The impossibility of isolating the satisfactions does not prevent the utilitarian from abstracting them from the overall social reality and then treating them as the basis for the social structure itself. Marx and Engels criticized utilitarianism on just this point: ' . . . the category of "utilization" is first of all abstracted from the actual relations of intercourse . . . and then these relations are made out to be the reality of the category that has been abstracted from them themselves, a wholly metaphysical method of procedure' (Karl Marx and Frederick Engels, *The German Ideology*, p. 110).

5   Welfare functions that do not involve simply adding individual utilities, but which still do not address the problem raised here, are discussed by Sen, *On Economic Inequality*, pp. 20–21, 39–41.

6   *Labor-Management Relations Act*, Public Law 101, 80th Cong., 1 Sess., 61 Stat. 136, Section 1.

XX

Revolutionary Ethics

IT is not the good of society as a whole but class tendencies that are the touchstone of morality. In any society where there is significant inequality, advancing what is called the good of the whole society would inescapably advance the domination of the ruling class within that society. With class tendencies as the touchstone of morality, the lower classes under capitalism have *revolutionary rights*—rights to take steps directly designed to abolish lower classes altogether. For the tendencies of such classes remain largely unrealized within the context of continued domination by the ruling class. Members of the working class and of other lower classes have, then, a right to do what is appropriate to realize the need for a new form of society. What is appropriate will vary considerably with circumstances.

Many reasons have been given for denying revolutionary rights. This concluding chapter examines reasons for denying revolutionary rights that might be relevant from the standpoint of the working class. It ignores reasons for denying revolutionary rights that explicitly express only the interests of the existing ruling class. Such reasons have been used to support laws like the Smith and McCarran Acts, which denied even elementary civil rights to dissidents.

1   Reform and revolutionary rights   There are two familiar ways revolutionary rights are denied. On the one hand, there is the 'conservative' view that reform measures which do not threaten the existing sum group are the best way to satisfy people's needs. There is no right to any action directly or indirectly weakening the existing economic or political system. The working class is then to be restrained when its demands might weaken capitalism. The state must be allowed to perpetuate the relations of domination within the capitalist sum group. This is the majority position of both the Democratic Party and the Republican Party in the US and of both the Labour Party and the Tories in Britain.

On the other hand, there is the view of 'gradualism'. The gradualist believes that step by step reform can lead beyond capitalism to a workers' democracy. At no step is it necessary to aim explicitly at the change to socialism. This change will take place of itself in the course of aiming at changes within capitalism. This view has the effect of denying revolutionary rights, for there is no occasion on which it is appropriate to act directly to change the society from one with a capitalist ruling class. That change will come about of itself as a result of a sequence of reforms. The majority voting its preference for socialism will be a reflection of this change and not a revolutionary act.[1]

One scenario for gradualism is a strictly parliamentary one. Through legislation the rights of private owners are gradually eaten away. How much, for what, and where they invest become matters over which owners have less and less control. At some stage it is pointless to continue speaking of private ownership and then the system has been transformed.[2] Another scenario for gradualism has been devised by the so-called Eurocommunists in response to the weaknesses of the strictly parliamentary one. It calls for reform activity on two fronts, within the state apparatus and by the spontaneous mass organizations of the lower classes and the oppressed groups. With pressure from the mass organizations coming from without and with pressure from leftist public servants coming from within, the state apparatus is gradually transformed into one appropriate for a changed mode of production.[3]

The gradualist approach, in one form or another, is that of the Socialist Party and the Communist Party in a number of advanced capitalist countries. Their approach satisfies the need for a socialist vision but confounds the need for effective action to realize that vision. They deny revolutionary rights by counterposing reformist programmes to revolutionary movements.

Both the conservative and the gradualist denials of revolutionary rights are based on the idea that reform within the system is the outer limit for deliberate change. On the one hand, conservative reform promises the lower classes and oppressed groups a perpetuation of domination. On the other hand, the gradualist has yet to present a convincing case for breaking the existing system of domination through step by step reform.

The case for gradualism would be convincing if one could assume that the dominant class would gracefully step down when it senses its power is being eroded by a sequence of reforms. Yet the dominant class always fights any threat to its power. It would stop such a sequence of reforms even if this meant replacing the democratic process with some form of authoritarian rule. Thus General Augustin Pinochet's authoritarian regime replaced the Popular Unity government of Salvadore Allende in Chile in 1973.

To forestall a right-wing coup, some gradualists slow the reform process down, hoping thereby to avoid antagonizing the international capitalist class. Thus Italian Communist Party leader Enrico Berlinguer promoted a compromise with the capitalist Christian Democratic Party for the purpose of strengthening capitalism in Italy during the economic crisis of the late 1970s. This slowing down of reform ends with the cooptation of the gradualists by capitalism. In the absence of some new defence against either a right-wing coup or cooptation, gradualism does indeed confound the need for effective action toward socialism.

Why do so-called progressive people deny revolutionary rights if denying them leaves the forces of domination without an effective challenge? There are several reasons, which we will list here even if we cannot discuss them fully. Merely listing them does, though, point up some of the defects of the reformist position of at least the conservative kind. (One of the reasons for accepting gradualism will be discussed in the next section.)

(1) There is the psychological aversion to changing the *status quo*. This aversion is widespread even among working people. Among them, it is rooted in the insecurity of life within the profit system. When fellow workers are being laid off, when minorities are demanding scarce jobs, when the security of retired life seems to depend on the continuity of the state, when the bank has a mortgage on the house—when all of this is hanging over one's head life seems insecure indeed. The least shock will bring personal ruin. Anyone who threatens to rock the boat appears as a personal enemy. It is this insecurity that gives fascism an entering wedge within the working class when there is a strong challenge to the state from the left. Denying revolutionary rights to everyone is an expression of this insecurity.

(2) There is among professionals and intellectuals little trust in the possibility that the majority of people in the lower classes have a potentiality for self-governance. They accept the necessity of rule by an elite. Since one elite has, they reason, about the same capacity for abusing the people as another, why not support the status quo? A revolution is a lot of trouble merely for the purpose of replacing an elite of bankers and industrialists by a bureaucratic elite that controls a nationalised economy. So there are no rights to actions designed to overthrow the capitalist system.

The alleged inferiority of the lower classes fails to fit the facts. There is enough evidence of worker ingenuity in self-governance to demolish the necessity of elites. Workers initiated and ran governments within governments during the general strikes of 1934 in the US.[4] After the overthrow of the Czar in February 1917,

Russian workers formed factory committees that ran plants without bosses.[5] In the second half of 1936, the revolutionary workers of Barcelona controlled communications, produced materials for the anti-fascist armed forces, and fought the fascist forces themselves.[6] In 1973, 1,300 workers at the Lip watch factory in Besançon, France, took control of their plant after the owners threatened closure. Despite subsequent harassment by the state, the workers showed again that bosses are expendable in industry. The French capitalist class was considerably exercised over this denial or transformation of property rights.[7] Village communities in China were capable of reorganizing themselves to overcome the tyranny of the landlords and to place power in a Village People's Congress, which contained delegates from various lower classes.[8]

It has not been the incompetence of people of lower classes to govern themselves that has put an end to their self-governance. Self-governance has been terminated by counter-revolution brought on by an aspiring elite or by an established government. For example, the Popular Front government used repression to take control away from the workers of Barcelona in May 1937. It justified this counter-revolution by saying that the fascist leader Franco had to be defeated before the revolution could take place. But the demoralization of the workers by the counter-revolution contributed to Franco's ultimate victory.

(3) There is the optimist who believes that, for all of its limitations, capitalism, which has raised the standard of living so much since the eighteenth century, can continue to improve life. The objective conditions for revolution are thereby removed and with them the right of revolutionary action.

It would be foolish to deny that capitalism has performed an important historical mission in raising the standard of living. But to give it a new lease on life because of its past successes would be a mistake. In the first place, even the great boom after World War II was unable to change significantly either the relative inequality within the US or the proportional amount of poverty. Doubling the buying power of workers in that period was accompanied by putting the necessities of life in new forms that were considerably more expensive. Since the proportional amount of poverty has not changed for some time, there is reason to deny that mid-twentieth century capitalism is still genuinely raising the standard of living and is thus still truly progressive.

In the second place, the human, social, and ecological costs of maintaining the system have become excessive. The loss of life in wars has become all the more clearly the responsibility of a social system of domination struggling to preserve itself.[9] The military overhead for the search for profits through overseas investment has, in addition, been a serious drag on raising the standard of living. There is also the unabated use of internal violence to break strikes and to stop many forms of dissent. And, finally, perpetuating capitalism is subsidized by ever larger sacrifices of the environment, sacrifices that lower chances for a healthy life.

Those who blink at these enormous human, social, and ecological costs do so either because of the special privileges they enjoy from the system that incurs these costs or because their own insecurity within the system leads them to support stability at all costs.

(4) Capitalism is, according to a widely held view, no longer a system in which the possessors of capital are the ruling class. A managerial elite has supposedly ousted the capitalist from highest power. This well-educated elite is more sensitive than was the capitalist to human needs. It will reduce the social costs of capitalism thereby making capitalism a habitable system even for the lower classes.[10] There are, then, no revolutionary rights since there is no need to get beyond capitalism.

Whether a managerial elite could ever have a humanizing effect that would reduce these costs of capitalism is far from clear. What is clear is that the increased role of the manager and the technician inside the firm should not be confused with the relinquishing of power by the possessor of capital. Capitalists are in fact still on top, and managers must subordinate their schemes to the aim of capitalists, which is capital accumulation.

The importance of private capital can be demonstrated through the importance of financial institutions. In 1968, financial institutions—banks and insurance companies—were providing 42 per cent of the investment funds for non-financial corporations and, in 1965, they either owned or administered through trusts 40 per cent of the stocks of the non-financial corporations. This vast interest of the financial establishment in the non-financial corporations is advanced by the presence of representatives of financial corporations on the boards of directors of the non-financial corporations. Each bank board, for example, is interlocked, on the average, sixteen times with the boards of other corporations. The financial establishment has but one aim, increasing private capital. Thus its importance is an indication of the importance of private capital. The power of the financial establishment, through credit and stock, over the running of non-financial corporations puts that of the industrial manager and the technician in the shade.[11]

2　Social change and absolutism　One of the biggest stumbling blocks to according revolutionary rights comes from an absolutist conception of ethics. Absolutism often lies behind the gradualist claim that, though at some point workers will have political and economic power, they do not have the right to act directly to overthrow the present system. Without convincing practical arguments for the denial of revolutionary rights, some gradualists ultimately rest their case for this denial on the view that a *class* is not the basis for rights but *humanity* is. Workers must then join with all other humans to change society from within the present system. To press for revolutionary rights would be to press their own class interests at the expense of other humans.

For gradualist Eduard Bernstein, workers do not have the right to form a new society until they are unified with all classes. To realize this unity they need the right to vote, which gives rise to a 'virtual' partnership in the community, one that 'must in the end lead to a real partnership'. His reason for requiring unity is that morality is for him based on the freedom of every human being.[12] To realize this universal human nature, no one group can assert itself at the expense of any other. And thus one may advance into a new society only after a partnership between classes has been established through electoral politics. Then all classes can advance together, arm in arm, into socialism. Revolution as a deliberate break with capitalist domination is unnecessary; its place is taken by the peaceful transformation through reform of the institutions of society. Yet it is not surprising that 'from the point of view of "eternal truths" revolution is of course "antimoral". But this merely means that idealist morality is counter-revolutionary, that is, in the service of the exploiters'.[13]

Bernsteinism is not a mere intellectual throwback to the rationalism of the eighteenth century.[14] It has been the ideology of millions in the twentieth century who think of themselves as socialists but also as universalist humanists. This ideology reflects the circumstances of the middle classes, which, because of their lack of coherence, cannot be the organized core of a social revolution, but which can claim to possess the universalist vision of humanity that others should follow. They believe they possess an ethics that is a final arbiter, whereas the other classes flounder about in the mire of self-interest. In expressing this middle-class view, Reinhold Niebuhr says he finds the exaltation of class 'charged with both egotism and vindictiveness' and claims that proletarians 'may fail to recognize some rational and redemptive forces in society'.[15]

The case against an ethics founded on a universal and non-social conception of human nature was made in Chapters VI and VIII. Bernstein and his gradualist followers have nothing to offer against such criticisms other than pious ejaculations about freedom. Those who no longer appeal to Bernstein appeal to the young Marx when he talks of the human essence as a capacity for conscious self-activity.[16] We noted that this capacity is present in humans in view of the presence of the survival need for deliberation (Chapter VIII, Section 2). Yet it along with the other survival needs do not constitute a full human nature. Since rights are relative to social persons and not to survival needs alone, the basis for rights cannot be the universal fact that humans are capable of conscious self-activity. Rather than recapitulate the discussion of the social nature of the person, it is more important now to dwell on the political implications for the lower classes of the universalist humanism so common among gradualists.

Bernstein correctly saw that a universal human nature was a good antidote to lower class 'egotism and vindictiveness' and was a good motive for the peaceful, parliamentary road to socialism. Belief in a universal human nature also promotes belief in the 'rational and redemptive forces' of discussion and persuasion in a forum open to all classes. The ruling class will not, though, limit itself to parliamentary debate. While discussion and persuasion go on among elected representatives, those parts of the state that are most important to an owning class—the so-called regulatory agencies, the upper administration, the judiciary, the federal reserve bank, the army, and the police—continue to protect the profit system. Lower officials who attempt to make the state support movements of the exploited and oppressed are systematically isolated or eliminated. Should a parliamentary majority propose measures threatening the dominance of the owning class, these agencies of the state are prepared to defend the owning class. Unless the ruling class is denied the use of state power, parliamentary victories will exist only on paper. A mobilization of the lower classes and oppressed groups behind institutions created by them for their own interests is necessary to sap the power of the capitalist state.

These problems of the universalist view of humans should be explored by looking at some concrete defeats, which can only be listed here. Despite the parliamentary successes of the German Social Democratic Party, militant sections of the German working class were defeated in the revolution of 1918.[17] The Spanish workers suffered defeat in 1937 through the compromises of various leftist parties.[18] The Chilean workers and peasants were defeated with the fascist overthrow of a duly elected Socialist-Communist government.[19] Thousands were killed by Pinochet to pay the left for having relied on the 'peaceful' road of parliament rather than on the organizations of the lower classes themselves. The self-organization of the lower classes is indeed their only 'rational and redemptive' force.

An absolutist ethics does not prepare people for the struggle to overcome domination. It creates illusions about the efficacy of persuasion and attempts at cooperation with other classes. These illusions have more than once left the lower classes naked to military violence. R. H. Tawney points to both the illusion and the danger of the reformist approach to realizing socialism in the following quip: You can peel an onion layer by layer, but you can't skin a tiger claw by claw. Denying that people have revolutionary rights leaves them at the tiger's mercy.

3 **Socialism and democracy** Another important cause of the denial of revolutionary rights is the belief that socialism is essentially anti-democratic. The inequality, the murderous wars, and the alienation of capitalist society is, it is argued, balanced by its respect for a wide range of liberties. There are always exceptions; among capitalist countries basic liberties are being denied in the late 1970s in West Germany, South Africa, the Shah's Iran, Chile, and so on. Yet it is claimed to be the rule that the lower classes are denied basic democratic liberties in socialist countries. This is because socialism involves in its very conception a centrally planned economy that inevitably leads to the denial of liberties.

As to what are here called socialist regimes, let us note that whatever follows capitalism in time need not be genuinely socialist. There is a post-capitalist society on this globe that exists, with important variations, in the USSR, China, North Korea, Cuba, Poland, Hungary, and Vietnam. In these places the means of production are, by and large, controlled by a state bureaucracy through its own central plan. They are controlled neither by private owners, as is the case in most western countries, nor by industrial, clerical, service, and agricultural workers, as would be the case under genuine socialism. Even at the shop level, the control of the bureaucracy is insured through its control of both plant directors and, where they exist, plant committees. The priorities of the overall economy are set by the bureaucracy, not by institutions whose make-up is determined from below. Since these are the relations between people within the productive process in such a society, it is wrong to attribute to socialism the limitations of such a society.

In many of these countries there was a need for industrialization and for building up a class of productive workers out of a population that was predominantly peasant. Without a socialist revolution in a more advanced country, this need made the construction of a society in which the class of productive workers would be a ruling class either highly improbable or an immediate impossibility. One important aspect of the historical purpose of bureaucratic planned economies in these countries now appears to have been to build an industrial base and a working class in areas where capitalism had retarded such a development. Through this process numerous aspects of the lives of lower class people have been improved. But these lower classes are dominated—in ways and degrees that vary importantly—by a bureaucratic class. For a workers' democracy to emerge this domination must end. It has already been challenged by the Hungarian revolution of 1956, repeated worker revolts in Poland, and the Shanghai Commune in 1967.

The major capitalist and post-capitalist countries have succeeded in great feats of industrial growth and have by now large working classes. There is the capacity to produce goods abundantly and to educate intensively on a mass scale. Under these conditions a mode of production becomes feasible that is no longer organized by and for the few, be they owners or bureaucrats. A mode of production that involves decisions by the producers themselves on *what* is produced and *how* it is produced is feasible for East and West alike. Central control of the economy can be exercised by the class of producers themselves. There may be periods when it is decided that the market rather than a central plan should exercise more control, but this decision will be made by the producers.

Socialism is defined here as just such a distinctive mode of *production*. Worries about democracy under socialism arise when socialism is defined as a distinctive mode of *distribution*. The primacy of production over distribution was already noted in Chapter XVIII, Section 4. But some people still think it is possible to generate the cooperative production relations needed for socialism by engineering a distribution of more and more free goods. They think this would reduce competition, and thus overcome the individualism needed for capitalism.[20] But who decides how many more consumer goods to make free; who decides the allocation of resources to machines? Of themselves, state ownership and free distribution do not make a workers' democracy. The whole thing could be engineered undemocratically by a bureaucratic class in a way that entrenches its own power. Once this possibility is recognized, one immediately sees the possibility that a free distribution of goods merely transforms without destroying competition. For what could be better than to win the scholarships and the production-quota prizes that would land one a powerful position in the bureaucratic ruling class that makes decisions regarding free distribution? To avoid these non-socialist outcomes, the mode of production must give workers themselves the production decisions. Only then is there assurance that the working class is in power.[21]

Spokespersons for the capitalist ruling class have a vested interest in identifying present post-capitalist society as socialist. They can then pillory socialism as a system of rule over the working class by a bureaucracy. But no system of rule over the working class is a workers' democracy—that is, socialism.

4   Ethics without class   The first stages in the development of socialism will be characterized by class antagonisms. Among other things, antagonisms will break out within the alliance of the various lower classes that was put together in order to make the working class a ruling class. Ethics will remain relativist in nature throughout these stages.

The basis for these antagonisms will have been weakened from the onset of socialism due to changes in the productive process. Antagonisms between productive and unproductive workers disappear when need satisfaction replaces profits as the goal of production. Productive workers were so-called because they produced what capitalism aimed at—profits. Unproductive workers provided a back-up role for profit making through education, banking, sales, research, garbage collecting, and security. The antagonism between the two was rooted in this asymmetry: unproductive workers were paid entirely out of the surplus generated by productive workers, whereas productive workers did not make a comparable gain from the efforts of unproductive workers. This is because most of these efforts went to perpetuating the system of private investment for profit and not to satisfying workers' needs.

Once, however, need satisfaction and not profit is the aim of the economy, the antagonism begins to vanish, and since classes are antagonistic the two groups lose their status as distinct classes. Some unproductive jobs that are important for the antagonism simply disappear. Jobs tied to the market realization of profits through advertising disappear entirely, as does the job of strike breaking performed by the police and militia. Others do not disappear but are redirected to satisfying workers' needs rather than remaining a back-up for the profit system. Technical research will not be preoccupied with devices for more control over labour.

There will be an end to a two-tiered system of education which leads to narrow skill training for the working class and broader learning for higher income levels.

Antagonisms give way in other places too. Antagonisms between office workers and office managers are overcome by collectivizing decision making within offices thereby eliminating the need for managers as anything more than coordinators of work. The seeds of the abolition of classes altogether are, then, present in what began as the rule of the working class. Production ceases to imply unequal control and begins to imply cooperation on a footing of equality.

Class relativist ethics becomes irrelevant to the resulting classless society. Could one salvage ethical relativism by saying that, since there will be conflicts between groups in the classless society, ethics will be relative to these groups? Group conflicts are, though, on an entirely different base than in a class society. They no longer involve the domination of one group by another. One group might have a temporary advantage over another but such an advantage would not endure within a genuinely cooperative organization of production. In an advanced society, a persistent and systematic domination—whether occupational, ethnic, sexual, or racial—would require an exclusion of the dominated group from equal control over the means of production. Yet such an exclusion is ruled out by the very idea of a classless society, which involves cooperative control of the means of production. There are then no sub-groups to which ethics can be relativized. Either there is no ethics in a fully socialist society, or its scope of application is everyone in the society. Does this mean that an ethics for a socialist classless society is an absolutist ethics?

There will be an important role for ethics since there will still be conflict in a socialist classless society. Moreover, ethics will then be justified on the basis of a human nature that is similar throughout the society—a universal human nature. This means that ethics will itself be *universal within this society*. It does not mean, though, that ethics becomes *absolute*. It would be absolute only if the human nature on which it is based were an unchanging human nature. In fact, the human nature important here is a historical product of a long period of class struggle. The internal historical needs of people in a classless society that results from class struggle will be the basis for an ethics that is universal only in the narrow sense that it applies to everyone in that society. It is not universal in the broad sense that it applies to everyone at any time and in any society. Only an ethics that is universal in this broad sense would be absolute. Even the narrowly universalist ethics of socialism is, as

Engels put it, 'a really human morality'.[22] It gets beyond class and applies to all humans in the society. Since this really human ethics is not an absolute ethics, there is no basis for rejecting ethical relativism because of the possibility of a classless society. This ethics develops naturally out of class relativist ethics. It is relative to the society and not to a sub-group in it. It will then reflect the basic change in the economic structure of society from production controlled by the few to cooperative production by all.

Notes

1 One of the originators of this view was Eduard Bernstein, *Evolutionary Socialism* (1899), trans. E. C. Harvey, Schocken, New York, 1967, p. xxx.
2 Such a reformist path to socialism is defended by a leader of a group that emerged from the US Socialist Party, Michael Harrington, in *Socialism*, Bantam, New York, 1973, Chs. XII–XIV.
3 Nicos Poulantzas, 'The state and the transition to socialism', *Socialist Review* (US), No. 38, March–April 1978, pp. 9–36.
4 Irving Bernstein, *Turbulent Years*, Ch. VI.
5 John Reed, 'Soviets in action' (1918), *International Socialism*, Vol. LXIX, May 1974, pp. 19–25.
6 Felix Morrow, *Revolution and Counter-Revolution in Spain*, Pioneer, New York, 1938, Ch. III.
7 'The Lip Watch Strike', *Radical America*, Vol. VII, No. 6, Nov.–Dec. 1973, pp. 1–18.
8 William Hinton, *Fanshen*, Ch. LX.
9 A summary of the bill of tragic particulars is given by David Horowitz, *Empire and Revolution*, Vintage, New York, 1969.
10 John Kenneth Galbraith, *The New Industrial State*, Signet, New York, 1968, Chs. V–VIII.
11 This type of critique of the managerialist thesis has been developed by Bernard Gendron, *Technology and the Human Condition*, Ch. XI.
12 Eduard Bernstein, *Evolutionary Socialism*, pp. 144, 151. Not all gradualists, though, explicitly claim to rest their case on universalist humanism. Eurocommunist literature still does not contain its chapter on human nature. Yet with their emphasis on democratic freedoms, which are not tied to class, and their emphasis on maintaining an electoral consensus, even when this means advocating austerity, Eurocommunists would be acting in character to put a universalist view of human nature to work in justifying their denial of revolutionary rights. See Santiago Carrillo, *Eurocommunism and the State*, trans. N. Green and A. M. Elliot, Lawrence Hill, Westport, Conn., 1978, pp. 97-8, 146-7.
13 Leon Trotksy, *Their Morals and Ours* (1938), Pathfinder, New York, 1969, pp. 36–7.
14 In a conversation with Sidney Hook in 1929, Bernstein cheerfully admitted to being a 'methodological reactionary'—'I am still an eighteenth century rationalist' (Sidney Hook, *Towards an Understanding of Karl Marx*, John Day, New York, 1933, p. 21. n. 5).
15 Reinhold Niebuhr, *Moral Man and Immoral Society*, pp. 156, 167.

16 Marx, 'Alienated labour', *Karl Marx: Selected Writings*, ed. D. McLellan, p. 82.
17 Paul Frölich, *Rosa Luxemburg*, trans, J. Hoornweg, Pluto Press, London, 1972, Chs. XIII–XIV.
18 Felix Morrow, *Revolution and Counter-Revolution in Spain*, Ch. VIII.
19 Paul M. Sweezy, 'Chile: the question of power', *Monthly Review*, Vol. XXV, No. 7, December 1973, pp. 1–11.
20 This point is defended by Howard Sherman, *Radical Political Economy*, Basic Books, New York, 1972, Ch. XXIII.
21 On the question of the primacy of production over distribution in defining socialism, see the exchange between Paul M. Sweezy and Charles Bettelheim, *On the Transition to Socialism*, Monthly Review, New York, 1971, pp. 3–76.
22 Frederick Engels, *Anti-Dühring*, Ch. IX, p. 105.

INDEX

Ability to do otherwise, 184; weak sense, 185, 190; strong sense, 185

Absolutism: ethical, xv, 30; spatial, 30; Kantian, 30–32; based on survival needs, 130; for virtue, 151; in rationality, 177; regarding freedom and responsibility, 196; history of morality irrelevant to, 212; denies revolutionary rights, 255; *see also* Relativism

Ackerman, Frank, 236n

Action, 3, 149; not automatic response to social force, 160; conditions of, 160; physical events and human, 160–1; causes of relative to ends, 161; structure of, 166; deliberation puts back on course, 181; free, 184; compulsive, 188, 192; voluntary, 192

Advocacy of overthrow, 207

Affluence: myth of, 224; with inequality, 226, 234; not a reality for the majority, 227; inequality as condition of, 229; *see also* Poverty

Agitation, 166; *see* Propaganda

Alienation: and historical needs, 123; defined, 124; origin in production, 126; obligatory to work against, 129, 205

Allen, Robert L., 54n, 223n

Alternatives, 171, 174, 181, 185, 188

Anderson, C.H., xxn

Aristotle, xvii, 105n, 118n, 170n, 183n, 212, 223n; on the nature of ethics, vii; on categorizing, 93f; holds wickedness defeats communism, 96–7; sees emotions with needs, 100; on virtue, 150–1, 153, 157; on ends in themselves, 172; on intellectual virtues, 177; calls freedom praxis, 187, 197n; bases rights on stations, 215

Arrow, Kenneth J., 173, 183n

Atomism, 9–10, 17, 108, 135, 201

Austin, J.L., 90n, 197n

Authority, 5, 20–1, 251

Baier, Kurt, 132n

Benevolence, 23, 70, 109

Bentham, Jeremy, 57, 67n, 167, 170n

Bernstein, Eduard, 89, 255–6, 261n

Bernstein, Irving, 132n, 261n

Bettleheim, Charles, 262n

Blackburn, Robin, 54n, 145n

Blacks: needs of, xv; personal needs and liberation of, 26; and self-identity, 46; consciousness of, 47; and their own values, 47; capitalism for, 48; labour of, 49; doctrine of inferiority of, 50; as nation, 221–3; *see also* Racism

Bolsheviks, 209

Bottomore, T.B., 118n

Bowles, Samuel, 132n

Boyd, Richard N., 170n

Braverman, Harry, 54n, 118n

Budget: modest but adequate, 227, 232

Bureaucracy, 210, 230

Burke, Edmund, 97, 105n

Burnette, Robert, 54n

Calculation, 57–9, 179

Cantor, Arnold, 236n

Capital: private, 229; collective, 230

Capitalism, 113, 142; classes in, 49; and oppression, 50; origins of, 74–5; source of jobs, 123; rationality within, 180; right to change, 205; and origin of idea of rights, 214–15; individualist ideology of, 215; structural need for inequality in, 218, 227ff; defenses of, 227–31; and investment, 229; limits of system of, 247; reform to preserve, 250; allegedly protects liberties, 257

257; universalist ethics of, 260
Society: not homogeneous, xiv, 114;
as sum group, 42, 113; capitalist,
74–5, 226; essential roles in, 113–
14; changed by dealienation, 124;
affluent, 224; classless, 260
Sociobiology, 102, 119
Solidarity, 25, 43, 219–20
Solzhenitsyn, Alexander I., 211
Spartacus revolt, 213
Speech: ideal situation, 178; free,
206–7
Stability, 10, 41–5, 48, 213–14, 247
Stalin, J.V., 209–10
Standards: dominant, 4; ethical, 13;
meta-ethical, 15; relative, 32; of
choice, 171
State: power, 208–9; apparatus, 251,
256
State of nature, 14n, 76–8
Steel industry: discrimination in, 54;
call for productivity by, 60
Stevenson, C.L., 90n
Strikes, 173–6, 194–5, 216
Structuralism, 116
Structure: opposed to quantity, 80–1,
240; as basis for good, 82; as social,
83, 111; in dialectic with results,
84–5; overarching, 243–4; primacy
of, 244
Struggle: and self-knowledge, 22; gaps
in, 131; undercuts imposed needs,
138, 180–1; as method opposed to
reflection, 140–3; unending, 142;
against inequality, 219–20; for high-
er income, 233; and social entities,
244–5
Subjectivism, 38–9, 155
Subsistence level, 232
Suicide, 7–8
Sum group, 42, 150
Support, 98; in family, 111; in work,
115
Surplus, 113–14
Survival needs, 12; as universal, 102;
as basic, 102
Sweezy, Paul, 262n

Taft-Hartley Act, 246, 249n
Tawney, R.H., 257
Taxation, 225
Teamsters, 206–7

Technology, 135–6
Teleology: defined, 80; and GNP, 81;
one-sided, 84; of human action,
161–2
Tendencies, xvi; group, xiv, 29, 39;
capacities plus conditional likeli-
hoods, 29; absolute set of, 30–1;
historical, 120; advancing, 244–5;
see Interests
Thompson, Frank, xix
Toleration: in sum group, 45;
principle of, 86–7; absolute, 87–9;
of Nazis, 89
Totalitarianism, 12, 202
Trotsky, L.D., 145n, 209, 261n

Unions: historical need for, 121; leaders of, 125, 233; alienation in,
125; bureaucratic control of, 127;
craft and industrial, 150; have lost
class conception of rights, 233
Universality: and the categorical imperative, 30–2; of survival needs,
102; of goods and virtues, 158
Upton, Lititia, 236n
Utilitarianism: defined, 57–8; hedonistic, 61; psychological, 65; group-
relative variant of, 240; incompatible with Marxism, 240

Validity: empirical, xvi; of ethical
principles, 21, 30; relative, 28, 37;
universal, 32; time-bound, 36, 41;
and position in domination, 43;
ostensible, 44–5, 47; on basis of
contract, 68–9
Value-freeness, 156, 172, 180
Values, 46, 60, 156; as preference
rankings, 173; expected, 174; comparability of, 175; clear sets of,
177–8; and rationality, 178–9; conflicting, 179
Violence, 31, 194; in overthrowing
government, 206–7; right to use,
206–7
Virtue, 149; and function, 150; as
capacity, 150; relativist view of, 151;
basis for goodness, 153; and pleasing sentiment, 154; subjective view
of, 155; universal, 158; as a good
motive, 167; intellectual, 177;